Home-Based Business For Dummies, 2nd Ed

D0795918

Ten High-Tech and High-Touch Ways to Earn Your Living From Home in the 21st Century

If you like to work with computers and the latest technology, the list on the left includes five hot high-tech businesses that you can start at home. Not techy? The list on the right includes five non-technical home-based businesses.

- Computer consultant for small and home businesses
- Technical writer
- Virtual assistant
- Webmaster
- Web merchant and auction trader

- Bodywork or massage therapy
- Elder services
- Financial advisor
- Pet sitter
- Tutor

Five Tips for Building an Effective Web Site

Your business's Web site may look great, but if it's not helping you sell more of your company's products and services, it's a waste of your time and money. Here are some tried-and-true ways to build a Web site that can be a real asset to your business:

- **Be easy to find.** Don't make it difficult for your clients to find you.
- **Advertise your new address like crazy.** One of the best ways to get the word out about your Web site is to include its address on your business cards, letterhead stationery, invoices, marketing brochures, and anyplace else you can possibly fit all those letters and dots.
- **Give your visitors a reason to visit — and to come back again and again.** If your site is boring, your client or prospect will click out of the site just as quickly as he or she clicked in.
- **Capture contact information.** Encourage your visitors to give you contact information that you can use in your organization's marketing and promotional efforts.
- **Check Web stats and visit your site regularly.** Make your Web site your Internet browser's home page so you check it every time you go online.

Five Ways to Get Referrals for Your Business

For many home-based businesses, referrals are the most effective marketing tool available. Here are some ideas for getting more referrals:

- Do great work for your current customers.
- Build a mailing list of all customers and prospective customers.
- Keep your mailing list informed.
- Always send a thank-you note to customers who refer you.
- Send work to others by making referrals yourself.

For Dummies: Bestselling Book Series for Beginners

Home-Based Business For Dummies, 2nd Edition

Cheat Sheet

Five Ways to Avoid Work-at-Home Scams

Although the vast majority of direct-selling opportunities are legitimate, plenty aren't. The following are some tips to help you avoid the scams:

✔ **Identify a company or product that appeals to you.** Check with the Direct Selling Association (DSA) for a list of member companies or look in your local phone book.

✔ **Take your time deciding.** Does "getting in on the ground floor" mean that everyone joining after you will be less satisfied or happy? A legitimate opportunity won't disappear overnight. Think long-term.

✔ **Ask questions.** Ask about the company, its leadership, the products or services, start-up fees, realistic costs of doing business, average earnings of distributors, return policies, and anything else you're concerned about. Get copies of all company literature. And read it!

✔ **Consult with others who have had experiences with the company and its products.** Check to see if the products or services are actually being sold to consumers.

✔ **Investigate and verify all information.** Don't assume that official-looking documents are accurate or complete or even produced by the company. (They may be created by the person trying to recruit you.) See Chapter 13 for more information.

Ten Commandments for Working from Home

Home-based businesses are real businesses. The following are the Ten Commandments for working from home:

✔ Maintain a professional attitude.

✔ Use technology to leverage your time and yourself.

✔ Locate your office in its own space.

✔ Set regular business hours.

✔ Avoid distractions.

✔ Set goals and track your progress.

✔ Don't become a prisoner to your home office.

✔ Stay organized.

✔ Set up a separate phone line, dedicated computer, and other equipment and systems.

✔ Have fun!

For Dummies: Bestselling Book Series for Beginners

Home-Based Business

Business

FOR

DUMMIES®

2ND EDITION

Home-Based Business

FOR

DUMMIES®

2ND EDITION

by Paul and Sarah Edwards
and Peter Economy

WILEY

Wiley Publishing, Inc.

Home-Based Business For Dummies®, 2nd Edition

Published by
Wiley Publishing, Inc.
111 River St.
Hoboken, NJ 07030-5774
www.wiley.com

Copyright © 2005 by Wiley Publishing, Inc., Indianapolis, Indiana

Published simultaneously in Canada

For general information on our other products and services, please contact our Customer Care Department within the U.S. at 800-762-2974, outside the U.S. at 317-572-3993, or fax 317-572-4002.

For technical support, please visit www.wiley.com/techsupport.

Wiley also publishes its books in a variety of electronic formats. Some content that appears in print may not be available in electronic books.

Library of Congress Control Number: 2004117579

ISBN: 0-7645-7763-8

Manufactured in the United States of America

10 9 8 7 6 5 4

2O/RU/QS/QV/IN

WILEY

About the Authors

Paul and Sarah Edwards's self-employment and career books have sold over a million and a half copies. They write monthly columns for *Entrepreneur* and *The Costco Connection*. They hosted *The Working From Home Show* on HGTV, have been regular commentators on CNBC, and appear frequently on radio and TV shows across the country. Since 1988, they have produced and co-hosted an hour-long show *Working From Home*, which currently airs on The Entrepreneur Radio Network at www.wsradio.com/entrepreneur_homebasedbiz/. Occasionally, their show, broadcast from their California home, is enriched by the barks of Billy, their toy Manchester Terrier.

Paul and Sarah provide a wealth of ongoing information, resources, and support, including updates, marketing tips, and excerpts from their sixteen books on self-employment at www.workingfromhome.com.

Peter Economy, who lives in La Jolla, CA, is a home-based business author and the coauthor of *Why Aren't You Your Own Boss?* with Paul and Sarah Edwards, *Managing For Dummies* and *Consulting For Dummies* with Bob Nelson, and *Writing Children's Books For Dummies* with Lisa Rojany Buccieri. Peter is also Associate Editor for the award-winning magazine *Leader to Leader*.

Peter combines his writing experience with more than 15 years of hands-on management experience. He received his bachelor's degree in economics from Stanford University and is pursuing his MBA at the Edinburgh Business School. Peter invites you to visit his Web site (www.petereconomy.com).

Dedication

To the millions of home-based businesspeople whose entrepreneurial spirit shines as a beacon, inspiring those around you and lighting a path to the success you so richly deserve.

Author's Acknowledgments

We give our sincere thanks and appreciation to our original publishing team: Kathy Welton, Mark Butler, and Tere Drenth. For the current edition, we thank Stacy Kennedy, Corbin Collins, and Beverley Williams.

Paul and Sarah also extend their thanks to Peter Economy for his dedication to this project.

Peter thanks Paul and Sarah Edwards for the opportunity to work with them on this dynamic topic, and for sharing their extensive experience and wisdom with him. Together, we rediscovered the joy of doing the work that we truly love and the power of teamwork.

Publisher's Acknowledgments

We're proud of this book; please send us your comments through our Dummies online registration form located at www.dummies.com/register/.

Some of the people who helped bring this book to market include the following:

Acquisitions, Editorial, and Media Development

Project Editor: Corbin Collins

Acquisitions Editor: Stacy Kennedy

Technical Editor: Beverley Williams

Editorial Manager: Michelle Hacker

Editorial Supervisor: Carmen Krikorian

Editorial Assistants: Courtney Allen, Nadine Bell

Cover Photos: Rob Melnychuk/Getty Images/ Taxi

Cartoons: Rich Tennant, www.the5thwave.com

Composition

Project Coordinator: Maridee Ennis

Layout and Graphics: Andrea Dahl, Lauren Goddard, Joyce Haughey Stephanie D. Jumper, Barry Offringa Heather Ryan, Julie Trippetti

Proofreaders: Leeann Harney Jessica Kramer, Joe Niesen, TECHBOOKS Production Services

Indexer: TECHBOOKS Production Services

Publishing and Editorial for Consumer Dummies

    Diane Graves Steele, Vice President and Publisher, Consumer Dummies

    Joyce Pepple, Acquisitions Director, Consumer Dummies

    Kristin A. Cocks, Product Development Director, Consumer Dummies

    Michael Spring, Vice President and Publisher, Travel

    Brice Gosnell, Associate Publisher, Travel

    Kelly Regan, Editorial Director, Travel

Publishing for Technology Dummies

    Andy Cummings, Vice President and Publisher, Dummies Technology/General User

Composition Services

    Gerry Fahey, Vice President of Production Services

    Debbie Stailey, Director of Composition Services

Contents at a Glance

Table of Contents

Introduction

● ●

*W*ho doesn't dream of starting one's own business and being one's own boss? Increasingly, this dream is becoming a reality for the millions of people who have chosen to start their own businesses at home. And it's not just a pie-in-the-sky dream; starting a home-based business is a reality that has created wide-open opportunity and success for those who decided to take the plunge — just as it can for you.

Home-Based Business For Dummies, 2nd Edition, presents and explains an incredibly wide variety of information — all of it aimed at ensuring your home-business success. Whether you need information on choosing the right business opportunity, avoiding scams, marketing your business, pricing your products and services, keeping accounts and books, understanding legal do's and don'ts, or growing your business, you'll find it here.

This book provides you with the very best ideas, concepts, and tools for starting and successfully operating your home business. Apply them, and we're convinced that you'll be able to create exactly the kind of business you have always dreamed of and find exactly the level of success that you have always wanted.

About This Book

Home-Based Business For Dummies is full of useful information, tips, and checklists for everyone who aspires to start a successful home-based business. Your current level of business experience (or lack thereof) doesn't matter. Don't worry about not having years of it under your belt or about not knowing the difference between *direct selling* and a *franchise.* For a fraction of the amount you would pay to get an M.B.A., this book provides you with an easily understandable road map to today's most innovative and effective home-based business techniques and strategies.

The information you'll find here is firmly grounded in the real world. This book isn't an abstract collection of theoretical mumbo-jumbo that sounds good but doesn't work when you put it to the test. Instead, we've culled the best information, best strategies, and best techniques — the exact same ones that are taught in today's top business schools. This book is a toolbox full of solutions to your every question and problem.

This book is also fun — it reflects our strong belief and experience that running a business doesn't have to be a bore. We even help you maintain a sense of humor in the face of the challenges that all home-based businesspeople face from time to time, because we've been there, done that!

And one more thing: The Internet has forever changed the world of business, and that includes home-based businesses. This book contains the latest information on e-commerce and on starting and operating a successful business on the Internet. It's also chock full of our own personal Internet bookmarks for the best home-business resources the Web has to offer.

How This Book Is Organized

Home-Based Business For Dummies is organized into five parts. The chapters within each part cover specific topic areas in detail. Because we've organized the book this way, you can easily find the topic you're looking for. Look in the index or table of contents for your general area of interest and then find the chapter that concerns your particular needs. Whatever the topic, odds are it's covered somewhere in this book.

Each part addresses a major area of the hows, whats, and whys of starting your own home-based business. The following is a summary of what you'll find in each part.

Part 1: Beginning at the Beginning

For most people, starting a home-based business is a big undertaking. But every great journey begins with some small first steps. In this part, we take a look at what you need to know about starting a home-based business and take you on a tour of the very best home-based business opportunities both for today and tomorrow. We consider the ins and outs of effective marketing. Finally, we discuss how to make the Web work for you.

Part II: Managing Your Money

Money is the blood that keeps any business running: It's how you pay for your supplies, your computer, and other equipment and how you put something aside for a rainy day. In this part, we take a close look at transitioning from a regular job into your own home-based business, as well as keeping track of your money and deciding how much to charge. We examine getting health insurance and planning for your retirement — and how to use the tax laws to your advantage.

Part III: Avoiding Problems

There's more to starting a business than simply announcing that you're "in business." You have to choose and register a business name, consider zoning regulations, and set up and equip your home office. In this part, we present the most common legal considerations for home-based businesspeople and discuss which kinds of business relationships are most important to establish and how you can establish them. Finally, we give you our best advice on avoiding scams and ripoffs.

Part IV: Making It Work: Moving Ahead

Creating a successful home-based business requires more than a good idea; you need the ability to separate your business from your personal life and to know when to mix the two and when to keep them apart. In this part, you find out about establishing a serious business attitude and how to ensure that your business coexists peacefully with those people you share your home with. We also take a look at how to successfully grow your business, if you so choose.

Part V: The Part of Tens

In this concise and lively set of condensed chapters, you can find tips to help start and maintain your home-based business. We show you how to succeed in your home-based business, what to do when times get tough, and much more.

Icons Used in This Book

Icons are handy little graphic images that are meant to point out particularly important information about starting your own home-based business. You'll find the following icons in this book, conveniently located along the left margins.

This icon directs you to tips and shortcuts for making your home-based business a success.

We've seen some pretty interesting things while working with home-based businesses, including our own. This icon points out some of our stories.

Sometimes you need advice that goes beyond what we can provide in this book. When that's the case, it's time for you to see a professional.

Remember these important points of information, and your home-based business will be all the better for it.

Danger! Ignore the advice next to this icon at your own risk!

Paul and Sarah Edwards provide insightful answers to a variety of home-business questions.

Where to Go from Here

If you're new to business, you may want to start at the beginning of this book and work your way through to the end. There is a wealth of information and practical advice awaiting you. Simply turn the page, and you're on your way! If you already own and operate your own home-based business and are short of time (and who isn't short of time?), turn to a particular topic to address a specific need or question. Regardless of how you find your way around *Home-Based Business For Dummies,* we're sure that you'll enjoy getting there.

Part I
Beginning at the Beginning

The 5th Wave By Rich Tennant

BOB'S HOME-BASED BOWLING

In this part . . .

Starting your own home-based business can be a very exciting time — not only for you, but for those around you. Before you can start on your journey, though, you'll need to take your first step. In this part, we present an overview of the home-based business process and delve into the questions of which business is best for you and what opportunities offer the greatest rewards. We then move on to the basics of marketing and how to make the Web work for you.

Chapter 1

What You Need to Know about Home-Based Business

In This Chapter
▶ Defining the home-based business
▶ Understanding the basics
▶ Dealing with the good and the bad news

Congratulations! You've decided to start a home-based business. We welcome you as you join with millions of others who have already made a decision to start a home-based business. According to the Small Business Administration (SBA), there are about 23.7 million businesses in the United States today. Of this total, 99.7 percent are small businesses (defined by the government as businesses with fewer than 500 employees), or about 23.6 million. Of these, just over half — about 11.8 million — are home-based businesses.

That's a *lot* of home-based businesses!

Take it from us: Owning your own home-based business may be the most rewarding experience of your entire life. And not just in a financial sense (although many home-based businesspeople find the financial rewards to be significant), but also rewarding in the sense of doing the work you love and having control over your own life.

Of course, every great journey begins with the first step. In this chapter, we provide you with an overview of this book, taking a look at the basics of home-based business — including getting started, managing your money, avoiding problems, and moving ahead. Finally, we'll consider some of the good news — and the bad — about starting your own home-based business and knowing when it's time to make the move.

Paul and Sarah's journey home

Paul and Sarah began working from home before it was fashionable for anyone other than people in the construction trades, writers, artists, and craftspeople to do so. In fact, the neighbors wondered whether Paul was unemployed. (Paul's first home business was doing political and public-affairs consulting.)

Sarah actually led the way home, to set up a psychotherapy practice as a way of reducing the stress she felt in her prior government positions and to actively raise Paul and Sarah's young son. Says Sarah, "I didn't feel I had many choices as a working mother. Juggling a successful career and motherhood meant being exhausted most of the time and not being able to do either job with the dedication I wanted. I was determined, however, to have both a career and a family, so I did my best in a difficult situation." Doing her best meant a trip to the hospital with a stress-related illness where the doctor told her she would die if she didn't change her lifestyle — that was her wake-up call. She left her secure government job and opened a private psychotherapy practice in her home. In the 25 years since she did that, Sarah hasn't regretted her decision for even one day.

For Paul, the decision wasn't an easy one, and it took some time for him to get used to the idea of having a home-based business. "Initially, I was hesitant about working from home," Paul says. "I had concerns about the image it might create and worried that I wouldn't get my work done. So when I started my own consulting firm, I opened a downtown office and hired a secretary." As time went on, Paul spent less time at his downtown office and more time working at home. Eventually, he decided to close the downtown office altogether and invited his secretary to join him in his home office.

At first, Paul and Sarah's businesses were separate, but in 1980 they decided to write a book about working at home. They wished such a book had existed for them when they got started. More and more people were asking them how they did it, indicating they wanted to work at home, too. That book, *Working from Home,* is now in its fifth edition, and they've written 15 others. For excerpts from those books, as well as daily messages, tips, and support, visit their Web site at www.working fromhome.com.

Home-Based Business Defined

A *home-based business* is, not surprisingly, a business based in your home. Whether you do all the work in your home or on customers' or third-party premises, whether you run a franchise, a direct-sales operation, or a business opportunity (described in the next section), if the center of your operations is based in your home, it's a home-based business.

The Basics of Home-Based Business

Each part of this book is dedicated to a specific aspect of the home-based business process. In the sections that follow, we take a peek at the topics to be covered within each of these parts.

What kind of business will it be?

Once you decide you're going to start your own home-based business, you're left with two questions: Exactly what kind of home-based business should you start, and what's the best way to market your products or services?

There are two major types of home-based businesses: businesses you start from scratch and businesses you can buy. The latter category of home-based business is further split into three types: franchises, direct selling, and business opportunities. Whether you prefer to march to your own drummer or get a business-in-a-box depends on your personal preferences: whether you like to create systems (or follow those of others) and how much structure you like.

The advantage of a business you start from scratch is that it can be molded to your preferences and to existing and emerging markets, and thus provides a boundless variety of possibilities. Businesses started from scratch account for the majority of viable, full-time businesses — in other words, they tend to be more successful over the long run than businesses you can buy. (In their book *Finding Your Perfect Work*, Paul and Sarah provide an appendix with characteristics of over 1,500 self-employment careers and hundreds of examples in the book of unique businesses that people have carved out for themselves.)

Each type of home business that you can buy, on the other hand, has its own spin. Here are examples of the three different types.

Franchise

A *franchise* is an agreement in which one business grants another business the right to distribute its products or services. Some common home-based franchises include the following:

- American Leak Detection (water/gas leak detection)
- Merry Maids (cleaning service)
- Kinderdance International (teaching dance to preschoolers)

✓ ServiceMaster (cleaning service)

✓ Terminix Termite and Pest Control (pest control)

Direct selling

Direct selling involves selling consumer products or services in a person-to-person manner, away from a fixed retail location. There are two main types of direct-selling opportunities:

✓ **Single-level marketing** is making money by buying products from a parent company and then selling those products directly to customers.

✓ **Multi-level marketing** involves making money through single-level marketing and by sponsoring new direct sellers.

Some common home-based direct-selling opportunities include the following:

✓ Amway/Quixtar (household cleaning products)

✓ Discovery Toys, Inc. (toys)

✓ Longaberger Company (baskets)

✓ Mary Kay, Inc. (cosmetics)

✓ Nikken, Inc. (wellness technology)

Business opportunities

A *business opportunity* is an idea, product, system, or service that someone else develops and offers to sell to others to help them start their own, similar business. (One way to think of a business opportunity is that it's any business concept you can buy from someone else that's not direct-selling or a franchise.) Your customers and clients pay you directly when you deliver a product or service to them. Here are several examples of business opportunities that can easily be run out of one's home:

✓ Balloon Wrap, Inc. (balloon gift wrap)

✓ Cardservice International (transaction service provider)

✓ Home Video Studio, Inc. (video studio)

✓ Rhino Linings USA, Inc. (truck bed liners)

Interested in finding out the names of more companies and how to get in touch with them? *Entrepreneur* magazine (at www.entrepreneurmag.com) and gosmallbiz.com also have extensive information on business opportunities you can buy. You can also do an online search for companies on Google (www.google.com), using the keywords *business opportunity*.

So once you decide on a business and get it started, you've got to market your products or services and persuade people to buy them. You can choose conventional methods of promotion, such as advertising and public relations, or you can leverage new selling opportunities, such as the Internet, to your advantage. Or you can (and probably should) do both. It's your choice — you're the boss! Check out the rest of Part I for more information on choosing and marketing your business.

Managing your money

Money makes the world go 'round, and because this is your financial well-being we're talking about, it's very important to have a handle on your money. This means you've got to do the following:

- ✔ **Find the money you'll need to start up your business.** The good news is that most home-based businesses require little or no money to start up. For the rest of you, there are lots of sources of start-up capital, including friends and family, savings, credit cards, bank loans, and more.

- ✔ **Keep track of your money.** For most of us, this means using a simple accounting or bookkeeping software package, such as QuickBooks, Quicken, or Microsoft Money, to organize and monitor your business finances.

- ✔ **Set the right price for your products and services.** Set your prices too high, and you'll scare customers away; set them too low, and you'll be swamped with customers, but you won't make enough money to stay afloat. Be sure to charge enough to cover your costs while generating a healthy profit.

- ✔ **Obtain health insurance, and plan for your retirement.** When you've got your own business, you're the one who needs to arrange for health insurance and setting up IRAs, 401(k)s, or other retirement plans for the day when you're ready to hang up your business and ride off into the sunset.

- ✔ **Pay taxes.** As someone famous once said: *The only things you can count on in life are death and taxes.* Well, taxes for sure.

Be sure to check out Part II of this book for lots of detailed information on managing your money.

Avoiding problems

Eventually, every business — home-based or not — runs into problems. As the owner of your own business, it's very much in your interest to avoid problems whenever possible and to deal with them quickly and decisively when they can't be avoided. Some of the problems you'll potentially deal with include the following:

- ✓ **Legal issues.** After a good accountant, the next best friend of any business owner is a good attorney. Keep one handy to help you deal with the inevitable legal issues when they arise.

- ✓ **Working with support services.** Finding skilled and reliable outside support services — lawyers, accountants, bankers, business consultants, and insurance brokers — is not necessarily an easy task, especially if your business is in a small town where you're pretty much stuck with what you've got.

- ✓ **Scams and ripoffs.** There are loads of home-based business scams out there, and it seems that more appear every day. Part of avoiding scams and ripoffs is remembering these words: *If it looks too good to be true, it probably is!* Don't rush into any business opportunity; take your time and fully explore it before you sign on the dotted line.

Want to avoid problems in your home-based business? Good. Simply move on to Part III, and you'll be well on your way to doing just that.

Moving ahead

One of the best things about owning your own business is watching it develop, mature, and grow. A growing business is the gift that keeps on giving — all year 'round, year after year. So to keep your business moving ahead, consider doing the following:

- ✓ **Maintain a serious business attitude.** Just because your business is located at home instead of in a big office building downtown, that doesn't mean that you shouldn't treat it like the business it is. While you can have fun and work all kinds of creative schedules, don't forget that business is serious, too, and that you've got to treat your business like a business if you hope to be successful.

- ✓ **Institute a truce with your friends and family.** Moving forward with your business requires that you minimize disruptions caused by loved ones, neighbors, friends who work in regular jobs, and anyone else who can distract you from your work. Do whatever it takes to avoid the negative impacts of such disruptions to your business.

- ✓ **Grow.** For many businesses, growth can turn an operation that is doing well financially into an operation that is doing *great!* Growth allows you to take advantage of economies of scale that might be available only to larger businesses, to serve more customers, and to increase profits. For these reasons and more, growing your business should always be on your agenda.

Peter's personal journey to independence

When Peter Economy graduated from Stanford University with majors in human biology and economics, he had no idea what he wanted to do for work, aside from some vague notion that he should "get into business." He worked a number of jobs, starting in the federal government as a contract negotiator and then moving into the private sector for many years as an administrative manager before ending up back in local government. As time wore on, working for others became less and less palatable to him, and becoming his own boss became a seductive proposition. In 1990, Peter was fortunate to be approached by his good friend Bob Nelson to write a book on the topic of negotiation. Although Peter had no real desire to write a book, a bit of gentle persuasion (and the promise of a $2,500 advance) helped bring him around. This first book, *Negotiating to Win*, started him on a new career as a business writer.

In time, Peter was able to seriously consider devoting himself fully to starting a home-based business as a professional writer. In 1997, he got the kick in the pants he needed to make the move when he was told that, due to funding cuts, he would be laid off from his local government job. And although a week later his employer found additional funds and asked him to stay, he already had one foot out the door, and there was no turning back.

Today, Peter runs his own home-based writing business. He works harder than he ever has before but has the satisfaction of knowing that every bit of work he does has a direct payoff for him and his family — not some distant company owners or shareholders. But although he works harder than ever, he also gets to spend far more time with his wife and kids than he ever did before, and the commute to his office has been reduced from half an hour each way to about 30 seconds. Is he happy? Yes. Would he go back to working a regular nine-to-five job? Not on your life!

Do you have specific questions or comments for Peter? He'd love to hear from you. Visit his Web site at www.petereconomy.com, and drop him a line.

To discover in-depth information on these particular topics, be sure to check out Part IV sooner rather than later.

Should you leave your full-time job and ramp up your part-time business?

Ask yourself several questions:

- ✔ Has there been a steadily growing flow of new customers over your time in business?

- ✔ Has your business, even though part-time, been producing a steady flow of income through seasonal or other cycles typical of the business?

- ✔ Are you turning away business because of limits on your time? If not, can you see that if you had the time to market or take on more customers, they would be there?

If you can answer at least two out of these questions in the affirmative, it's a good sign that it would be safe to leave your job. Of course, you should also be aware of any developments that could worsen the outlook for your business to grow, such as pending legislation, new technology, the movement of the kind of work you do outside the United States *(outsourcing)*, or the decline of an industry your business is dependent on.

If your work has been providing you the contacts you have used to build your part-time business, it's important you find ways to replace these.

Breaking the umbilical cord of a paycheck is an uncomfortable step for most people. So the closer the current income from your business is to producing the money you need to pay your basic business and living expenses, the more confident you can be.

The Good News and the Bad

Surprise, surprise: There's both good news and bad when it comes to starting your own home-based business. The good news is that the good news probably outweighs the bad for most of us. So in the spirit of putting our best foot forward, let's start with the good news.

Reasons to start a home-based business

When you start a home-based business, you're leaving behind the relative comfort and security of a regular career or 9-to-5 job and venturing out on your own. How far out you venture on your own depends on the kind of home-based business you get involved in. Many franchises provide extensive support and training, for example, and *franchisees* (someone like you) are able to seek advice from experienced franchisees or from the *franchisor* (the party selling a franchise opportunity) when and if it's necessary. This support can be invaluable if you're new to the world of home-based business.

At the other end of the spectrum, some business opportunities offer little or no support whatsoever. If you're a dealer in synthetic motor oil, for example, you may have trouble getting the huge, multinational conglomerate that manufactures the oil to return your calls, much less send you some product brochures. Training or extensive, hands-on support if you run into the inevitable snags? Nope — that's not going to happen.

Which brings us to the good news about starting and running your own home-based business:

✔ **You're the boss.** For many owners of home-based businesses, just this is reason enough to justify making the move out of the 9-to-5.

✔ **You get all the benefits of your hard work.** When you make a profit, it's all yours. No one else is going to try to take it away from you (except, perhaps, the tax man — see Chapter 10).

✔ **You have the flexibility to work when and where you want.** Are you a night owl? Perhaps your most productive times don't coincide with the standard 9-to-5 work schedule that most regular businesses require their employees to adhere to. And you may find that — because interruptions from co-workers are no longer an issue and the days of endless meetings are left far behind — you're much more productive working in your workshop than in a regular office. With your own home-based business, you're the one who decides when and where you work.

✔ **You get to choose your clients and customers.** The customer may always be right, but that doesn't mean you have to put up with one who mistreats you or gives you more headaches than they're worth. When you own your own business, you can fire the clients you don't want to work with. Sounds like fun, doesn't it? (Believe us, it is!)

✔ **You can put as much or as little time into your business as you like.** Do you want to work for only a few hours a day or week? No problem. Ready for a full-time schedule or even more? Great! The more effort you put into your business, the more money you can make. You get to decide how much money you want to make and then you can work the kind of schedule that will help you meet your goal.

These reasons to be on your own are just the tip of the iceberg. When you add it all up, you're left with one fundamental reason for owning your own home-based business: freedom.

Admittedly, starting a home-based business isn't for everyone. In fact, for some individuals, it can be a big mistake. If, however, you have an entrepreneurial spirit, and you thrive on being independent and in charge of your life, a home-based business may be just the thing for you.

You have only one life to live. If you're tired of working for someone else, being second-guessed by your boss, or having your creativity stifled; if you're full of great ideas — ideas you know will lead you to success if you have the opportunity to put them into practice; if you long for something better, we have a message for you: There is something better. It's called a home-based business. And when you find the business that's right for you, it can change your life and the lives of those around you.

The pitfalls of home-based businesses

Starting a home-based business is not the solution to every problem for every person. Although many home-based businesses are successful, and the people who started them are happy with the results, more than a few home-based businesses end up causing far more headaches than their owners anticipated. Starting your own business is hard work, and there are no guarantees for its success.

So the next time you're lying on your sofa, dreaming of starting your own home-based business, don't forget some of the potential pitfalls:

- **The business is in your home.** Depending on your domestic situation, working in your own home — a home filled with any number of distractions, including busy children, whining spouses or significant others; television; loaded refrigerators; and more — can be a difficult proposition at best.

- **You're the boss!** When you're the boss, you're the one who has to get you motivated to work hard every day — there's no one standing over your shoulder (except maybe your cat) watching your every move. For some people, focusing on work is very difficult when *they* are put in the position of being the boss.

- **A home-based business is (usually) a very small business.** As such, you will likely be more exposed to the ups and downs of fickle customers than larger businesses are. Not only that, but also, if a customer decides not to pay, it could be devastating to you and your business.

- **You might fail or not like it.** There are no guarantees that your business is going to be a success. Failure might cost you dearly, including financial ruin (no small number of business owners have had to declare bankruptcy when their businesses failed), destruction of personal relationships, and worse. Not all small businesses close due to financial problems. The Small Business Administration has found that at the time of closing, one out of three businesses is financially sound.

Regardless of these potential pitfalls, starting a home-based business remains the avenue of choice for an increasing number of people. Are you ready to join them?

Understanding when you're ready to make the move

Many people talk about starting a home-based business, and many dream about becoming their own bosses. Making the transition from a full-time career to self-employment, however, is a big change in anyone's life. Are you really ready to make the move, or should you put the idea of having your own home-based business on the back burner for a while longer?

To help you decide, take the following quiz. Circle your answer to each of these questions, add up the results, and you'll know for sure!

1. How strong is your drive to succeed in your own home-based business?

   A. I can and I will be a success. Period.

   B. I'm fairly confident that if I put my mind to it, I will succeed.

   C. I'm not sure. Let me think about it for a while.

   D. Did I say that I wanted to start my own business? Are you sure that was me?

2. Are you ready to work as hard as or harder than you have ever worked before?

   A. You bet — I'm ready to do whatever it takes to succeed!

   B. Sure, I don't mind working hard as long as there's something in it for me.

   C. Okay, as long as I still get weekends and evenings off.

   D. What? You mean I'll still have to work after I start my own business? Isn't that why I hire employees?

3. Do you like the idea of controlling your own work instead of having someone else control it for you?

   A. I don't want anyone controlling my work but me!

   B. That's certainly my first choice.

   C. It sounds like an interesting idea — can I?

   D. Do I have to control my own work? Can't someone control it for me?

4. Have you developed a strong network of potential customers?

   A. Yes, here are their names and numbers.

   B. Yes, I have some pretty strong leads.

   C. Not yet, but I've started kicking around some ideas with potential customers.

   D. I'm sure that as soon as I let people know that I'm starting my own business, customers will line up.

5. Do you have a plan for making the transition into your home-based business?

    A. Here it is — would you like to read the executive summary or the full plan?

    B. Yes, I've spent a lot of time considering my options and making plans.

    C. I'm just getting started.

    D. I don't believe in plans — they crimp my style.

6. Do you have enough money saved to tide you over while you get your business off the ground?

    A. Will the year's salary that I have saved be enough?

    B. I have six months' expenses hidden away for a rainy day.

    C. Three months' worth.

    D. I'm still trying to pay off my college student loans.

7. How strong is your self-image?

    A. I am self-esteem!

    B. I strongly believe in my own self-worth and in my ability to create my own opportunities.

    C. I feel fairly secure with myself; just don't push too hard.

    D. I don't know — what do you think?

8. Do you have the support of your significant other/family?

    A. They're all on board, an integral part of my plan, and have been assigned responsibilities.

    B. They're in favor of whatever makes me happy.

    C. I'm pretty sure they'll support me.

    D. I'm going to tell them about it later.

9. If it's a necessary part of your plan, will you be able to start up your home-based business while you remain in your current job?

    A. Sure — in fact, my boss wants in!

    B. If I make a few adjustments in my schedule, I can't see any other reason why I can't.

    C. Would you please repeat the question?

    D. Maybe I'll be able to work on it for a couple of hours a month.

10. What will you tell friends when they ask why you quit that great job?

    A. I'm free at last!

    B. That the benefits clearly outweigh the potential costs.

    C. I don't know; maybe they won't ask.

    D. I'll pretend that I'm still working for my old organization.

Tally up the numbers, and compare your result with the ranges of numbers below. Give yourself 5 points for every A answer, 3 points for every B, –3 for every C, and –5 for every D.

By comparing your total points with the points contained in each of the six following categories, you can find out whether you're ready to jump into your own home-based business:

25 to 50 points: Assuming you were honest with yourself as you answered the preceding questions (you were, weren't you?), you're ready! What are you waiting for? There's no time like the present to take the first step on your journey to success with your own home-based business. Whether you decide to drop your day job or work into your new business gradually, you're ready to give it your all. Read this book from cover to cover for tips on making your endeavor a raging success.

1 to 24 points: You're definitely warming up to the idea of starting your own home-based business. Consider starting your own business in the near future, but make sure to keep your day job until you have your venture well under way. Read this book from cover to cover to get a better idea of how to make a relatively painless and successful transition from your present career to owning a home-based business.

0 points: You could go either way on this one. Why don't you try taking this test again in another month or two? Our advice? Read this book cover to cover before you begin your own home-based business.

–1 to –24 points: Unfortunately, you don't appear to be quite ready to make the move from career to your own home-based business. We strongly recommend that you read this book from cover to cover and then take this test again in a few months. Maybe working for someone else isn't the worst thing that can happen to you.

–25 to –50: Forget it. You were clearly born to work for someone else. Take this book, and sell it to a co-worker.

More than 50 or less than –50 points: Hmm . . . we have a problem. Either you're getting a little rusty in your addition tables, or you hit the wrong key on your calculator. Try again!

Keeping up with the scuttlebutt

Q: I've never regretted starting my own business, but the one thing I do miss is being in the middle of the corporate buzz. How can I can stay connected with what's going on downtown?

A: The first step is to figure out just what you're missing from being in the buzz of corporate life. Being part of the daily routine of an organization provides people with a whole array of experiences. Some, like office politics and dreadfully dull meetings, are a joy to get away from. But others leave a void that you must find ways to refill, such as the following:

✔ **Feeling like you're part of the downtown business community:** Even when you're working from home, it's important to get out of the house and participate in the business world. Join the chamber of commerce, and go to luncheons, after-work mixers, or evening meetings. Get active in various civic and charitable activities in your community. These can lead to valuable business relationships while keeping you up with what's going on in town.

✔ **Getting in on the inside information and latest scuttlebutt in your field:** You can replace this need by becoming active in a local chapter of your professional or trade association or by participating in their online listserv or forum. To find professional and trade associations in your field, do a search on the keyword *association*.

✔ **Establishing the esprit de corps from being part of a group that's working together toward a goal:** If you crave experiences like this, affiliate with others and work on joint projects instead of working strictly solo.

✔ **Finding moral support and positive peer pressure to stay focused — someone to bounce ideas around with, celebrate victories, and commiserate disappointments with:** To fulfill this need, form a group of colleagues with whom you can meet weekly over lunch and call regularly to spur one another on toward your goals.

✔ **Seeking out the expertise of superiors you can turn to for advice, getting honest feedback, or talking over strategies and crucial decisions:** If you're missing this type of interaction, seek out a mentor, form an advisory board for your business, or hire a consultant whose experience you respect. Some professional associations have formal mentor programs that offer this kind of contact. If yours doesn't, suggest that they consider adding such a service — or even volunteer to help organize it.

✔ **Using the Web:** Though it's not a substitute for face-to-face contact, you can use the Web to locate other individuals, networks, and organizations in your own community through, for example, the message board operated by a trade or professional group you belong to.

Are you ready to make the move to starting a home-based business? If the quiz indicates otherwise, don't worry — plenty of opportunities will be out there in the future. When you're ready for them, they'll be ready for you. If you're ready, congratulations! The rest of this book shows you what you need to do to make owning a successful home-based business a reality.

Chapter 2

Mirror, Mirror on the Wall, What's the Best Business of All?

. . . .

In This Chapter

▶ Starting a new business from scratch

▶ Buying an established business

▶ Considering your options

▶ Specializing to find your niche

. . . .

So once you have decided that starting a home-based business is right for you, what's next? Choosing which kind of home-based business to start. Although on the surface that may seem like a fairly easy proposition, for many people it really isn't. There are thousands and thousands of businesses to choose among, each with its own set of pros and cons. And an opportunity that's hot today can be as cold tomorrow as a Minnesota winter.

Before making your decision, research your options thoroughly. And above all, listen to your heart. Be sure that the opportunity is right for you, that it's truly something you will love doing, and that it is going to provide the potential for long-term success. This is your future we're talking about (and, perhaps, the well-being of you and your family or loved ones), and the things you do today to prepare for it will pay off in a big way down the road.

In this chapter, we take a close look at many different home-based business options available to you.

ASK PAUL & SARAH

Top ten home-based business opportunities

The following are Paul and Sarah's picks for the top ten home-based businesses:

- ✔ Bodywork or massage therapy
- ✔ Computer consulting for small and home businesses
- ✔ Elder services
- ✔ Financial advising

- ✔ Interim or contract executive
- ✔ Pet sitting and other services for animals
- ✔ Technical writing
- ✔ Tutoring
- ✔ Virtual assistant
- ✔ Web merchant and auction trader

Starting Something from Scratch

There is a certain amount of pleasure in making something from scratch with your own two hands. It's the same pleasure a sculptor gets from creating a beautiful piece of art or a violinist gets from mastering a difficult piece of music. You may not get it right the first time — after all, it took Thomas Edison thousands of tries before he hit upon the right material for light bulb filaments — but when you do find the right formula for success, the feeling of satisfaction you'll experience will be hard to beat.

Perhaps the quickest and least expensive way of starting your own home-based business is to do so from scratch. No need to fill out a bunch of applications or save up money to buy into a franchise, or take weeks or months to learn some complex, proprietary way of doing business. If you really wanted to, there's no reason you couldn't start your business from scratch — right now.

TRUE STORIES

A number of years ago, Peter's wife, Jan, started a successful medical-billing business out of their home. She built it from scratch. After deciding to start her business, the first thing she did was create a simple flyer on the family computer, print 100 copies, and distribute them throughout the neighborhood. Although her original idea — and indeed, the offer in Jan's flyer — was to do typing and desktop publishing, when her next-door neighbor, a psychologist, suggested that she take on the billing for his thriving practice, a new business was born!

If you decide to start a home business from scratch, you're in good company. Did you know that some of today's largest, most successful companies were started that way? There's no reason in the world that you can't enjoy the same level of success, if that's what you desire. Here are a few notable examples:

- ✔ With $538 in working capital, Bill Hewlett and David Packard started their fledgling company in Packard's garage in Palo Alto, California. Today, Hewlett-Packard is a multinational corporation with sales in excess of $73 billion a year.

- ✔ In 1950, Ewing Marion Kauffman started Marion Laboratories, Inc. (now known as Marion Roussel Hoechst) in his basement with a total investment of $5,000. When the company merged with Merrell Dow in 1989, it was doing more than a billion dollars a year in sales.

- ✔ Jeff Bezos, founder and CEO of Amazon.com, started his business in his rented, two-bedroom house in Bellevue, Washington. To make room for his new home-based business, Bezos converted his garage into a workspace. And to save money — of which he had precious little in those early days — he built three desks out of three wooden doors, some 2×4s, and a handful of metal brackets. The cost? Sixty dollars per desk. Today, Amazon.com rakes in more than $5 billion a year — enough to pay for all the desks that Jeff Bezos would ever want to buy.

Of course, these home-based business success stories are exceptional, but many home-based business owners find exactly the level of success they are seeking — while paying the bills, doing exactly the work they want to do, and serving the customers they want to serve. The real beauty of owning your own home-based business is that it is first and foremost *your* business. When you start a business from scratch, you write the rules, and you decide what's important. You might grow your business into the next Apple Computer (a former home-based business, started in the garage of cofounder Steve Jobs's parents' house), or you can simply enjoy a bit of extra income to supplement your earnings from a full-time career or other sources.

Here are a few examples of people who have found exactly the level of success they wanted by starting their own home-based businesses:

- ✔ Dan Dorotik of Lubbock, Texas, started his own successful business — Career Documents, a résumé-writing service — when he left his job to move to a different city with his fiancée and found himself out of work. Says Dan, "When I saw the money coming in, I realized that if you're really good at something — and if you're smart at the business and marketing side of it while maintaining the quality of the work — you can make a very good living for yourself."

- ✔ Tim and Wendy Eidson dreamed about moving out of the big city and enjoying a simpler, more relaxing small-town lifestyle. But instead of just dreaming, they got to work; left their secure, lucrative jobs behind; and started selling hot sauce out of their garage in San Luis Obispo, California. Tim and Wendy created the popular mail-order hot-sauce business, Mo Hotta-Mo Betta.

> ✔ In high school and pregnant, Alexis knew that she would have to find some way to support herself and her child. She started her El Cajon, California-based business — Demko Demolition Warehouse, which specializes in recycling and selling items such as light fixtures and cabinets salvaged from building demolition projects — on a shoestring. She has done so well with her business that she was named entrepreneur of the month by *CosmoGIRL!* magazine.

When starting a business from scratch, you can use one of two main approaches: Choose to do the same kind of work you have been doing in your regular job or career, or choose to do something totally different. In the following sections, we take a closer look at each approach and the advantages that each offers you.

Doing what you have been doing in a job

As you consider the different options available to you in starting your own business, one of your first thoughts will undoubtedly be to do what you've already been doing in a job.

And why not? You know the job, you're already experienced in it, and you know exactly what to expect. You also know what your customers want and how to give it to them. You may even have a network of potential customers waiting to sign up for your products and services. Doing what you've been doing has the following advantages:

> ✔ You can start up your business more quickly (like right *now*!) and more easily than if you choose to do something you've never done before.

> ✔ There is little or no learning curve, and there's no need for time-consuming and expensive training courses or workshops.

Ten more home-based business opportunities

Entrepreneur magazine (www.entrepreneurmag.com) keeps track of the ten best ideas for new businesses (all of which, coincidentally, can be home based). Here's its most recent list:

✔ Consulting service

✔ Financial planning

✔ Patriotic products

✔ Referral service

✔ Personal trainer

✔ Tech consulting

✔ Online games

✔ Maternity clothes

✔ Online learning

✔ Life coach

Why women want to start their own businesses

There are a variety of reasons why people want to start their own businesses; one of the most compelling is when regular 9-to-5 jobs and careers don't provide workers with the things that they expect and want. A recent survey of women by Roper-Starch (reported in *USA Today*) found that

✔ 33 percent want equal pay.

✔ 20 percent want more affordable health care.

✔ 15 percent want more flexibility at work.

✔ 11 percent want more equal chores between spouses.

✔ 8 percent want more affordable day care.

✔ 8 percent want a four-day work week.

Many women — and men — have found that by starting their own businesses, they become the boss, and they get to decide how their businesses will be run. And isn't that, ultimately, what we all dream about?

✔ You'll be much more efficient and effective because you've already discovered the best ways to do your job, along with time-saving tricks of the trade.

✔ You can capitalize on your good reputation, which may be your most important asset.

✔ You can tap into your network of business contacts, clients, and customers (when ethically appropriate) and generate business more quickly than doing something new and different.

For many people, doing something they've been doing is the best choice. Because it is often the quickest and least expensive avenue for starting your own home-based business, be sure to take a close look at this option before you consider any others.

Doing something new and different

Although doing what you've been doing in a job offers many advantages, doing something new and different has its own set of advantages. If you're burned out on your current job, and you dream of making radical changes in your career or lifestyle — for example, trading your high-pressure career as an attorney for a much more relaxing home-based massage business — doing something new and different may well be exactly what the doctor ordered.

The following are some key advantages to doing something new and different:

✔ Getting a fresh start in your career can be an extremely energizing experience with positive repercussions for every aspect of your life, opening up exciting new possibilities and opportunities for you along the way.

✔ Tapping into new career options allows you to find work that may not have even existed when you first started your career — for example, designing Web sites or computer-network consulting.

Many successful home-based business owners have created businesses that have nothing to do whatsoever with what they had been doing as a full-time job. If you're sufficiently motivated, nothing can stand between you and success, no matter which business you choose. If you're looking to shake up the status quo or to make a break from the past, this may well be the best option for you.

Buying a Business

For many people, buying a ready-made home-based business is the way to go. Instead of learning how to run a business the hard way — through trial and error — when you buy a business, you buy a proven product, system, and support organization. Of course, you have to pay for these benefits, but the investment — if you choose wisely — can easily be eclipsed by the financial rewards of your new business.

As you consider different home-based business opportunities, keep the following in mind:

✔ **Be sure there's a fit between you and the business.** Some franchises and network marketing opportunities require that you adhere to strict rules and procedures, including the clothes you wear and the way that you present yourself and your business. If you're not comfortable with these kinds of restrictions, avoid such businesses.

✔ **Be sure a market exists for the product or service you plan to offer.** Talk to others who have bought the business you're interested in, and ask for their honest and candid feedback on the attractiveness of the opportunity. And don't just rely on a list of happy people provided by the company — do some research, and find people who may be more willing to tell you the real story.

✔ **Be sure the company you select is credible and viable.** This may very well be the most important thing to consider. Upward of 90 percent of businesses that offer franchises, direct selling, and business opportunities (all described in the following sections) go bust within five years, leaving their owners high and dry (and sometimes bankrupt and out of work). Be sure that any company you're considering has been in business for five years or more.

Four options for finding a new opportunity

Many paths lead to finding the home business that's right for you. Over the past two decades, Paul and Sarah have interviewed thousands of self-employed individuals to discover exactly how they found the path that ultimately led them to their chosen destination. As a result of these interviews, Paul and Sarah found that the roots for new businesses come from four sources: talent, mission, passion, or assets. Successful home-based business owners invariably tap into one or more of these.

- **Talent:** Each person has one or more innate talents or skills at which he or she excels. When you're able to tap into this talent or gift, and others value it and are willing to pay for it, developing a business around it can be rewarding, both financially and emotionally. About one in six home-based business owners become successful by taking advantage of their special talents or skills.

- **Mission:** Those who follow a higher purpose — to make a positive difference in the people and the world around them — are following a mission. Although fewer than one in six people take this route in creating their home-based businesses, for those who do, the personal rewards of seeing the impact of their work on others can be profound.

- **Passion:** For some home-based business owners, the passion they feel to be their own bosses or to pursue the work that they truly love is so strong that it creates success in and of itself. For the person with a fire in his belly, no obstacle stands between him and the successful achievement of his goals. About one in four home-based business owners have chosen this path to success.

- **Assets:** Everyone brings assets when starting a home-based business. In some cases, these assets may take the form of previous work experiences; in other cases, they may take the form of a network of friends or business contacts. While almost one of every two people who start a home-based business tap into their assets to do so — making it the most popular route by far — these businesses typically don't fare as well as those based on talent, mission, or passion. Why? Assets by themselves don't create excitement, intensity of purpose, or motivation, and absent these kinds of emotions, the business owners don't feel much drive to succeed.

Clearly, your business has a much greater chance of success if it is built on a foundation of talent, mission, or passion. Although asset-based businesses can also succeed, the chances are less that they will.

As you review potential business opportunities, be aware of your own talents, mission, or passion, and keep them foremost in your mind, because your success will be directly proportional to the motivation that you bring to your work.

The major categories of home-based businesses that you can buy are franchises, direct-selling opportunities, and business opportunities, covered in the three following sections.

Ten different ways to do what you love

Can you honestly say that you love your job? If not, have you ever thought about what you would do for a living if you had the opportunity? Guess what? You do have the opportunity to do what you love! Millions of home-based business owners are doing just that and creating incredible success for themselves in this process. Here are ten ways that you can do what you love:

✔ Provide a service to others who do what you love.

✔ Focus on doing just the things you love.

✔ Teach others to do what you love.

✔ Write about what you love.

✔ Speak about what you love.

✔ Create a product related to what you love.

✔ Sell or broker what you love.

✔ Promote what you love.

✔ Organize what you love.

✔ Set up, repair, restore, fix, or maintain what you love.

Home-based franchises

If you've ever eaten at a McDonald's restaurant, you know what a franchise is. No matter which McDonald's restaurant you visit, whether it's in Iowa, England, or Hong Kong, you can be fairly certain that your cheeseburger and French fries are going to look, feel, and taste the same. In a world attracted to corporate icons such as the golden arches, franchising has taken the world of business by storm. According to a report published by the International Franchise Association (www.franchise.org), franchises employ more than 9 million people and produce more than $600 billion of economic output a year, just within the United States.

Although popular franchises such as Subway, Curves, Quiznos, and Burger King are easy to think of, if we asked you to identify a popular home-based franchise, you would probably have a harder time. Although many home-based franchises are out there, you may not be aware that franchises are available in an incredible array of sizes, shapes, and styles. From cleaning services to babysitting to photography studios, a home-based franchising opportunity to fit most anyone's needs is out there.

What's a franchise?

A *franchise* is an agreement in which one business grants another business the right to distribute its products or services. Typically, the company that grants the franchise has developed a successful and proven business model that is easily replicated by others. According to franchising expert Gregory Matusky, three elements define a franchise company:

- Use of a trademark or a trade name
- Payment of fees or royalties
- Significant assistance provided by the franchisor

As the old saying goes, "It takes two to tango." Similarly, every franchise agreement involves two key parties:

- **Franchisor:** The company that owns the franchise trademarks, trade secrets, and successful business model.
- **Franchisee:** The individual or other entity who pays the franchisor for use of trademarks, trade secrets, and successful business model.

Of course, all the trademarks, successful business models, and assistance come at a price. Fees are paid by the franchisee to the franchisor in the form of one or more of the following:

- A one-time payment
- An ongoing flat-fee payment
- Ongoing sliding-scale payments
- Ongoing royalties
- Advertising fees

The fees paid by the franchisee to the franchisor vary considerably from opportunity to opportunity. For example, the initial fee to buy into a McDonald's franchise is around $45,000. However, actual startup costs (leases, building, equipment, labor, supplies) for a location run from $400,000 to more than $1 million. On top of that, franchisees are required to pay a royalty rate of 12.5 percent or more on every dollar that they bring in. Despite all these fees, McDonald's franchises — though certainly unsuitable for a home-based business — are considered to be among the most desirable of all.

On the other hand, Jani-King, a popular home-based business franchise that specializes in commercial cleaning services, has an up-front franchise fee of between $8,600 and $16,300, startup costs of $3,000 to $18,000, and an ongoing royalty rate of 10 percent. This is a substantially more affordable investment than the bricks-and-mortar opportunity presented by a McDonald's franchise, *and* you can run the business out of your own home. Of course, each has its pluses and minuses — you have to decide which is best for you.

For an extensive listing of franchising opportunities, both home based and not, check out *Entrepreneur* magazine's franchise 500 list on its Web site at www.entrepreneurmag.com. If you're the slightest bit interested in buying a franchise, chances are you'll find this list to be interesting reading!

Legal issues in franchising

As with many areas of business, franchising is chock-full of laws and regulations. In addition to the usual bevy of federal laws, many states have their own stringent rules and regulations that supercede federal laws. Keep in mind that most franchising laws and regulations actually protect the franchisor, not the franchisee!

✔ **The uniform franchise offering circular:** In states that don't have their own specific franchising laws, the Federal Trade Commission (FTC) has established a comprehensive code of regulations that are often referred to as the *franchise rule*. As a part of the franchise rule, franchisors are required to provide prospective franchisees with a detailed disclosure statement, called the *uniform franchise offering circular* (UFOC).

Before you think about buying a franchise, be sure you get a copy of the company's UFOC and study it carefully. It contains valuable information that can have a dramatic impact on your decision not to buy into a particular franchise opportunity. If you have any questions, ask the franchisor for clarification.

A UFOC contains the following valuable information:

- The franchisor's name

- A complete and accurate description of the business

- A listing of people affiliated with the franchisor

- Background information on the franchisor and principals in the company, including business experience and track record

- The franchisor's financial information

- Detailed information on the number of franchises, their failure rate, and their termination rate. (Failure is a matter of closing a company's doors, usually for financial reasons. Some franchise operators prevent this from happening by reacquiring the franchise from the franchise holder. The franchise is therefore terminated but technically not a failure. This helps keep those statistics about success in franchising looking good.)

- Bankruptcy and litigation histories of the franchisor and principal officers

- The franchise fee

- Ongoing fees, royalties, and other payments to be paid to the franchisor

- An itemized list of goods and services that must be purchased, rented, or leased directly from the franchisor

- Terms of franchisor-provided financing (if applicable)

- Restrictions on how you are to operate the business

- Training programs available to the franchisee

- Information on the renewal, cancellation, and termination of the franchise

For further information on franchising laws and regulations, consult your state attorney general's office, or contact the Federal Trade Commission at www.ftc.gov.

✔ **The elements of a franchising agreement:** Franchises depend on *franchise agreements* — contracts setting forth the rights and the obligations of the franchisor and the franchisee — to define the legal relationship among all involved parties. A franchise agreement is negotiable. Be sure to read and understand it thoroughly before you sign. Even better, have a competent lawyer who specializes in franchise law take a look at it. Believe us: A few hundred bucks invested in a legal review up front may save you many thousands of dollars (and countless headaches) down the road.

Here are the most common elements of a franchising agreement:

- **Grant of franchise:** Defines the nature of the franchising agreement.

- **Use of trademark(s), patents, and copyrights:** Spells out exactly how you can use the franchisor's trademarks, patents, and copyrights.

- **Defining the parties:** Lists the parties to the agreement and sets forth the independent relationship between the parties.

- **Payments:** Spells out the franchise fee and any other required royalties or payments.

- **Term of agreement:** Enumerates the length of time that the agreement will be in effect. About half of all franchise agreements run for ten years, while a large percentage have five-year agreements.

- **Renewal of franchise agreement:** Details the mechanism for renewing the agreement.

- **Developing and opening:** Details the length of time that you have to open your business after signing the agreement, usually 90 to 120 days.

- **Territory:** Spells out any restrictions on the areas in which you may operate. Generally, the larger the territory, the larger the franchise fee payable.

- **Advertising:** Sets forth requirements for using the franchisor's logos, advertising designs, trademarks, and so on in advertising.

- **Equipment and supplies:** Spells out what supplies and services must be purchased directly from the franchisor.

- **Franchisor-provided training and assistance:** Details training offered by the franchisor, as well as any ongoing support and assistance.

- **Assignment of franchise:** Describes any special rules for transferring ownership to another person or entity, should the franchisee decide to sell the business.

- **Termination of franchise agreement:** Sets forth the legal requirements for terminating the agreement.

Be absolutely sure that you understand every part of your franchising agreement — and agree with its terms and conditions — before you sign it. We don't mean that you should just read it over and be generally familiar with the opportunity; we mean understand *exactly* what every sentence means and how it will impact the way that you do business, as well as your rights and obligations now and in the future. You have your greatest leverage as you're considering a variety of franchising opportunities — but not after you've signed your agreement.

Franchising pros and cons

Buying a franchise brings potential positives and negatives. When deciding whether buying a franchise is the best way to start your own home-based business, weigh these pros and cons, and discover the best path for you. Here are some of the elements that franchises often have in their favor:

- Buying into a franchise that has a proven track record and ongoing training and support can translate into a quick startup phase and almost immediate cash flow. And don't forget: Happiness is a positive cash flow.

- Established, successful franchises are proven systems that are almost guaranteed to meet your financial expectations. As long as you play the game by the franchisor's rules, it's hard to lose.

- Many people who start up a home-based business have never actually owned or run a business before. A good franchisor provides extensive training in how to operate and market the business.

- You have access to a network of other franchisors who are in a business just like yours. Many franchisors sponsor special Web sites, conferences, or conventions that get franchisees together to talk shop and share their experiences.

- Many franchisors provide opportunities for regional and national cooperative advertising — saving you money while giving your business more exposure than you would probably get on your own.

Of course, you want to think about the downsides to buying a franchise. Before you sign on the dotted line of that franchise agreement, be sure that you can tolerate these potential negatives:

- ✔ You're required to follow someone else's system and procedures. For some prospective owners of home-based businesses, the whole point of starting a business is to get away from following someone else's rules.

- ✔ You work without a great deal of supervision and direction. No one's going to get on the phone to wake you up if you're late to work; no one's going to constantly urge you to work harder or sell more. If you're not a self-starter, or if you lack the confidence to sell yourself and your products or services, this could be a very real problem, and it could jeopardize your prospects for success.

- ✔ You may be required to pay an ongoing fee or royalty to the franchisor for the life of your business. Of course, if you're making lots of money, this likely won't be a problem. But if your business is marginal, franchise fees and royalties can quickly become an anchor that drags you and your business down with it.

- ✔ Ultimately, the franchisor is still the boss. You have to follow the franchise's policies and procedures whether you agree with them or not. If you don't, you may be in violation of your franchise agreement — potentially resulting in nasty lawsuits, loss of income, and the termination of your business.

- ✔ There are no guarantees. Your business may or may not be a success, despite all your hard work, all the money you invest, and all the time you devote to it. Any business is a risk, and a home-based business that you own makes that risk a very personal one.

- ✔ The franchise agreement may not protect you against competition from other distributors, particularly those using the Internet. Long story short, you may make less money than you thought or were led to believe.

What kind of people do best with franchises? Research indicates that a number of personality traits come into play, including a person's influence with others, his willingness to comply with company rules, and his ability to think on his own two feet. To take a detailed test to see if your personality traits match those of the people who have been most successful in franchises, check out Paul and Sarah's book *Home Businesses You Can Buy*.

If you decide that franchising is something you would like to explore further, thoroughly research all the possible opportunities to find the one that is the best fit for you. After you identify an opportunity that you wish to pursue, talk to current owners of the franchise, and get their candid opinions of the opportunity — both the good and the bad. And be sure to see what kinds of information you can find about your prospective franchise on the Internet. Disgruntled franchisees are often not very shy about telling others about their bad experiences, and some post their stories on a variety of Web sites. Some even set up their own Web sites specifically to warn others. Just be sure that you take such stories with a grain of salt until you can verify that they are indeed true.

Buying and operating a franchise will likely require a lot of money and a lot of your time and effort over a long period of time. It's in your best interest to be absolutely sure — before you sign the franchise agreement — that it's the best one for you.

Direct-selling opportunities

Direct selling means selling a consumer product or service in a face-to-face manner away from a fixed retail location. According to the Direct Selling Association (www.dsa.org), this kind of business has taken the world by storm. In a recent year, 13 million people sold more than $28 billion worth of products through direct-selling opportunities. The kinds of products sold included home and family care products, such as cleaning supplies, cookware, and cutlery; personal care products, such as cosmetics, jewelry, and skin care products; wellness products, including weight-loss products and vitamins; and leisure and educational products, such as encyclopedias, toys, and games.

And the companies that offer direct-selling opportunities are household names: Nu Skin, Discovery Toys, Amway, The Fuller Brush Company, Tupperware, Nikken, Primerica, and many others.

There are two main types of direct-selling opportunities:

- ✔ **Single-level marketing:** Single-level marketers make money by buying products from the parent company and selling them directly to their customers.

- ✔ **Multi-level marketing:** Multi-level marketers make money both by buying products from the parent company and selling them to customers and by sponsoring new direct sellers.

What is single-level marketing?

Single-level marketing is simple: A direct seller buys products from a parent organization and sells them directly to his or her customers. Home-based businesspeople have been pursuing single-level marketing for years, and you'll probably recognize the names of some of the most successful organizations:

- ✔ Avon
- ✔ Electrolux
- ✔ Tupperware
- ✔ Kirby

While much of the media spotlight that shines so brightly on the direct-selling industry tends to focus on multi-level marketing organizations, single-level selling produces about 20 percent of direct-selling revenues, or just under $6 billion in a recent year.

What is multi-level marketing?

From its humble beginnings in California in 1945, when Lee Mytinger and William Casselberry formed California Vitamins to sell their vitamin supplement (called Nutrilite), *multi-level marketing* (MLM) — also known as *network marketing* or *person-to-person marketing* — has grown to an incredible $22 billion in sales a year in the United States alone, employing more than 10 million people.

What makes multi-level marketing special is its unique system of selling, in which salespeople take on two key roles:

✔ **Distributor:** As a distributor of a product, your job is to buy product from the parent company and sell it directly to the public — usually to friends, relatives, and work associates. Every time you sell an item, you make a profit.

✔ **Recruiter:** As a recruiter, you sign up other distributors to work for you. Every time your distributor buys an item from the parent company, you receive a percentage of the profit.

Multi-level marketing gives you two ways to make money — by selling products as a distributor and by signing up new distributors and taking a portion of their product sales. As you sign up new distributors, you create what's known as a *downline:* all of the people you sponsor into the program, as well as the people they sponsor, and so on. In multi-level marketing, an *upline* is a distributor's sponsor, as well as the other sponsors above him or her in the organization.

The most highly successful multi-level marketers make far more money through their downlines than they do actually selling product themselves. Because of this, many multi-level marketers focus most of their efforts on recruiting new distributors to join their downline and motivating the individuals in their downline to recruit new distributors.

Warning! It is against U.S. law for a multi-level marketing organization to only recruit distributors — and collect fees from them — without also selling products. Such an arrangement is called a *pyramid scheme,* and it is set up specifically to make its creators rich while relieving everyone else of their hard-earned money. Be particularly careful about so-called opportunities where you sell something that has little or no intrinsic value, such as a "special" report on how to make money on the Internet. Such thinly veiled pyramid schemes will land you in very hot water if you are caught.

ASK PAUL & SARAH

Finding a home-based business that's compatible with a military career

Q: I am currently an active Navy member looking for a business to take me out of the Navy. I need something with low startup costs and overhead — a business that could start as a part-time venture and bloom into something full time. I have been searching for a while. Please give me any suggestions.

A: Many full-time businesses can be started from home, on the side. In fact, that's the preferable way to start out on your own. You can test the viability of your idea and go through the learning curve while you still have income coming in. The best sideline businesses don't require a lot of marketing or administrative tasks, leaving you free to devote your limited time to income-producing work. So you want to choose a service or product that's in high demand and easy to sell. Also, your business will need to have flexible hours so you can run the business after or around your current working hours.

Whatever business you choose needs to be something you truly enjoy doing, something you know enough about to do well (or are willing to invest time learning while you still have a job), and something for which you can identify a specific market that you can easily reach.

Often, the best solutions are quite unique to the business owner.

✔ A woman who wanted to be at home with her children had an inspiration: Because her husband collects bow ties, she decided to become a Web merchant selling handmade bow ties through the Internet.

✔ An aerospace engineer had been an avid amateur photographer for years before starting a sideline photography business. By the time his job was downsized, he already had a growing clientele.

These businesses certainly won't work for everyone, but each was an ideal match for its owner. Look closely at your interests, skills, and assets, and think of how you could use them to meet the needs of specific individuals or companies who would gladly pay for your help. Pay attention, also, to some factors that are particular to starting a business while on active duty. If you live in military housing, you need to get permission to use your home for your business from your local command, although this is usually granted.

Also be sure you're clear on the ethical limits of doing business with other members of the military. Many military personnel go into business with their spouses so that their businesses get developed without conflicting with their military duties. Keep in mind that soliciting to other members of the military of a junior ranking is a no-no. This includes their spouses and dependents. Primarily, then, you may be building in the nonmilitary population. After you're consistently earning enough income from a part-time business to cover your bare-minimum living and business expenses, you're ready to make the jump to full time. Be sure to check out Chapter 5, though, for several steps to take before turning in your resignation.

The pros and cons of direct selling

According to the enthusiastic sales pitches of recruiters for many direct-selling opportunities, signing up to sell their products will put you squarely on the road to riches. Although that may very well turn out to be the case (every direct-selling opportunity has its successes, often people who got into the business early and established a large downline), it also may not be. Of course, no kind of business can guarantee profits — direct selling included.

Direct-selling opportunities are geared to the home-based businessperson, and the right opportunity may be just what you're looking for. Here are some of the positive attributes of direct selling:

- ✔ Because startup costs are generally low, you have little financial risk if the business fails — certainly lower than most franchises and business opportunities. (Beware of direct-selling opportunities with high startup costs — these are often scams!)

- ✔ High earning potential is possible (although relatively few people actually make six-figure incomes). Mary Kay, Inc. really does give out pink Cadillacs to its top salespeople. If you're the right person in the right place at the right time, the sky really is the limit.

- ✔ Most direct-selling programs are designed specifically to be home-based businesses and are often geared to women (66 percent of U.S. direct sales distributorships are one-person distributorships, owned by a woman).

- ✔ Your direct-selling parent company generally provides you with sales and promotional materials, as well as bookkeeping, sales tracking, and commission data.

- ✔ You can work as many or as few hours as you like. Part time, full time — all kinds of work arrangements abound in direct selling. In fact, the clear majority of people who have chosen direct-selling opportunities work part time, some while working other, full-time jobs.

Because of the need of those in multi-level marketing to continuously recruit a downline of new distributors — to replace those who fall by the wayside, as well as to grow their own organizations — competition for recruits can be quite lively. This tends to put a lot of pressure on those being recruited. Aside from these kinds of minor indignities, you may experience a number of negatives with direct selling. Here are a few:

- ✔ Many direct-selling businesses are here today, gone tomorrow. While a number of companies have been around for years and will likely be around for years to come (including such companies as Amway and Mary Kay), far too many direct-selling firms have lifespans that can be measured in months.

✔ Direct selling has a poor reputation with many people, often making recruiting new distributors (and selling products) a difficult proposition.

✔ Motivating your downline to sell more products and sign up new distributors can require more of your time and attention than you may imagine. And the more distributors you sign up, the bigger the job.

✔ Few people in direct selling make enough money to make it a full-time profession. According to industry figures, about 90 percent of the individuals working in direct sales do so on a part-time basis. Of this number, about half make $500 or less a year; the other half makes *up to* $5,000 per year in direct sales. It is indeed the rare direct salesperson who makes enough money in her own business to support herself and a family.

✔ Friends, relatives, and coworkers may quickly tire of your constant attempts to sell them products or recruit them into your downline. If they cross the street or duck behind a tree when they see you coming, you're pushing too hard.

Business opportunities

If the ready-made company you're thinking of buying into isn't a franchise and isn't direct selling, chances are it's a business opportunity. Although franchises and direct-selling opportunities have well-defined, unique structures, business opportunities come in all flavors, shapes, and sizes. In general, however, a *business opportunity* can be defined like this:

> *An idea, product, system, or service that someone has developed and offers to sell to others to help them start their own, similar businesses.*

Business opportunities can take most any form, but they all fall into one or more of the following eight categories:

✔ **Broker:** A broker is someone who buys or sells products or services for a parent company, often acting as an agent. Common examples include real estate and insurance brokers. Although brokers are independent contractors, they are generally paid commissions by the parent company for their efforts.

✔ **Dealer:** Dealers represent lines of products, which are purchased from a parent company and sold directly to consumers. An example of this is someone who sells windows or wooden doors that are produced by several different companies to local home builders and uses his or her home as a base of operations.

✔ **Distributor:** Distributors buy products from wholesalers (and sometimes from manufacturers) and resell them to direct-sales organizations, brokers, and dealers. Distributors generally don't sell directly to consumers or end users.

Is that direct-selling opportunity real or not?

As with any other business that you may be considering, check it out before making a commitment. Unfortunately, direct selling has a bit of a reputation as being fraught with less-than-reputable opportunities and — in some cases — outright fraud. The Direct Selling Association (DSA) at www.dsa.org offers the following advice for checking out any direct-selling opportunity before you buy into it:

✔ **Identify a company and product that appeal to you.** Check the DSA list of member companies, or look in your local phone book.

✔ **Take your time deciding.** Does "getting in on the ground floor" mean that everyone joining after you will be less satisfied or happy? A legitimate opportunity won't disappear overnight. Think long-term.

✔ **Ask questions.** Ask about the company, its leadership, products or services, startup fees, realistic costs of doing business, average earnings of distributors, return policies, and anything else you're concerned about. Get a copy of all company literature. And read it!

✔ **Consult others who have had experiences with the company and its products.** Check to see if the products or services are actually being sold to consumers.

✔ **Investigate and verify all information.** Don't assume that official-looking documents are accurate or complete or even produced by the company, as opposed to the person trying to recruit you.

✔ **Need help evaluating a company?** Check the list of Direct Selling Association members at www.dsa.org, or call your Better Business Bureau, state attorney general, or consumer-protection offices.

✔ **Licensee:** Licensees buy the right to sell, market, produce, or use established product brand names, technologies, or systems. A bit like a franchise, licensees have much greater freedom to run their businesses as they see fit.

✔ **Mail-order business:** Mail-order businesses take orders for products (and, in rare cases, services) over the phone, or via e-mail or the Internet, and send those products to end users. In some cases, mail-order businesses can have products shipped directly (sometimes called *drop shipped*) from their manufacturers, removing the need to maintain a product inventory and dramatically improving cash flow.

✔ **Vendor:** Vendors sell materials and supplies to other companies for their own consumption (for example, office supplies), for use in their own production processes (for example, titanium ingots), or for resale to consumers or other companies.

✔ **Manufacturer:** Manufacturers build and produce products that are eventually sold to consumers. Manufacturers can sell directly to consumers in a variety of ways (direct sales, mail order, or the Internet) or to brokers, dealers, wholesalers, and others.

✔ **Wholesaler:** Wholesalers buy products directly from manufacturers, mark up the price, and sell them to retailers — the people who deal directly with the end consumer. In most cases, wholesalers don't sell directly to the public.

Although some of these categories overlap to some degree, each represents a unique facet of the total universe of business opportunities available to you. As you can imagine, the kind of business opportunity that you select has a significant influence on how you do business, whom you sell to, and the way you market your products and service your customers.

For many people, business opportunities are exactly the right choice for a home-based business. Is a business opportunity the right choice for you? Take a look at the pros and cons of business opportunities, and decide for yourself. The following are some of the things that make business opportunities attractive propositions:

✔ Business opportunities are not as strictly managed by parent companies as are franchises or network marketing businesses. This provides the owner with substantial independence and freedom to run the business as he or she sees fit.

✔ Many business opportunities offer good, steady income. The upside may not be as dazzling as some network marketing opportunities, but the chances of your succeeding on a full-time basis are much greater.

✔ Many business opportunities are suitable as home-based businesses.

✔ Startup costs are generally far less than most franchising opportunities.

✔ You can work whatever hours as you like. Part time, full time — all kinds of work arrangements abound in business opportunities. Many pursue a home-based business opportunity with a full-time job.

Of course, business opportunities also have their potential problems. Here are some things to consider before you sign on the dotted line:

✔ The independence of most business opportunities can be a disadvantage if you don't already have some experience in sales or running your own business. Few business opportunities provide the level of support that good franchises or direct-selling opportunities do.

✔ There's little regulation of business opportunities by the federal government, and state and local regulations vary. Beware of scams! There are plenty. If it sounds too good to be true (getting rich stuffing envelopes, clicking Web sites), it probably is.

✔ Most owners of legitimate business opportunities work far harder than they ever did in a regular 9-to-5 job. Chances are, you will, too.

✔ There is always a possibility that your business will fail. Be sure to have the financial resources available (in other words, sufficient savings in the bank) to weather a serious business setback or misfortune.

As in any other business, thoroughly explore all your options before you invest your hard-earned money in a particular business opportunity. Most business opportunities require little in the way of an up-front payment — so even if things don't work out how you planned, you can change course and give a different one a try. For more on different kinds of home-based businesses, many of which may be right for you, pick up Paul and Sarah's book *Home Businesses You Can Buy* (co-authored by Walter Zooi).

Identifying Which Option Is Best for You

Between creating your own business from scratch and buying a business, you can find an amazing array of options and opportunities. In fact, all your choices may be a little overwhelming. How can you decide which option is the best one for you and be sure you don't make the wrong choice?

Although you can never be 100 percent sure how a particular path will turn out until you embark upon it, use the following indicators to help you gain a better sense of which option will be the best one for you to pursue:

- **Desire to sell:** Some people naturally love to sell. Do you? Most direct-sales and business opportunities require a lot of selling — no sale, no income. Does the opportunity you're considering (and the style of selling you have to adopt to be successful) fit with your natural selling ability and desire? If not, this option may not be the best one for you.

- **Ideas you already have:** You may already have some idea of the business you want to start and how to run it. You have more freedom to pursue your own unique ideas if you start it from scratch or if you pursue a business opportunity. Franchises and direct selling generally require that you closely follow the parent company's established system.

- **How independent you are:** Do you relish the idea of being your own boss and calling your own shots, or would you rather have the comfort that comes from following someone else's direction? Either approach is fine, so long as it matches your own personality. When you start a business from scratch or buy into a business opportunity, you're pretty much on your own and really are your own boss. Most franchises require that you follow strict policies and procedures, and take direction from the parent company. Direct-selling organizations are usually somewhere in between. You won't find a right or wrong answer here — you have to assess which situation you're most comfortable with.

- **How much money you want to make:** Do you just want a little extra money for a rainy day, perhaps on a part-time basis? Or do you want to make enough money to pursue your business full time? Your answers point you toward certain businesses and away from others (for example, about half of the people in direct-selling opportunities such as Avon or Mary Kay Cosmetics make $500 or less a year).

✔ **How unique you want to be:** Do you want to stand out from the crowd, or would you be happier blending into a well-established corporate identity? Starting a business from scratch allows you to be as unique as you want to be. Franchises, direct-selling opportunities, and business opportunities allow you to closely affiliate with an established corporate identity. This is a source of pride for some but stifling for others.

✔ **How much control you want:** Different work options have dramatically different levels of control. A business you start from scratch may put you in full control, and buying a franchise may mean little control over how the business is marketed and run. Be sure you're aware of the level of control you want and that the business you choose provides it.

✔ **Your long-range goals:** Is your goal to make lots of money? Meet interesting people? Work as little as you possibly can? Retire early? Whatever your long-range goals, be sure that the opportunity you select is compatible with and helps you achieve them. Check with other people who have invested in your prospective opportunity, and see where they are in their lives. Were they able to leave their careers behind? Are they now independent and able to have that little cabin on the lake that they always dreamed of? Were they able to retire early? What is the reality behind the sizzling sales pitch for your particular opportunity?

Finding Your Niche by Specializing

People need to know what business you're in — there shouldn't be any question in their minds or yours. If you try to be everything to everybody, you end up pleasing precious few customers. The best way to avoid this is to find a business niche and specialize in it. An expert is worth a lot more to clients than someone without experience. Would you rather have your silk shirt cleaned by someone who has years of experience working with silk or by the local laundromat? Chances are you would be willing to pay more for someone who specializes in cleaning your delicate (and expensive) silk shirt.

It's the same way in any business. People want to work with people who know what they're doing. Be one in a million, not one of a million.

The specialist pyramid, shown in Figure 2-1, shows the relationship between expertise and the amount of money you can command. As your expertise increases, you make more money and make yourself easier to market.

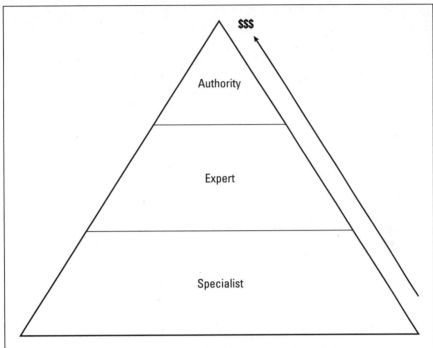

Figure 2-1:
The
specialist
pyramid.

There are eight ways to find your niche by specializing:

1. **Assess and outline your current expertise.**

2. **Identify your strengths and weaknesses.**

3. **Build on your strengths, and fill in the gaps in your experience.**

4. **Articulate a point of view (in writing) for how you work.**

5. **Collect evidence to support your point of view.**

6. **Review and begin documenting your experience.**

7. **Identify the patterns suggested by your experience.**

8. **Explain (in writing, to yourself) what you've discovered.**

Chapter 3

Hot Opportunities Now and for the Future

. . . .

In This Chapter

▶ Understanding demographic trends

▶ Considering the impact of globalization

▶ Looking into the future of security and health care services

. . . .

*O*ver the years Paul and Sarah have found that when it comes to hot new businesses, what's hot today is cold tomorrow. So in selecting businesses to profile for their *Best Home Businesses* books, the most recent of which is *The Best Home Businesses for People 50+,* they rely on scouting long-range trends. That's what we'll do in this chapter. We will look down the decade and relate both what's warm now and growing hot, as well as what we think may become hot. Our journey is organized around ten trends.

1. The Maturing Population

Because two of your three authors are in the 50+ age group, we prefer calling the burgeoning number of people reaching 50+ the *maturing* rather than *aging* population. But whatever you call it, the population of the industrialized world is getting older. In the United States, by the year 2020, one in every six people will be over age 65, and nearly seven million people will be over 85 years old. The number of Canadians aged 65 and over is predicted to grow to 6.9 million by 2021.

An older population means potential customers for many businesses that can be run from home. Bodywork and massage therapy, for example, will grow along with other, newer services designed to meet the needs of an older population, such as daily money management and senior relocation services. Let's examine some specific needs of this population and the kinds of home businesses they will foster.

Daily needs

- **Daily money management.** Although older adults are able to live independently longer, many need assistance with tasks such as making bank deposits; paying bills; balancing checkbooks; reconciling bank, credit card, and charge account statements; organizing taxes and other paperwork; and filing medical claims. This business has grown from the fact that adult children often no longer live in the same community as their parents, and even when some do, they're too busy to help manage their parents' day-to-day financial affairs. Resource: American Association of Daily Money Managers, Inc., (301) 593-5462, www.aadmm.com.

- **In-home care.** Many seniors need help with the *activities of daily living* (ADLs), such as cleaning, cooking, driving to medical appointments, grooming, laundry, medication reminders, organizing closets, and running errands such as picking up prescriptions and especially shopping. In-home, nonmedical caregivers provide these services, as well as much-needed companionship. House cleaning is especially important, because many seniors lose their visual acuity and simply can't see dirt in kitchens and bathrooms that would appall them if they could. These services enable elders to continue to live in their own homes, avoiding placement in nursing homes. Also, because of the growing size of the senior market, research and development is creating new products and medical technology that should enable more elders to live at home with the assistance of people who lend a helping hand and in the process help control health care costs. Training as a nurse's aid is helpful for this work. Resource: National Alliance for Caregiving, http://caregiving.org.

  In-home health care is a separate service that is typically operated on a larger scale than can be done from home; however, smaller in-home health care providers in rural areas are sometimes home based. In-home health care is usually paid by Medicare or Medicaid, but sometimes families pay for in-home health care directly. Resource: National Association for Home Care and Hospice, (202) 547-7424, www.nahc.org.

- **Personal-chef services.** Personal chefs bring the groceries and their own utensils and equipment to cook in their clients' kitchens. Typically, personal chefs who cook for seniors come in once every two weeks and package meals to store in the refrigerator or freezer for use until their next visit. Resource: United States Personal Chef Association, (800) 995-2138, www.uspca.com.

- **Pet services.** Seniors love their pets, and research has proved pets are healthy for them. For example, seniors with dogs go to the doctor less, have lower triglyceride and cholesterol levels, and engage in conversation and social interaction. Thus, seniors are frequent customers for pet sitters and other pet services such as dog and cat training, mobile pet grooming, nonanesthetic dental cleaning, pet transportation, and pooper-scooper services. Resource: National Association of Professional Pet Sitters, (856) 439-0324, www.petsitters.org.

Professional services

✔ **Geriatric care management.** These professionals specialize in assessing the needs of seniors whose situations require special attention in order for them to continue to live independently. Geriatric care managers also coordinate needed services and negotiate their delivery with agencies. Because of certification requirements, being credentialed in gerontology, nursing, social work, or psychology is required in this field.

✔ **Professional advice.** Professionals of all kinds — including accountants, clergy, financial planners, insurance brokers, lawyers, independent nurse practitioners, real estate agents, and psychotherapists — are specializing in working with elders. Professionals and others can become Certified Senior Advisors by the Society of Certified Senior Advisors, (303) 757-2323, www.society-csa.com.

Special services

✔ **Relocation services.** When life circumstances change due to health or finances, downsizing one's home is something seniors often do, trading a now too-large or hard-to-maintain home for a smaller one. But moving is both physically and emotionally daunting. This has given rise to relocation specialists, who handle everything from packing to unpacking and setting up the new living space to make its new resident(s) feel at home. Resource: National Association of Senior Move Managers, www.nasmm.com.

✔ **Retirement counseling.** A recent Gallup survey found 54 percent of American adults do not have a long-term financial plan and that 74 percent of these do not expect to have enough money to retire. This means a lot of work for retirement counselors to do. Certification is possible through the College for Financial Planning (800-237-9990, 303-220-1200, www.fp.edu), which offers a Chartered Retirement Planning Counselor, and the International Foundation for Retirement Education (806-742-6100, www.infre.org) offers a Certified Retirement Counselor (CRC) designation to financial planners and individuals with human resource and finance work experience in corporations or government.

✔ **Tour packaging.** Travel is a high priority for the maturing population. When people approaching retirement age are asked what kind of travel they look forward to, travel that combines intellectual and physical stimulation scores high. So a home-business–based tour packaging business does more than make travel arrangements; it's also about fulfilling aspirations for adventure for both mind and body. Most tour operators find niches — novel and unique tours or subjects focused on food, art, history, or other special interests, sometimes exotic, that require particular knowledge and expertise in order to create a satisfying tour. Unlike travel agents, who are in an increasingly difficult field, tour packagers generally do not sell tickets to their customers; they either pay for the transportation such as renting a bus, which is included in the tour package, or the customers make their own travel arrangements. The tour package consists of the itinerary, hotel accommodations, food, and guide services. Resource: United States Tour Operators Association (USTOA) has a client insurance program, (212) 599-6599, www.ustoa.com.

✔ **Virtual Retirement Communities.** This form of retirement community enables seniors to stay in their homes by providing them with access to needed services at preferred costs from reliable vendors. Beacon Hill Village in Boston is a prototype for this type of organization. It "contracts for household services (repair, cleaning, errands), transportation (to friends, airports, doctors), concierge services, meals and grocery shopping, and home health care." Residents pay less than $1,000 a year to belong. This developing addition to community services makes possible two different business roles: organizing virtual communities and operating the resulting associations. Example: Beacon Hill Village, www.beaconhillvillage.org.

2. Great Migration South and to Smaller Places

Americans and Canadians are on the move — generally southward! In *American Demographics,* business futurist Stuart Bradford forecasts that as many as 50 million people may move to the South over the next 20 years. The migration south is being led by boomers surging past 50, but where the population and money are, work is too, so younger people and families are heading south as well.

Geographical shifts are not limited to the South. Smaller cities such as Burlington, Vermont; Columbia, Missouri; Fargo, North Dakota; Iowa City, Iowa; Northampton, Massachusetts; and Rochester, Minnesota are growing, too, as people choose less stressful environments to live in. Also emerging are *micropolitan* areas with one or more towns at their core and at least 10,000 but fewer than 50,000 people, surrounded by growing populations in adjacent counties. These core towns have names most people don't recognize: Edwards, Colorado; Rio Grand City, Texas; Daphne-Fairhope, Alabama; and Elko, Nevada. They draw people because the core towns have basic infrastructure, and the adjacent areas offer lower-cost real estate.

New population growth creates many home-based business opportunities. A home-based service business that is pressed to make ends meet in a slow-growing area such as Cleveland, Detroit, Milwaukee, Philadelphia, or Toledo, after having relocated to a fast-growing area such as Phoenix, Atlanta, or Las Vegas, may have so much work, it finds itself turning customers away or raising its prices to screen out bargain hunters. In fact, a northern work ethic may be sought after by customers in places where "native boys" are known to work only when they "get round to it."

What kinds of businesses will do best? Although geography no longer plays the dominating role for many businesses as it did when the mantra was *location, location, location,* local clienteles can be important in that they provide face-to-face interaction with colleagues and suppliers. Places with growing populations and expanding economies are most apt to provide both. So virtually all the businesses described for the other nine trends will find fertile ground in growing areas.

In addition, businesses that involve homes and real estate do well in growing areas, including things that can be done at or from home, such as

- Cleaning services
- Drafting/design using CAD
- Handyman work
- Home inspection
- Insurance sales and independent adjusting
- Landscape and garden design and installation
- Real estate sales and specialties such as staging homes for sale and the video work needed for virtual tours that appear on Web sites
- Real estate appraisal
- Remodeling contracting

But what if you live in a city or region that's losing population, and because of family or other reasons, you don't want to move? With population loss, businesses that formerly were operated in storefronts and in offices retreat home, lowering their overhead. At the same time, acceptance of businesses located in homes rises, because this may be the only way of having goods and services available nearby. Would-be competitors may have followed the crowd and moved away, leaving you king or queen of the hill, though one that may continue to shrink in size.

3. Universal Connectivity: the Electronic Environment

Universal connectivity has gone from dream to pricing plans. The appliances needed to connect to the world and to access virtually anything from virtually anywhere keep decreasing in size. New software coming onto the market, combined with wireless transmission of electronic waves, will enable communication over a broad range of frequencies, bandwidths, and transmission standards while maintaining a constant Internet connection even when traveling from state to state or nation to nation.

The emerging fabric of wireless broadband connections, the Global Positioning System (GPS), and radio frequency identification tags (RFID) led Ed Zander, CEO of Motorola, to declare in *USA Today*, "The big change is going to be when the Internet follows you, not you trying to follow the Internet. It's just there. Your life is just affected the way it's affected today by the lights in a room." Or as Carly Fiorina of Hewlett-Packard told *PC Magazine,* "Every process . . . is going to be digital, mobile, virtual, personal."

What are the implications for home-based businesses? First, the self-employed, particularly consultants, will have the equivalent of a support staff for tasks such as making travel arrangements, presentations, and getting needed information delivered automatically wherever they are. This will lower overhead costs and equalize the playing field between the one-person company and larger companies. Second, for more people home will be anywhere or nowhere, making it possible to live and work in an RV or out of a suitcase, as well as respond to instant work opportunities, such as the demand for construction tradesmen, insurance adjusters, and others following a natural or manmade disaster. We'll be able to freely follow the markets for the kind of work we want to do and live in the variety of places we want to live.

A business that has already emerged and that has continuing growth potential is selling what you have, make, or acquire on the Web from this trend. If you have a product to market or are a collector of anything from toasters to toilet seats, you can make the world your market on the Internet as a *Web merchant/auction trader*. Ask anyone to name five businesses that have thrived beyond the dotcom meltdown, and eBay would come up high on everyone's list. Although it's the most popular trading site, eBay isn't the only auction site being used by collectors, merchants, liquidators, and hundreds of thousands of home-based sellers. Other sites include Bidville and Ubid and the auction sections of Amazon, Yahoo!, and Overstock.com. Another way to be a Web merchant is to operate a virtual storefront of your own on a Web site or within a mall. Check out www.auction-sellers-news. com for a free newsletter.

4. Economic Globalization

Do you remember Ross Perot in 1992 describing the "giant sucking sound" of manufacturing jobs exiting the United States? It's turned out that a lot more than factory jobs are leaving. A study by University of California at Berkeley estimates that 14 million U.S. service jobs are vulnerable to offshoring. Some economists view this relocation of work as positive. Whether this facet of economic globalization turns out to be good or bad for the economy as a whole, here are the significant ways it is affecting home-based businesses:

- First, some work that formerly went to home-based businesses, in fields ranging from medical billing and claims processing to programming, is now being done in countries like the Philippines, India, Russia, and Romania. Home businesses making products like baskets, ceramics, and quilts sometimes find their products underpriced by inexpensive imports sold by the bin in places like Wal-Mart and Target. This means the opportunities for craft-oriented home businesses lie with unique or personalized creations not available for less. See Trend 10, later in this chapter.

- On sites such as `elance.com` and `guru.com`, bidders from around the world are competing for all kinds of work — from Web design to writing. This means home-based businesses could have new competitors they didn't have in the '90s, but it also means we, too, have access to a world-wide market. It can be a quick route to obtaining one's first customers.

- Third, what some home-based businesses can charge for what they do has been dampened by offshoring and a worldwide market. Medical transcription is an example. The rate paid per line has dropped from an average of 18.5 cents in 1985 to 14 cents in 2004, while the cost of the technology needed to run such a business has gone up. Nevertheless, because of rising demand, medical transcription remains a viable home business.

So in considering what's going to be a good business for you, determine as best you can whether what you will be doing is something that might be off-shored. Obviously, there's no danger of this if you're providing facials or being a handyman, particularly in communities not hard hit by job losses.

If you're wondering whether offshoring will continue and whether there any bright signs on the horizon, the answer to both of these questions is quite probably *yes.* New technologies are coming along that will reduce or elimi-nate the advantages of offshoring. This makes watching for emerging tech-nologies a way to spot the home businesses of the future.

For example, one revolutionary technology that could hold promise is mecha-tronics. What's that? Think replicators aboard the *Star Trek* "Enterprise." *Mechatronics* can be thought of as first-wave replicators, using ink-jet printing technology to build products that have movable parts and working circuitry. Cartridges filled with polymers and other materials will produce ready-to-use items of all kinds.

Imagine having a mechatronic printer or two as the basis of a home-based business or enabling someone in a remote location to fabricate automotive parts; consumer electronics; and medical, household, and office items. This could be a technology that, by changing the nature of manufacturing, could return to domestic production items now produced abroad. If you're interested in mechatronics, watch for developments from Cornell University, MIT, and UC Berkeley, as well as manufacturers moving forward with this emerging technology.

Another technology capable of doing tabletop manufacturing is called *molecular manufacturing*. It is based on advances in nanotechnology. Organizations tracking this development are The Institute for Molecular Manufacturing, www.imm.org, and the Foresight Institute, www.foresight.org.

5. Increasing Numbers of Self-Employed

In his best-selling 1989 book, *Age of Reason,* Charles Handy first foretold the reorganization of corporations into what he called *cloverleaf organizations* functioning with three types of personnel: (1) a small core of employees, (2) outsourced contract workers and services when needed, and (3) strategic alliances with other corporations. Since then, we have witnessed this very phenomenon in how organizations are now being structured.

A contingent workforce comprised of temporary workers and independent contractors has grown to an estimated one out of three workers. These contingent workers are not just assembly-line and administrative workers, they're also attorneys, doctors, and professors. Their numbers are growing at a galloping rate. Many in this growing contingent workforce are in the market for the services of other small businesses and self-employed individuals on both a cash and barter basis (see Chapter 12).

Following are some businesses that can grow from increases in self-employment:

- ✔ **Computer consultants.** Most small and home-based businesses are dependent on technology, but they don't possess the skills or the inclination to deal with problems of installation; upgrading; compatibility; repairs; and being disabled by malware, spyware, viruses, and worms. They need computer consultants. They may call a computer consultant even when they're eligible for the manufacturer's technical support if, at that support, they can talk only to someone who is reading a script or who has difficulties with English. Toward the end of the decade, computer consultants may also be applying their problem-solving skills to robotic appliances. Resource: Independent Computer Consultants Association, (800) 774-4222, www.icca.org.

- ✔ **Interim or contract executives.** One consequence of the imminent retirement of the baby boomer generation and the much smaller generation that's replacing it is that corporations are willing to contract out for top executive roles. Thousands of companies are seeking out *interim, contract,* or *short-term* executives from CEOs, CFOs, and CIOs to marketing, purchasing, and other managerial roles. Sometimes these interim assignments are part-time, and sometimes full-time, but they are usually limited to from several months to several years. Resource: `www.the phoenixlink.com`.

✓ **Virtual assistants (VAs).** Growing in lockstep with virtual organizations are the bundling of many office functions into a grab bag of roles for *virtual assistants* — who do executive assisting, secretarial work, meeting and travel planning, project managing, and coordinating logistics. Virtual assistants often specialize by working with a specific profession, occupation, or industry, and of course, the tasks they provide are tailored to the needs of their clients. So for a virtual assistant working for a psychiatrist, managing the appointment schedule could be a key job, whereas for a startup company, the VA may be busy finding sources of insurance or outfitting an office on a minimum budget. Stacy Brice, one of the founders of the field, offers VA training at AssistU (`www.assistu.com`).

6. Living off the Grid

Not a week and often not a day goes by in which someone doesn't write or say to us, *I'd sure like to get off the grid.* By that, they mean becoming independent of utilities such as electricity, water, gas or propane, usually in rural settings. Solar, wind, hydro, geothermal, and wireless are among the technologies that are actually enabling increasing numbers of people to live independent of pipes and wires and rising utility bills.

The increasing cost of energy plus improving technology, such as plastic instead of silicon solar panels, is stimulating what will become a new way of life for perhaps hundreds of thousands of people. An estimated 30,000 to 40,000 people are already living off the grid in the United States today. Although solar power is not the only technology enabling people to live virtually anywhere they choose, its growth may be an indicator of what's to come. Revenue spent on solar power equipment and installation is forecast to rise from under $5 billion in 2003 to over $30 billion in 2013.

One type of home-based business that will grow from this trend is *alternative energy installation.* Homes of people wanting to live off the grid and homeowners who want backup energy available on standby constitute the largest part of the customer base for alternative energy installers. Other customers for alternative energy equipment and installation are RV and boat owners, and commercial entities such as radio stations, bed-and-breakfast inns, and large resorts, all wanting backup power. This is a business that requires mechanical abilities and the willingness to climb roofs and towers. Resource: Solar Energy Installation Businesses, `http://energy.sourceguides.com`.

7. Rising Physical and Property Security Needs

How many of us have transitioned from breathing a sigh of relief at security check-ins, to getting irritation at the lines and hassle, to accepting it as part of everyday reality? This is reflected in the finding that three out of four adults believe it likely that the United States will suffer more major terrorist attacks.

The challenges of both protecting ourselves and our assets from terrorists, crooks, and exploiters of computer vulnerabilities while maintaining an open society have created pressing demands for a variety of security needs. The result is industries, such as data recovery, that require special training; other industries involve adapting one's existing experience and know-how to new niches in the security field. Specializing in this field is important because it enables a home-based businessperson to more easily identify, reach, and gain the respect of clients, be they accountants, architects, attorneys, or any other industry needing security services. Here are some existing specialties:

- **Security consulting.** Some security consultants sell products from which they earn commissions; others provide expertise and are paid by the hour or on a per-project basis. They write plans and design and install systems. Areas of specialization include

  - Customer theft and product piracy

  - Electronic security systems

  - Employee theft

  - Intangibles like client lists and proprietary technology

  - Real estate and tangible property

- **Site consulting.** Security is an issue for virtually every building and office, from high-tech industrial complexes to distribution centers, retail stores, self-storage facilities, housing developments, hotels, resorts, casinos, parking lots, and hospitals. Site consultants help businesses and institutions address security concerns about their facilities. They evaluate the physical design of buildings and spaces. They determine what security problems a sites poses and recommend countermeasures, from guards to electronic security with cameras and electric lights, or a combination of such methods and policies.

- **Systems design.** Security system designers prevent security problems before they begin by developing specifications and providing architectural or engineering support during the design phase of a security consulting project. Systems designers may also develop new electronic security tools to be used at specific locations.

> ↙ **Forensic consulting.** Forensic security consultants step in after security problems have already occurred. They serve as expert witnesses in trials in which security breaches are at issue, such as those involving fires, thefts, break-ins, and so on. Forensic consultants may focus on any of the security specialties.
>
> Resource: ASIS International is an association that provides certification. 703-519-6200, www.asisonline.org.

8. Education for Youth and Adults

An increasingly skilled workforce is needed to staff a 21st-century civilization. *Pardon My Planet* made this point humorously in a recent cartoon. A young boy says to his father, "Dad, you really should help me with my homework while you still can. Next year I enter the 4th grade." Children today must learn more far sooner than their parents did when they were growing up.

Yet despite the United States spending more on education per student than any country in the world, American students score below students in other advanced economies in every way that educational achievement is measured. High school graduates are less prepared for college, 28 percent of freshmen are enrolled in remedial math or English, and fewer than half of freshmen entering college graduate with a degree after four years.

Yet a healthy information-age economy requires workers who can lead and meet the demands of fast-changing workplaces. Many dads and moms who see that their kids need help if they are to pass demanding courses and tests and to succeed in a competitive job market are creating a growing need for a business that has traditionally been done from or at home.

Although for years, parents vitally interested in their children doing well have provided the impetus for tutoring, the emphasis on testing is creating additional reasons for parents to hire tutors. The pressure on children is described as horrendous. Tutors may be hired by parents or obtain funding under the No Child Left Behind Act. Even in Canada, whose students score markedly ahead of American students, tutoring in English as a second language and mathematics is not uncommon. In addition to academic tutoring of youth, tutors also work with adults, teaching carpentry; plumbing; and sport and hobbyist skills such as tennis, golf, and dancing. Resource: National Tutoring Association, (866) 311-6630, www.ntatutor.org.

Adults are feeling challenged, too. Only one in five adult Americans has the work skills or education to be competitive in the global economy, according to MIT economist Lester Thurow. The speed of technological change is increasing, resulting in new products and information, as well as training in how to use and service them. Some people maintain — and we agree — that remaining economically viable requires a lifelong learning process. These challenges provide the basis of several other education-oriented types of home-based businesses:

- ✔ **Continuing education and training.** Although continuing education may not be a full-time home-based business in itself, teaching continuing education classes offered by college and university extension programs and adult learning companies such as the Learning Annex are a way to attract clients to any number of businesses, from consulting and financial counseling to personal chefing, photography, and home improvement. Many people decide what they learn to do themselves from a class is more difficult than they anticipated and are sufficiently impressed with the instructor to hire him or her to carry out the task they were hoping to learn how to do. Training is increasingly becoming an Internet-based phenomenon, usually called *e-learning,* which provides another role for professional trainers, as well as for people who design e-learning courseware and experiences. Resource: American Society for Training and Development, www.astd.org.

- ✔ **Technical writing.** Changing technology always requires the creation of materials to introduce it to its probable consumers, sell it, explain how to use it, service it, assemble it, install it, and so on. The pace of innovation has been accelerating for over a hundred years, and there's every reason to believe it will continue as innovation shifts abroad, particularly to China, which is investing heavily in science and technology. Technical writers also will find work making technologies created abroad understandable and usable by English-speaking sales engineers and technicians. Resource: Society for Technical Communication, (703) 522-4114, www.stc.org.

9. Health Care: Up in Demand and Cost

Spending on health care increases as people grow older, contributing in part to U.S. health-care costs soaring — by 59 percent since 2000. That's five times the increases in both wages and inflation. One consequence of this is that heath-care providers work hard to lower their costs, sometimes by outsourcing back-office services to small independent services, specifically for medical coding, billing, and transcription.

At the same time, the high price of traditional health care and the inability to simply get services from traditional health-care providers is spurring the growth of alternative medicine both for prevention and treatment. More than one in three Americans use some kind of alternative or complementary health care, such as natural products, breathing exercises, chiropractic care, yoga, massage, and diet-based therapies. Spending on organic foods, for example, is growing by 20 percent a year.

Home businesses in the health care field that can do well include the following:

- ✔ **Fitness trainer/coach.** Fitness training was already growing before serious efforts to make war on obesity began. Trainers work both from home and at home, depending on the trainer and the needs of the clients. Trainers who work from home work with clients in gyms or at their clients' homes. Trainers who work at home have their clients come to their homes or provide coaching over the phone or Internet. Because the best advertising to potential clients is the trainer's own health and appearance, coaches and trainers need to be physically fit. Yoga, which is being used for relieving stress-related conditions and fitness, is increasingly popular and can be done at studios or by going to clients' homes. Resources: Aerobic and Fitness Association of America (AFAA), (800) 446-2322, www.afaa.com; and The Yoga Site, www.yogasite.com, 877-964-2748 or 508-896-4456.

- ✔ **Medical billing service.** Though too frequently in the news because of FTC actions closing down medical billing business opportunity vendors, medical billing is a viable home business. Medical billing involves the ability to handle detail, because accuracy is critical. Medical billers prepare insurance claims using medical-billing software and then send them electronically to third-party payers for evaluation and payment. Health-care providers other than doctors also use medical billers, including chiropractors, ambulance services, dentists, home-nursing services, and massage therapists. Resources: Electronic Medical Billing Network of America, Inc., (908) 470-4100, www.medicalbillingnetwork.com and National Electronic Billers Alliance (NEBA), (650) 359-4419, www.nebazone.com.

- ✔ **Medical coding.** Between the treatment of a patient and the submission of a bill to a third-party payer, medical services provided to the patient must be translated into a standardized code. These codes are also used in record keeping and health-care statistical measurement by hospitals and various government agencies. Accuracy is imperative, as miscoding results in the health-care provider being fined. People with backgrounds in medical fields such as nursing are best suited to enter this growing field. Resource: American Academy of Professional Coders provides education and certification, (801) 626-2633, www.aapc.com.

- ✔ **Medical transcription.** Medical transcriptionists produce reports and documents from dictation that doctors, nurses, and other medical personnel have made regarding their patients. As medical personnel employ voice-recognition technologies, the transcriptionists' work becomes editing the documents on-screen. But they are still needed in this $50 billion industry based on the need for records on continuing patient care and to get paid for services from third-party providers, among other uses. Resource: American Association for Medical Transcription offers free information about the profession, (800) 982-2182, (209) 527-9620, www.aamt.org.

> ✔ **Growing organic food.** A growing appetite for healthy foods and the desire to avoid produce grown with the use of pesticides or irradiation is propelling market growth for organic growers. Much locally grown produce, fresh herbs, and edible flowers found at farmer's markets, roadside stands, and gourmet restaurants are grown by small growers who practice what is variously called *vest pocket* or *micro farming*. People living in warmer climates have the advantage of being able to grow several crops a year. Resource: ATTRA National Sustainable Agriculture Information Service, (800) 346-9140, www.attra.org.

Experts estimate that 30 percent of doctors' offices and other medical providers contract out their billing. Unhappily, some larger medical facilities are outsourcing their billing outside the United States. So the home-based medical biller needs to think of her or his market as smaller practices and medical providers that seek payment for services to their patients from third parties. These include commercial ambulance services, chiropractors, dentists, optometrists, home-nursing services, nurse practitioners, physical therapists, physician assistants, podiatrists, psychologists and other counselors, respiratory therapists, and speech therapists, among others.

The smaller office often has difficulty keeping and training an employee with sufficient skills to do their billing accurately. Thus, independent medical billers are more expert than office staff responsible for doing other office functions. An outside medical biller should be able to increase the revenue of their clients while reducing overhead.

To be a medical biller, what you must know has increased, however, in part because of security and privacy standards for handling medical data provided for in the Health Insurance Portability and Accountability Act of 1996 (HIPAA). Because these standards change, you must keep continually up to date.

You can acquire more background on new developments at the Electronic Medical Billing Network of America site at www.medicalbillingnetwork.com and the National Electronic Billers Alliance site at www.nebazone.com.

ASK PAUL & SARAH

Are medical billing businesses still hot?

Q: I am taking an at-home study course on medical billing. You've indicated that this is a good business. Is this still the case?

A: We've included medical billing as a "best business" since the first edition of our book

Best Home Businesses, despite the harm done to this field by the dozens if not hundreds of business opportunities that overpromised what they could deliver in preparing people to do medical billing.

10. Luxuries as Necessities

What's been called the *democratization of luxury* is evidenced by the fact that U.S. consumer spending on luxury items has grown four times faster than total spending. In 2003, luxury purchases accounted for about 20 percent of the $2.35 trillion American retail sales market, including many items and services that home-based businesses can make, sell, or offer as personalized and premium services. Although Canadians are more conservative in their expenditures, they also are spending more on things like clothing, personal-care products, and entertainment.

By buying basic goods at Costco, Home Depot, Lowe's, and Wal-Mart, shoppers are saving $100 billon a year, finds a Harvard study. At the same time, marketing analysts find spending on luxury goods and services is growing particularly among the 47 million households earning more than $50,000 a year. Surveys find that many people shop for bargains, clip coupons, and wait for sales on household items in order to splurge on luxuries and special treats for themselves or their loved ones.

What's motivating this spending? First, experts say that pampering oneself with luxuries is a way of compensating for hard work, long hours, and not having enough time for loved ones. In short, many people turn to luxury purchases to help themselves feel better. Other people seek new experiences, which translates into opportunities for tour operators offering exotic vacations and personal chefs who will introduce them to new culinary experiences.

For some customers, the important things about a luxury are superior quality and that it lasts a long time. These customers welcome information about a product, including what it's made of and how. Others buy luxuries as a reward for achievement; still others want things that make them feel good, both with their senses and emotionally. This creates a growing market for handmade and personalized items that can be made by skilled home-based artists and crafters.

For most luxury products, quality is more important than brand, and thus, what a home-based business produces has a *uniqueness cache*; nevertheless, establishing one's own brand, such as Amy's, Barbara's, or Bill's, can also be the route for some to growing a much larger business (Table 3-1).

Table 3-1	Luxury Products and Services Marketable by a Home-Based Business	
	Goods	*Services*
Personal care	Calligraphy	Facials and beauty treatments
	Clothing	Massage
	Costumes	Travel experiences
	Fragrances using essential oils	
	Handmade soaps, beauty products	
Edibles	Cake baking, decorating	Personal-chef services
	Herbs, foods, flowers	
For the home	Baskets	House cleaning
	Candles	Pet sitting, grooming, walking, training
	Ceramics	
	Handmade furniture	
	Home décor	
	Quilts	
	Window treatments	

One more thing. We've identified the trends we think will most affect home-based businesses and named some of the businesses we believe have the best potential to prosper. But one lesson from the past is that no one has a foolproof crystal ball. New opportunities from new technologies will continue to arise, some technologies that showed promise won't gain market acceptance, and established businesses will fade or require such retooling that they wouldn't be recognized by the same name. That's the process, the opportunity, and the price of an economy and an era in which change is normal and in which some dreams are put to rest as new ones arise.

How can I tell what work I should do?

Q: I've always heard people say, "Do what you love." That can be discouraging if you don't have any clue as to what you'd love to do. How does someone like me proceed?

A: We understand there's more to the choices people make than doing what they love. In fact, a study by Roper Starch Worldwide found that 29 percent of American adults choose work that pays well, even if they hate the work. Personally, we learned from interviewing hundreds of people while writing *Finding Your Perfect Work* that many don't choose a business based on work they love. We've identified four productive "paths" people take:

- Drawing on a talent, whether natural or acquired

- Building on a passion

- Following a sense of mission, which often grows out of a desire to right a wrong

- Capitalizing on an asset, such as equipment, contacts, or specialized training.

At the same time, we strongly advise against doing something you dislike. Although some people may be able to sustain a job they dislike due to the structure an employer provides, entrepreneurs lacking passion typically also lack motivation. Also, those who force themselves to do something chronically unrewarding may make themselves ill. Thus, you should score your business idea at least 7 on a "likeability" scale of 1 to 10.

If you still can't think of potential businesses, perhaps you haven't dug deep enough. We love the story of a woman in Los Angeles who liked watching TV and going to parties. She stitched together a business matchmaking celebrities with charitable events and good causes. Now she gets to watch TV to see who's "in" and then go to the parties she's helped line up celebrities for. You, too, may find an unlikely combination of things you like (if not love) and turn them into both an enjoyable and profitable livelihood.

Where You Can Learn about More Home Businesses

The following types of businesses are described in greater depth in other books by Paul and Sarah Edwards:

- Found in "Best Home Businesses for the 21st Century"

- **Found in "Best Home Businesses for People 50+"**

- *Found in both books*

Abstracting service

Advertising agency

Alternative energy installer

Antiquing

Aromatherapy

Association management service

Astrology

Background checking

Basket-making and chair-caning

Bed-and-breakfast inn

Bodywork and massage therapy

Bookkeeping service and bill-paying service

Business broker

Business network organizer

Business-plan writer

Cake-baking and decorating

Calligraphy

Candle-making

Caretaker

Caterer and personal chef

Ceramics

Chair-making

Cleaning services

Coach

Computer consultant

Computer programmer

Computer repair

Consulting to businesses and other organizations

Copywriter

Daily money manager

Desktop publishing

Desktop video

Direct seller/network marketer

Disc jockey service

Dog walking

Doula service

Drafter/Computer-Aided Design

Editorial services: editing, proofreading, indexing

Elder services: elder relocation service and other elder services

Environmental assessor

Errand services

Estate sales services

Executive search

Expert referral service/brokerage

Export agent

Facialist/aesthetician

Family child-care provider

Feng shui consultant

Financial planner

Fitness trainer

Fund-raiser

Gardening, growing flowers, food and herbs

Gardening service

Gift-basket business

Graphology

Handyman

Hauling service

Home inspector

Image consultant and personal shopper, clothing sales

Indoor environmental tester

Information professional/ broker

In-home health care

Interim executive

Interior designer/decorator

Leak-detection service

Mail order/Web merchant and antique and collectibles reseller

Mailing list service

Make-up artist

Manufacturer's rep/independent sales representative

Mediation

Medical billing

Medical claims assistance professional and hospital bill auditing

Medical coding

Medical transcription service

Meeting and event planning

Microfarming

Mobile notary

Mobile screen repair

Personal chef service

Mystery shopping

New media/multimedia production

Newsletter publishing

Personal historian **and scrapbooking**

Pet groomer

Pet party giving

Pet sitting and other services for animal lovers

Pet taxi

Pet training

Photography

Plant caregiver

Private-practice consultant

Professional investigator and security consultant

Professional organizer

Proposal and grant writer

Public-relations specialist

Quilting

Real estate appraiser and personal property appraiser

Red-tape expediter/complaint service

Referral service

Relocation expert

Remodeling contractor

Repair services

Restoration services

Résumé-writing service

Reunion planner

Rubber-stamp business

Scopist

Secretarial and office-support services

Sewing

Sign maker

Soapmaking

Tax preparation service

Technical writer

Tour operator

Training specialist

Transcript-digesting service

Translator/interpreter

Travel agent/outside salesperson

Travel consultant

Travel writer

Tutoring: computer tutoring/training, *scholastic tutoring*

Virtual assistant

Web site designer

Web merchant and auction trader

Webmaster

Wedding consultant and planner

Writing coach and writer

Chapter 4

Marketing 101: Getting Customers

*Y*ou've worked hard to start your home-based business and get it going. You've set aside some space in which to operate, and you've picked up a business license. You've purchased and stocked products to sell, or you've prepared yourself to deliver first-rate services to what you hope will be an eager throng of potential clients and customers. But before you can start enjoying the fruits of all your hard work, there's one thing you've got to do: You've got to convince someone to buy your products and services. You see, the greatest business idea in the world — the greatest products and services — are essentially worthless if no one is willing to pay you for them. For your business to be successful, you have to get good at marketing your products and services so that your prospective customers and clients hear about you and are encouraged to buy from you.

In this chapter, we help you identify your best customers and assess their needs. We take a look at different marketing methods — including *referrals,* one of the most effective marketing tools — and help you create a meaningful marketing plan. We also check in on the latest information about starting your own Web site for e-commerce.

Identifying Your Best Customers

Here's a secret that may make a very big difference in the amount of money you stand to earn from your home-based business: *Some of your potential customers are better than others.* That is, some (the ones who are willing to pay top dollar for your products or services with little intervention on your part) will earn you a lot of money, and some (the ones who nickel-and-dime you to death, complaining all the way) will actually lose you money. Because potential customers come in all sizes, shapes, and spending profiles — and because customers don't come with their profiles stapled to their heads — your very difficult job is to first figure out which ones are the most likely to become your best customers and then to figure out how to attract and reach them. Because your time and marketing dollars aren't unlimited, the best use of your money is to target them to specific people — the people most likely to buy your products and services. Instead of running expensive radio or newspaper advertisements day after day, hoping to get the attention of the customers you seek, you may find that targeted advertising in a specific magazine or Web site delivers a much greater payoff.

What does your ideal customer look like? Here are a few questions to ask as you create a picture. (Don't worry if you can't answer all of the questions right now — just give it your best shot.)

- Who do you think your best customers will be?
- Are they individuals or businesses?
- If they're individuals, what do they and don't they like?
- What are their needs and problems?
- How will those needs and problems be best addressed?
- What's most important to your best customers?
- What's least important to them?
- How will you provide more of the former and less of the latter?

Based on these questions, develop a written description of your best customers, and have some of your customers look it over to validate it or to make corrections. Here is a sample description of the ideal customer for a pet-sitting service:

> *My ideal customer is a single, working adult with one or more pets, including dogs, cats, or birds, that require daily care and attention. My ideal customer often travels, has sufficient income ($30,000 or more per year) to afford to hire a pet sitter, and prefers to keep his or her pet in its home environment rather than in a kennel or other offsite care situation. My ideal customer loves his or her pets and wants them to have the best care possible.*

The idea is to understand your best potential clients and customers inside out — to know what makes them tick and what motivates them. By knowing this, you can easily figure out which marketing approaches (direct mail, Web site, Yellow Pages, search engine listings, display advertisement, and so forth) has the highest probability of not only reaching your best customers, but also inducing them to want to find out more about what you've got to

Promoting a new business

Q: My sister-in-law and I have a home business together that offers complete medical billing for physicians. Our primary way of marketing is to visit physicians personally and present information on what we have to offer. Do you have any other suggestions on how to promote new business without spending too much?

A: Our interviews with owners of successful medical billing services for *The Best Home Businesses for the 21st Century* and again for *The Best Home Businesses for People 50+* confirm that what you're doing now continues to be the best way to get started in this field. Most startups begin by knocking on doors or making marketing calls by phone. To make getting through to doctors easier, we suggest warming up your sales contacts by mailing out brochures and letters and then following up with a personal contact for an appointment.

✔ Talk with your own doctors and other health-care providers whom you know personally, and ask for referrals.

✔ Collaborate with pharmaceutical salespeople, who regularly see doctors in their private offices. (Expect to pay a commission to reps who introduce you.)

✔ Don't limit your marketing contacts to medical doctors. You can also provide billing services to a wide range of other health-care practitioners, such as acupuncturists, dentists, chiropractors, commercial ambulance services, dentists, home-nursing services, massage therapists, nurse practitioners, occupational therapists, optometrists, physical therapists, physician assistants, podiatrists, psychologists and other counselors, respiratory therapists, and speech therapists.

✔ Contact local professional societies about offering discounts to their members.

After making contacts, follow up by phone to find out if you can provide additional information. Then keep your services top of mind (that is, in their minds) by sending periodic reminders in the form of timely tips and other useful information on postcards, flyers, or newsletters that you can send via mail, e-mail, or fax.

offer. (Check out the "Marketing: Different Roads to Meeting Your Goals" section later in this chapter for ideas on ways to market your products and services.)

Tapping Into Your Customers' Needs

Which do you think is the better approach — creating a product or service that you're not sure anyone will want to buy and then trying to sell it, or first finding out what people want to buy and *then* creating a product or service that responds to that? Here's a hint: If you build a business around a product or service that you're not sure will sell, you're taking a very big risk.

Creating a product or service in a vacuum, without the input of your clients or customers, is a recipe for disaster. You're designing a product or service that your prospects may neither need nor like, which means that you have to market much harder — or offer lots of incentives — to get your clients or customers to buy your products. Even then, they still may not buy.

Finding a need and filling it is one of the most basic marketing strategies. Your first step in marketing, therefore, begins before your product or service is available to the public, when you're designing and creating it. By tapping into your customers' needs early in the process, you not only build a product or service that your prospects truly want and need, but also, your marketing efforts take far less personal energy, time, and money to implement.

The WPWPF principle

Many home-based business owners are in love with the products and services that they sell, as well they should be. They are their own best cheerleaders, creating infectious excitement whenever they have the opportunity to talk to someone about their business or their products or services. The problem is that some home-based business owners fall so deeply in love with their products and services that they fail to notice that their prospective clients and customers aren't equally in love. They may not even be *in like*. And when this happens, a great idea remains only a great idea — not a great product or service.

Paul and Sarah have developed a test for home-based business owners who love their products and services. It's called the WPWPF (what people will pay for) principle. Your products and services are only as good as what people are willing to pay for them — no matter how beautiful, clever, or well thought out they may be, if your clients and customers don't want them, they aren't worth even a fraction of the time and money that you invested to create them, and you really don't have a business.

So what's the solution? How can you be sure that the products and services that you've been dreaming about delivering to your clients and customers are the ones that they truly want? It's actually quite simple: Ask them. That's all it takes. Here are a few simple steps for defining your target market and then asking the people in that market which products and services they really want and need (and will therefore be willing to buy):

1. **Decide which market you're going to target.**

   Who, potentially, are your best customers — the people in the market you want to target? Do you want to sell your products and services to busy businesspeople, to retirees who spend their winters in Florida or Arizona, to preschool children, or to people who like to go on extended vacations to exotic lands? Whichever product or service you hope to create, first decide who you're going to try to sell it to. All of the steps that follow depend on this one.

2. **Ask the members of your target market which products or services they want and need.**

   You can do this in person, over the telephone, via written surveys sent through the mail, or through your Web site. The key is to collect as much data about the wants and needs of your target market as you can — the more data, the better.

3. **Use the results of your survey when designing your products and services.**

   Using that great data from surveying your potential customers and clients, determine the design of the products and services you offer. Be sure that you address — and at least consider — every feature mentioned as important by the people you surveyed. Some may not make financial sense, but others may be essential to include, whatever the cost. Believe us: Not only do you end up with better products and services, but you also sell a lot more of them, because they match the wants and needs of your customers and clients.

4. **Test the market.**

   After your products and services are available — but before you roll them out to the public at large — test them out on a few selected people, businesses, or not-for-profit entities. What's their reaction? Are they satisfied with the results? Do your selected customers have suggestions for improvements or changes? What about price? Are your products and services priced realistically? Will your potential clients be willing to pay what you ask? Incorporate the feedback you get by tweaking your product or service or the prices you plan to charge.

5. **Market, market, market.**

   By going through the preceding four steps, you can be reasonably assured that you have a product on your hands that you can not only sell, but that you also can sell a lot of. Now get ready for the ride of your life!

Never bring out a product before you find out for sure that your target market really wants it enough to pay for it. Doing so may mean wasting far too much time and money — delaying your ability to create a positive cash flow while creating negative public opinion about your company. Better to wait a few months to fully explore your customer needs and wants than to rush through a great idea that ends up going nowhere.

Carving out a niche

In most economies around the world, competition is a good thing. More competition is better for consumers, causing companies to push technology to the limits while reducing prices to gain advantage over other competitors. But although competition is almost always a certain win for consumers, it can mean big problems for the businesses caught up in it — especially small and home-based businesses.

Why? Because small and home-based businesses are often thinly capitalized; in other words, there is not a lot of cash to spare, and so your marketing dollars as well as your time need to be aimed well.

To avoid the problems that come with competition, carve out your own niche by providing your clients and customers with unique products and services that they can obtain nowhere else.

Here are a number of tips for carving out a niche of your own:

- **Offer a product or service that no one else offers.** Do you remember the Pet Rock? If that little item is before your time, the Pet Rock — created by salesman Gary Dahl in 1975 — was a regular, everyday rock placed in a small cardboard box with a witty instruction manual entitled the *Pet Rock Training Manual.* After appearing on *The Tonight Show*, not once but twice, Dahl sold more than one million Pet Rocks at a price of $3.95 each. Dahl's creation — definitely a product that no one else offered — took the nation by storm and made its inventor rich many times over.

- **Specialize in only one business area or industry.** You can't be everything to everybody, and if you want to be successful, you shouldn't even try. Instead of spreading yourself too thin with too many unrelated products and services, focus on the one or two kinds of products or services that you do best. Peter figured this out a number of years ago when he decided to specialize in writing business books. Before then, in addition to writing business books, he had ghostwritten a book on how to pick up men through the personal ads (written from a woman's perspective!) and completely rewritten a book on dieting and nutrition.

- **Serve an unserved market.** Believe it or not, not every market has yet been tapped by companies eager to sell their products. If you take the time to identify these markets and serve them, you can carve out a niche that others will be hard pressed to match. Chances are you'll find yourself with little or no competition for months or even years.

When you carve out a niche in the market, you're doing nothing more than getting in touch with your potential clients and providing them with exactly the products and services that they want and need. And when you offer that market something that they really want and need, marketing your product will be easier than you ever imagined.

Marketing: Different Roads to Meeting Your Goals

The topic of marketing covers an incredibly broad spectrum of activities, all with one final goal in mind: to spur clients and customers to buy your products and services. When you start your home-based business, marketing should take up most of your schedule. After all, your business isn't going to get very far down the road until you start selling your products and generating the money that you'll need to give it life (and to pay yourself for all

ASK PAUL & SARAH

Growing a repair business

Q: Is my business doomed? I do carpentry and household repairs, and although I have some business, it's just not enough. I don't have any money left to do the kind of advertising I know I should do. I'm not much of a salesman. Is there hope?

A: Yes, there's hope. Many people don't have much sales and marketing experience before starting their first home business and can feel quite overwhelmed by the relentless chore of getting business. Surveys tell us that getting business remains the number-one concern of small and home-based business owners year after year.

Advertising is expensive because, to be effective, it must appear again and again in publications where your targeted customers are looking when they need your services. In a business like yours, if you can afford to, we advise getting an enhanced Yellow Pages listing and localized listings on Yahoo! Get Local and SuperPages. And (for free) you can list on the Craigslist for your city at www.craigslist.org. In addition, you can actively market yourself in several low-cost ways:

✔ **Build a list of all of the people who have regular interaction with potential customers who want and need services like yours right now — not "someday."** For example, real estate agents who have just

sold new homes or who have clients trying to sell a home but needing to make improvements to get their price may fill the bill. Or how about home inspectors who have discovered problems in the homes they inspect? Contact these people by phone or in person, and let them know about you and your service. You aren't selling when you contact them; you're just getting acquainted and making sure they know how to reach you.

✔ **Put these people's names into a database, and send them something monthly.** Consider, for example, a tips newsletter, a postcard about a special offer, or a news clipping related to home improvement.

✔ **Offer mini-workshops or seminars at hardware stores on do-it-yourself home improvements.** You may be surprised at how many people realize they need help after hearing about what they "can" do themselves — especially if your mini-workshops or seminars are free.

✔ **Arrange to leave a specially produced booklet or newsletter at hardware stores.** If you're not already familiar with the software necessary to produce a professional-looking booklet or newsletter, consider hiring a desktop-publishing professional to do it for you.

Four approaches to marketing

When marketing your products and services, an almost unlimited number of approaches are available. Each can be grouped within the following four categories:

✔ **Personal contact:** Whether knocking on your prospective customer's door to pitch your product's advantages face to face, cold-calling on the phone, or buttonholing an acquaintance at your local grocery store, when you market your products directly to your customers one-on-one, you've made personal contact. If you have a great personality (always a plus when you're trying to sell something), if your product is complex, or if your product is best demonstrated live and in person (like that incredible kitchen knife that slices tomatoes and 3-inch-thick steel bars with ease), personal contact is definitely the way to go.

✔ **Through others:** Although you can personally sell only a finite amount of products or services — after all, you only have 24 hours in a day — you can leverage your efforts and sell far more by selling through others. Selling through others involves creating a buzz around your products and services by getting people to talk about them (through word of mouth or through your promotional efforts), obtaining referrals from satisfied customers, and generating interest in the media.

✔ **Written communications:** Brochures, advertisements, newsletters, targeted e-mail messages, sales letters, proposals, and thank-you notes are all different ways of using the power of the written word to sell your products and services. If you're not comfortable selling your company's products and services personally, or if you would have difficulty giving your potential customers samples of your products and services (for example, giving a potential customer a sample of your car-detailing services without actually detailing his car), you should try selling your product through written communications. Again, properly used, written communications can leverage your own direct-selling efforts and generate far more leads and sales than personal contact alone could ever do.

✔ **Showing what you can do:** Sometimes a demonstration of a product or service can spark sales like nothing else. Product samples, videotaped demonstrations, Web sites, house parties, product displays, audio tapes, photos, and trial subscriptions are all ways of showing what you and your business can do for your clients-to-be. When your prospective customers want to try your product before they buy, or if you know that once your customers have a chance to actually use your products or services, they'll be hooked, showing what you can do is the right approach.

Which approach works best for you depends on a variety of factors, including the nature of your business, the likes and dislikes of your typical customer, your customers' buying habits, and the complexity of your product or service. Be sure to keep each of these considerations in mind as you decide which approach to take in marketing your own products and services.

your hard work). As you gain clients and customers — and start doing paid work — you can reduce the amount of time and money that you devote to marketing, but it should never be forgotten. When you own your own business and rely on it for your livelihood, it's important to keep a steady flow of new business in the pipeline, ready to pick up the slack as you complete your work for current clients. For most home-based business owners, plan on making an ongoing commitment of at least 20 percent of your time to marketing activities.

Why bother? Won't your products sell themselves? Few — if any — products truly sell themselves (and if someone trying to sell you on a business opportunity tells you otherwise, your internal lie detector should be on red alert). Selling your products and services requires constant marketing — you can't simply create something and hope it will sell.

The good news is that you can promote your business in a variety of ways. If you decide to tackle even just a few of them, you can easily create a successful marketing campaign for your home-based business that can propel your home-based business to the front of the pack. In the following sections, we show you some of the most popular and effective ways to do just that.

Word of mouth

Word of mouth means getting people to talk about you, your company, and its products and services in a positive light. Of course, the more people talk, the better your company looks as a result, and the better it is for your business. That's exactly why any good promotional campaign starts off with a heavy emphasis on generating positive word-of-mouth excitement. There's nothing like a little bit of buzz to get your sales to take off.

Here are some of the best ways to get people talking about your business:

- **Networking:** Everyone has a circle of friends and acquaintances — both in work lives and in nonwork lives. Or you might belong to a community-service or fraternal or sororal organization such as Optimists, Junior League, Rotary, BPO Elks, Lions International, or others. Your networks of friends and acquaintances are probably the first and best places to start a word-of-mouth campaign for promoting your business. They know you, they like you (at least, we hope so), and they will be willing to tell *their* friends and acquaintances about you (who will then tell others, and on and on). See the following section on referrals for more information.

- **Volunteering:** Why not give something back to your community by volunteering your time? Whether helping out at a local school, crisis center, animal shelter, or other community-based organization, you can be sure to meet a variety of people who may one day become your future clients and customers. Chances are, members of the board of directors and some volunteers are influential people who, if they like you and what you do, can give you business or refer business to you (see the following section for more on referrals).

✔ **Sponsorships:** Sponsoring a kids' baseball team, local charity, parade, or other special event can be another good way to generate word-of-mouth promotional opportunities. Be careful, though, that you're not just one sponsor lost in a flood of others — your message will be ineffective. It's far better to choose your opportunities so that your business is featured and particularly noticeable to your target audience.

✔ **Business cards and letterhead:** These are the mainstays of most businesses' promotional efforts. Your letterhead and business cards can convey a lot of information to your prospective clients and customers, and get people talking about your business. Invest a few dollars in a professional logo design, and you'll make a great first impression on your prospects while conveying the right kind of message to your current customers and clients.

Word of mouth costs your business little, but the payoff can be great. Look for opportunities to generate a buzz about your business wherever and whenever you can. If people aren't talking about your business, you can be sure they won't be buying from it, either!

Referrals

Getting *referrals* — when people you know direct clients and acquaintances to your business — is the number-one way that many home-based businesses obtain new business. Although current clients are your bread and butter, and the best possible sources for vital repeat business, new clients provide opportunities to grow your business while covering for financial shortfalls if current customers decide to shop elsewhere.

Referrals are extremely powerful because when they come to you, they have already been presold on your business and your products or services. Here are some other advantages:

✔ **Referrals are less expensive than many other kinds of marketing.** No costly Yellow Pages ads to run, no billboards to erect, and no extravagant mail-order campaign to launch. Referrals cost little or no money to obtain. And maintaining a favorable relationship with the people who give you referrals means simply doing good work for them and letting them know from time to time that you appreciate their business (perhaps with a discount on your products or services, a small gift, or some other token of your appreciation).

✔ **Referred customers trust you.** When people turn to their trusted friends and business acquaintances for advice on whom to hire for a particular job or to provide a particular product, they automatically tend believe the recommendations that they hear. As the saying goes, *You have only one chance to make a first impression.* When someone recommends you, you've already made a positive first impression with your client-to-be.

✔ **Referred customers are ready to buy from you.** When people ask their friends and business acquaintances for referrals, they're ready to buy. People wouldn't ask if they weren't. And because people trust the opinion of those they ask, most people go no further in their search for sources than the person or business recommended to them.

Identifying potential referrals

So where do you find referrals? Here are the most common places:

✔ **Family and friends:** If you don't yet have current clients, family and friends are a great place to start for getting referrals. Make sure that everyone you personally know is familiar with your new venture — what it is and what you do — and that you're looking for customers to help get it off the ground. Most will be more than happy to help.

✔ **Current clients:** If you're doing good work for your current clients (and you are, aren't you?), they will refer friends and business acquaintances to you when asked for recommendations. Just make sure you don't let your work with your current clients suffer as you take on new work — you need to walk a very fine balance in your business between delivering on your current work and developing new work.

To help ensure that your clients will want to share you with others (don't laugh; some may want to keep you all to themselves), be sure to meaningfully thank them for the referrals they make and consider providing additional incentives for providing them. Examples of incentives depend on the kind of business you have but could include half off their next order or a free automobile detail.

✔ **Business associates:** Vendors and other nonclient business associates can be another rich source of referrals. If you have a good reputation in your field, and if they like you, they will gladly tell their business associates about you. Of course, they will be equally happy if you send some business their way, too.

✔ **Other home-based businesses:** Many home-based businesses are one-person operations and, as such, can have a hard time dealing with the inevitable business peaks and valleys. Sometimes work is plentiful, sometimes not. In those times when another home-based business is overwhelmed, a good option is to farm the extra work out to a trusted and proven company — yours. Why not become the company of choice for other home-based businesses in your industry?

Getting referrals for your business

Okay, now that you know where to find your referrals, exactly how are you supposed to get them? Unless you find a genie in a lamp on the beach, the best way is simply to ask. When you do good work for a client, thank her for choosing you, and let her know that referrals are welcome and appreciated. The following is a list of five other great ways to get referrals:

- **Do great work.** By far the best way to get great referrals is to do great work. People are proud of themselves when they find businesses that provide them with above-average service and products, and they want to tell others of their good fortune (and their good business sense). Do great work, and your clients and customers will be the best marketing tools you could ever ask for.

- **Build a mailing list.** A mailing list of all your referrals can be a powerful tool in your promotional efforts. Because they are already presold on you and your business, your referrals will generally welcome hearing from you on an ongoing basis. List Builder (www.listbuilder.com) is a terrific Internet e-mail-based service that allows you to send periodic newsletters to your referrals for a nominal fee. Just one click of the button, and your message is sent to your entire mailing list — whether it consists of one person or a thousand — in a matter of seconds. Your clients can opt into and out of your mailing list easily and with the barest minimum of muss or fuss.

- **Keep your mailing list informed.** Many home-based business owners have discovered the value of keeping their referrals up-to-date with the latest news about their products and services. Not only do past and present clients enjoy reading such stories, but they also really enjoy reading about themselves. Make a point of playing up customer success stories as much as possible.

- **Always send a thank-you note.** People appreciate it when you take the time to thank them for sending you a referral. Whenever a new customer is referred to you, make a point of immediately sending a handwritten thank-you note to the referrer. It's far better to take the time to personalize your thank-you note than to just dash off a quick e-mail. Depending on the nature of your business, you can also send a small gift or a certificate good for a discount on your client's next purchase.

- **Make referrals yourself.** As your business grows, you'll soon find that people come to you seeking referrals. Pick out several high-quality and trusted companies to use for referrals, and be sure to let their owners know when you have sent a client their way. Not only will your clients be thankful for the referral, but the companies to which you make referrals will also be more likely to make referrals to you.

Public relations

In general, *public relations* (PR) means the release of information to the general public to favorably influence its opinion about you, your business, or your products and services. Because of the nature of PR — and the potential for information to be broadcast over a wide area through print or electronic media — its successful execution can lead to your message being communicated to an amazing number of people. If you handle your own public relations, the cost is minimal. If you farm it out to a consultant or PR firm, expect to pay $50 to $100 per hour or more.

Collaborating without getting lost

Q: We are a new small business. We offer public relations, marketing, and fund-raising. A local advertising agency has outsourced several small jobs to us. Now the owner wants to include our names on his marketing materials but doesn't want to use our company name. Is this standard business practice? It seems like he's using our services to market his business.

A: Business-to-business collaboration is *one of the major trends* increasingly common among small businesses today. In researching our book *Teaming Up,* we found that 65 percent of the business owners we interviewed — all of whom had been in business for more than five years — were teaming up in some way with other small businesses, and most wanted to do even more in the future. One message was clear, though: In creating such collaborations, there is no standard business practice unless it would be to say, "It's all negotiable."

We found ten types of strategic alliances that range from networking to virtual organizations. Many types of collaborations, such as joint ventures and mutual referral agreements, involve each company promoting its own identity. In others, like satellite subcontracting and interdependent alliances, the company that gets the business usually is the one whose company name is used on a particular contract. Here are the types of alliances we found:

- ✔ Networking
- ✔ Mutual referrals
- ✔ Cross-promoting
- ✔ Interdependent alliances
- ✔ Joint ventures
- ✔ Satellite subcontracting
- ✔ Consortiums
- ✔ Family/spouse collaboration
- ✔ Partnerships
- ✔ Virtual organizations

Kurt Zell, for example, has a production company through which he subcontracts work to independent camera and sound professionals. He gets the business and brings in independent professionals who work as part of his organization. They are paid by Zell's company, not by the client. In relationships like this, it would be highly unethical for a subcontractor to market his own business to clients brought in through the contractor.

In your situation, the ad exec evidently believes that including your names and expertise on his marketing materials will help him get more business. For you, this arrangement could mean an inflow of new business with no marketing costs. But you must determine if you see a downside to such an arrangement. If so, strive to negotiate a more desirable arrangement.

Among your options would be to suggest that you contribute to the cost of producing his business cards and marketing materials in return for including your company name. Then you can agree to pay a referral fee for any business that comes directly to you from these materials or simply agree to bring the agency in on any business project arising from these materials. Alternatively, you can include his services on your promotional materials as a way of helping you attract larger projects that include advertising.

- **Publicity (newspapers, magazines, Internet, and other media):** Have you ever seen a newspaper article about some hot new local business or a special-interest TV news story about the latest-and-greatest home-based business opportunity? Chances are it's no accident that that particular piece of news made it to your eyes and ears — the business that is its subject likely spent money to make sure it showed up on the media radar screen. The media thrive on interesting stories, especially human-interest ones with an uplifting message. By creating an interesting and positive story around your business — and getting it in front of the media — you can generate the kind of publicity you seek, drawing potential clients and customers in the process.

- **Press releases:** Press releases are brief summaries of company news that are specifically targeted at the media. The hope is that newspapers, magazines, radio, television, and other media outlets will find the press release newsworthy and give it exposure. Chances are they will. The good news is that if the media pick up on your press release and publicize it, you'll get wide distribution for free. To have the best chance of gaining the kind of reaction you seek from the media, be sure your press release is tailored to the particular interests of the media outlet that you seek. A pitch to *Oprah*, for example, is going to be quite different from a pitch to *Late Night with David Letterman*, which will be different again from a pitch written to your small, hometown weekly newspaper.

- **Letters to the editor:** Anyone can write a letter to the editor, about most any topic. It's easy, and it offers a unique way to get your message in front of thousands of readers at a price that's hard to beat: the price of a first-class stamp (or less, if you write via e-mail). If, for example, you own a home-based business that specializes in home security systems (alarms, deadbolt locks, and so on), you can comment on a recent article about a rise in crime rates while throwing in a plug for the products and services that your company happens to sell.

- **Speeches:** Have you thought about making a speech to a local service club — say, a Rotary or Lions Club — or to local business organizations? All kinds of business associations, clubs, and other organizations exist in every city, and they tend to have lots of meetings. And guess what every organization needs for every meeting? A speaker. Whether you speak to your local chamber of commerce, the Society for Human Resources Professionals, or a local software *special interest group* (SIG), you have a great opportunity to promote yourself and your company by sharing your expertise with others. And you just may get a free lunch or dinner out of it, too (but beware: they don't call it the rubber-chicken circuit for nothing).

- **Seminars:** Seminars are a terrific way to generate new customers and clients — and make a few bucks in the process. Home-based financial planners, for example, often use seminars to generate business. Here's how that works: You send out announcements for a free seminar, usually held at a nice local hotel, to prospective customers and possible referral sources. Rent out a meeting room at the hotel (much better than trying to jam 65 people into your living room), and arrange for the seminar to be catered with a light meal and refreshments. During the course of the seminar, you provide attendees with lots of usable information and pass out brochures, pamphlets, and other promotional material — all emblazoned with your company's name and contact information. After the seminar, guess who the attendees' first choice is whenever they have questions about the subject matter of the seminar or need help setting up their own personal financial plan?

One of the great things about public relations is that if you have a bit of time to spend, you can generate your own PR materials and make your own contacts. And the more PR you do, the better you'll get at it. Not only will you become more confident in your abilities and savvy in how the system works, but you'll also make contacts in the media and in your community that you can keep coming back to.

Direct marketing

Direct marketing means making direct contact with potential clients, most often by mailing, faxing, or e-mailing them promotional messages. However you do it, the point is to get your message squarely in front of a decision-maker in a way that will capture his interest in a moment. Any longer, and your prospect will likely throw your message in the trash — at no small expense to you and your business.

- ✔ **Direct mail:** Although direct mail — or, ahem, junk mail — can be a major headache for many who receive it, when it's targeted precisely to potential customers and clients, it can be a cost-effective way of getting your message in front of the people most likely to buy your products and services. You can target your prospects very precisely by renting mailing lists of people within specific demographic groups. Do you want to reach human resources managers only? No problem. People who live within a particular ZIP code? Easy. People who recently bought a house? Piece of cake. For a fairly reasonable fee, you can buy hundreds or even thousands of up-to-date mailing labels for exactly the kind of people you want to reach with your message. Regardless of how much people complain about receiving direct-mail solicitations, enough of them usually respond to make it worthwhile. For more information on direct-mail marketing, check out the Direct Mail Association Web site (www.the-dma.org).

- ✔ **Circulars and flyers:** With a computer and a printer or photocopier, you can create all the circulars and flyers you could ever want, make thousands of copies, and blanket your clients-to-be with them. Drop them in your direct-mail envelopes, or pass them around your neighborhood. With a little practice, you can create circulars and flyers in minutes, and the price is very easy on the budget. You probably won't get as good a response as you would from a direct-mail campaign, but it's certainly worth a try.

✔ **Giveaways and contests:** One of the tried-and-true methods of attracting the attention of potential clients is to give something away — the more attractive the prize, the more attention you'll get. And that's really the whole point of promoting your business: to attract your potential clients' attention long enough to show them the benefits of your products and services.

✔ **Incentives:** Businesses commonly use incentives to get prospective clients and customers to buy. Whether you offer two for the price of one or give a coupon for 10 percent off the next purchase, incentives are a standard tool in the marketing campaigns of many regular businesses, and they work just as well for home-based businesses.

✔ **Newsletters:** If you're ready to get a bit more sophisticated in your direct-marketing efforts, consider creating a newsletter. Businesses create newsletters to provide customers and clients with value-added tools and information while also serving as a platform for promoting the company's products and services. If you run a pet-sitting business out of your home, you can create a one- or two-page newsletter with the latest trends in pet care, along with plugs for your business. If you're a lawyer who specializes in employment law, you can keep your clients up-to-date on the latest developments in the field. Sending your newsletter by e-mail or fax lowers your costs and time investment.

One more thing: If you have neither the time nor inclination to create a quality newsletter yourself, consider hiring a home-based desktop publishing professional to do it for you.

You can spend as little or as much as you want on direct marketing, but the results you get will be directly proportional to the amount of money and effort you put into preparing your direct-marketing pieces and precisely selecting the individuals who receive your message. Investing some quality time and money now will pay off big-time later.

Advertising

When many people think about marketing, they are thinking about advertising. Advertising your products and services can be an effective way to get the word out, but it can also be expensive (and, frankly, a waste of money for many home-based businesses). The key is to be sure that your advertisements are specifically targeted and that you advertise in places where your potential clients are most likely to read or hear your message.

✔ **Yellow Pages ads:** For many businesses, running a Yellow Pages advertisement is essential. It can be expensive — in the thousands of dollars for an ad large enough to stand out — but effective. Can you imagine a successful plumbing, appliance repair, or tree-trimming business — home based or not — that doesn't rely heavily on the Yellow Pages?

✔ **Business directories:** Business directories are another good way to get the word out about your company, as long as your potential clients and customers are likely to see your listing. Most directories have traditionally been available in printed form, but an increasing number are now found on the Internet. With just a few mouse clicks, your clients-to-be will be able to find out more about your company and discover what it has to offer them.

✔ **Web site:** Creating a Web site to market your business and its products and services is a must for most businesses today, small and large. The good news is that starting up and maintaining a Web site is easier and less expensive than ever. (See the "Web sites and e-commerce" section later in this chapter and Chapter 5 for more information.)

✔ **Web site advertisements:** Although banner advertisements have long been the standard method for advertising businesses on the Web, a relatively new innovation is taking hold: targeted advertising on search engines such as Google (in Google's case, called AdWords) that is geared to specific keyword searches. If you're a home-based plumber, for example, you can have your business show up at the top of the list whenever someone does a keyword search for *faucet repair*. You don't pay unless the person doing the searching clicks your listing. Relative to print, radio, and TV ads (which are quite expensive), Web site advertisements are a bargain. Better yet is getting links to your site from as many other high-traffic Web sites as you can.

✔ **Your own radio or TV show:** Would you like to get your message out to thousands of people every week? Why not host your own radio or television show? If your business is interesting enough to generate public interest, you have a real shot at it. Paul and Sarah's radio show, "The *Entrepreneur* Magazine Home-Based Biz Show," on wsRadio.com reaches many thousands of listeners each week.

Web sites and e-commerce

More businesses than ever are moving to establish a presence on the Internet, and being e-commerce–capable is rapidly becoming the standard worldwide. Despite challenges facing an organization that decides to market itself on the Web (getting your site noticed in a sea of millions is just one challenge), having a Web site is still a great idea for many home-based businesses. If your company doesn't yet have its own site, chances are it soon will. The simple fact is that building and maintaining a Web site is now considered to be essential to any organization's marketing plan — just as important as printing brochures; placing ads in targeted publications; networking with potential clients; and performing other, more traditional marketing activities.

At its heart, a company Web site is nothing more than a glossy, full-color brochure — with a twist: The Web site is available to potential clients instantly, anywhere in the world, at any time of the day or night. It can be interactive, respond to visitor queries, communicate with clients in real time through online chats and message forums, and provide customers a place to research your products — and buy them.

Today, any business can have a Web site, including home-based businesses. Our advice is that if you believe your sales will benefit by establishing a Web presence for your business, make creating a Web site a priority.

Even if your business is a local, high-touch one, a Web site is important because:

✔ **It increasingly serves in lieu of a printed or mailed brochure — one that can be updated immediately.** A Web site is a much faster and generally more convenient way for your potential customers to get information about your products and services. Instead of waiting to receive a brochure in the mail, they can type in your Web site address and obtain the information in seconds.

ASK PAUL & SARAH

Is creating a Web site a good idea?

Q: I'm a photographer and sell most of my work through art fairs. Recently, more and more people are asking me if I have a Web site. I don't, but I'm starting to wonder if I should. What would the advantages really be, and would they be worth both the time and the money?

A: Having a Web site for any business is fairly common today. We just interviewed hundreds of home-based businesses for *The Best Home Businesses for People 50+* and found the majority of them have Web sites. This is about double the percentage when the first edition of this book came out in 2000. But there are some holdouts.

You won't be surprised to find out we think having a Web site is worth it. On the up side, we found many people, from interim executives to former brick-and-mortar shop owners, who get their business or do their business from the Web.

Because photographs are visual, selling yourself and them via a Web site is a natural. You can sell your images on your own Web site. However, we believe you should put up a Web site only when you are able and willing to keep it up. A Web address that yields a "Cannot find" message or is obviously out-of-date works against you, particularly if you're using your site to attract photography clients.

So if you're not ready for your own site, you can sell your images on such sites as Photographers' Portfolios at www.vsii.com/portfolio/homeport.html, Portfolios Online at www.portfolios.com, and Sell Photos at www.sellphotos.com.

We suggest visiting the sites of other photographers and talking with them about their experiences. For example, nature photographer Ernest Hori has a site at www.horizenfoto.com, and portrait photographer Mary Ann Halpin has one at www.goddesshood.com.

✔ **With a clear majority of homes and businesses having Internet access, increasingly people are going online to check out a business they have heard about or been referred to.** To not be there when they click is to ensure losing business. For this reason, it's a good idea to use your business name as your Web site address. Only a little over 10 percent of all Web sites are found in search engines, so you want to make finding your business on the Web as easy and intuitive as possible.

✔ **The Web is becoming the new Yellow Pages.** Getting listed in search engines and exchanging links with sites that people are likely to turn to when looking for your kind of business is good business for you.

But what if you know nothing about creating a Web site? How do you go about making one happen? Will you have to spend thousands of dollars to get your Web site up and running, or do you have more affordable options? These and other questions are addressed in detail in Chapter 5.

Developing a Marketing Plan — Now!

Whenever you want to achieve a measurable goal within a specific period of time, you greatly enhance your chances of doing so by having a plan. Plans make your goals real: They organize and prioritize your actions, and they tell you how far along you are toward achieving them.

If you've read through some of the earlier sections of this chapter, you're probably already thinking of lots of ways to start marketing your products and services. You may be ready to start up a Web site, seek referrals, or create an e-mail newsletter for your current customers and clients. A marketing plan is simply a written version of the many different ideas that are probably now spinning through your head. It's not the same as a business plan, which takes a much broader look at your business goals and plans, including marketing. A *marketing plan* summarizes all of your marketing goals and strategies, along with the actual methods you can use to achieve them, and states milestones and deadlines for achieving your goals. A marketing plan answers the following questions:

✔ Who are your target customers and clients?

✔ What are your unique product attributes and advantages in the marketplace?

✔ Where will you focus your marketing efforts?

✔ When will you implement each step in your marketing plan?

✔ How much revenue do you expect your marketing plans to generate, and how much will it cost you to generate that level of sales?

This marketing plan belongs to you, and you can make it as simple or as complex as you want. If you're just starting out, a one-page or even a one-paragraph plan may be just right. As your company gets bigger, you may see benefits in expanding your plan to meet its growing needs.

The following sections review the five key parts of a good marketing plan.

Part 1: Overview

Also known as an *executive summary,* the *marketing plan overview* provides a glimpse of your overall plan without bogging the reader down in the details that are presented later in the document. Upon reading the overview, a reader can get a pretty good idea about your overall marketing strategy, market focus, product focus, and the tactics and programs you plan to put into effect. *Projected revenues* — the estimated amount of money you intend to bring into the business during the period of the plan, as well as the budget required to achieve that level of sales — are also important parts of the marketing-plan overview.

Part 2: Marketing objectives

Marketing goals and objectives define the targets that you hope to achieve in your marketing efforts. Your goals may be modest *(To increase sales 10 percent a year for the next three years)* or quite ambitious *(To be the company of choice whenever anyone in the nation needs a dog groomed).*

This section of the marketing plan should, at a minimum, include:

- ✔ An overall objective for your marketing efforts *(To become the preferred source of Internet solutions for doctors and dentists).*
- ✔ Several specific marketing objectives, such as units sold, *market share* (the percentage of the overall market that your company commands), or distribution channels *(Twenty-five percent of sales will be through Target stores).*
- ✔ Basic financial objectives, such as total sales and profit for the year.

Part 3: Situation analysis

This part of the marketing plan reveals what's going on in the marketplace: who your competition is, which similar products exist and what their relative success is, market trends, and so on. The idea is to develop a good understanding of your customer base, its needs and wants, and your strengths and weaknesses relative to the competition. Be sure to include the following:

✔ A summary of the *demographics* (the characteristics of a population, such as age, gender, income, and so on), and economic, technological, and social trends that impact your customers. You can get this information through the Internet or the reference section of your public library.

✔ A list of your key competitors, including strengths, weaknesses, products and services, market share, and other key information. See Chapter 8 for how best to collect this kind of information.

✔ A brief discussion of your target customer, as well as his or her wants and needs. You should know your customer as well as you know the back of your hand — perhaps even better.

✔ A summary of your key products and services, along with a discussion of their advantages and disadvantages versus the competition.

✔ A discussion of your current distribution channels (if any) and how they help or hinder the product marketing process.

Part 4: Marketing strategies

For every key marketing objective listed in your plan (see "Part 2: Marketing objectives," earlier in this chapter), you should have one or more marketing strategies for achieving it. Include a minimum of the following:

✔ The specific features of your products and services that you can use to help you market them, such as convenience, speed, ease of use, and so on. Consider why people will buy your products and services instead of someone else's.

✔ A pricing strategy for your products and services. To find out more about the fine art of product pricing, check out Chapter 8.

✔ Specific strategies to promote your products. For ideas on promoting your products, see earlier in this chapter.

✔ Specific strategies for getting your products and services into the hands of your customers and clients. This, for example, includes using e-commerce and developing relationships with distributors.

Part 5: Financials

This part of the marketing plan takes all the words in the previous sections and turns them into numbers — specifically, dollars and cents. An annual marketing plan gives financial information for an entire year and may be broken down into months or quarters. Be sure to include the following:

> ✔ Detailed projections of anticipated revenues and percentage growth (or decline) — by product or service — from the previous period. For example, revenues of $55,000 for the year, reflecting 10 percent growth over the previous year.
>
> ✔ Detailed projections of expenses required to obtain the projected revenues. For example, attending industry conferences, including roundtrip airfares, hotels, taxis, and the cost of meals.

When putting your marketing plan into action, consider using Paul and Sarah's 5/5/5 approach to marketing. The *5/5/5 approach* involves using five different avenues for reaching prospects, and initiating and following through on five different activities every day, week, or month, depending on how much business you need (daily, if you have little or no business yet; weekly, if you have some but need more; monthly, if you have ample business and want to be sure you sustain it). This is the best way we've found to be sure you are doing the level of marketing activity you need to succeed. You can get further details in their book *Getting Business to Come to You.*

Putting an idea into action

Q: I've drawn up a plethora of sketches of blue jeans, and now I'm satisfied with one I think the public would rush to purchase. How do I proceed with manufacturing and finding a buyer?

A: Some business experts may view the idea of a solo novice designer like yourself going head-to-head in a highly competitive field of giants like Levi's and Lee to be a pipe dream. But we've seen too many people defy the odds to discourage you from proceeding if you're sufficiently passionate, committed, and determined. The novice designers we've seen succeed have done so in two ways: by carving out a highly specific niche, such as designing specialized clothing for yoga devotees, orthodox Jewish professional women, or people with physical disabilities; or, for a mainstream item like jeans, by starting small and building up an avid following for a unique design that makes their line desirable to sales reps and retail stores.

So before leaping into mass production here or abroad, we suggest offering your jeans directly to what you hope will be a mad rush of avid buyers by making (or hiring someone to make) several dozen and selling them yourself. You can do this at swap meets or sidewalk booths (as Ash Hudson did with his wildly popular Conart T-shirts) or by placing them in a few select boutiques (as Anna and Sarah Levinson did with their brightly colored Ripe Cosmetic nail polishes). After your jeans begin selling rapidly and attracting growing numbers of customers, you'll be ready to arrange for mass production and to contact reps or buyers — if they haven't sought you out already.

You can contact reps through the Manufacturers' Agents National Association (MANA) at One Spectrum Pointe, Suite 150, Lake Forest, CA 92630, (877) 626-2776, www.manaonline.org.

Chapter 5

Making the Web Work for You

*W*e've all heard about the tremendous opportunities that the Internet has opened up for businesses of all sizes, shapes, and locations. Today, even the smallest home-based business — located in the most remote location in the country (can anyone say Nome, Alaska?) — can sell its products and services to a worldwide base of customers via a Web site.

But there are a lot of other businesses out there, all trying to get noticed and all trying to become the next Amazon or Google. The good news is that you don't have to become a huge company to take advantage of the Internet — many small, home-based businesses are doing quite well, thank you, selling their products and services via the Web.

And you can, too.

In this chapter, we explore using the Internet to bid for work and how to get listed and noticed in online directories. We explore the best approaches and places for networking with others on the Net and take a look at participating in Web-based collaborations and teams. Finally, we consider the best ways to attract clients and customers with your Web site and how to build and maintain one that's first-class.

Bidding for Work

Something interesting has been happening on the Internet over the past several years — a number of freelance bidding sites have sprung up with the express purpose of getting independent, home-based businesspeople together with companies that need work done. Although some such sites may be scams (see Chapter 13 for more about those), more than a few offer legitimate opportunities to home workers.

Let's take a look at what you need to know to use the Internet to leverage your own business opportunities.

Sites that specialize in putting buyers and sellers together

So what, exactly, is a freelance bidding site? A *freelance bidding site* is a Web site where companies can list jobs they need done (anything from writing advertising copy to building Web sites to doing graphic design), and freelancers can bid on the work. The company needing the work selects a freelancer and assigns the work, the home-based businessperson does the work and pays the bidding site a commission (usually, between 5 and 10 percent), and everyone is happy.

In general, here's how freelance bidding sites work:

- ✔ Visit the site of your choice and register.

- ✔ Build your online résumé, adding your particular skills and experience to the site. Be specific!

- ✔ Conduct a search for projects that are suited to your experience. Look beyond the main categories at the subcategories and specialties.

- ✔ Bid on a project by providing an estimate of the price for the job and your time frame for completion.

- ✔ Negotiate a deal with an interested company; then do the work.

For someone with the right skills, this can be a relatively easy way to develop an ongoing stream of work that may be quite lucrative. Plenty of freelance bidding sites are out there, but be sure to check these out:

- ✔ www.scriptlance.com

- ✔ www.smarterwork.com

- ✔ www.ework.com

- ✔ www.elance.com

- ✔ www.prosavvy.com

For a very comprehensive (and up-to-date) listing of legitimate freelance bidding sites, click on over to the FreelanceMom site: www.freelancemom.com/gigs.htm.

Tips for winning bids

Guess what? You may be very well qualified in whatever it is that you do. You may have tons of experience and skills out the wazoo. But you're not alone. There are lots of other people with just as much experience — maybe more — and you're going to be competing with some of them when you decide to bid on a project. Here are ten tips on how to win that dream project:

✔ Become intimately familiar with how the freelance bidding site you're using works.

✔ Make your profile first-rate. In it, show your background in the field; your education, training, and credentials; the services you offer; and the range of your rates. If you need help with writing your profile, consider posting it as a job on one of the freelance boards for a writer to help you. You'll experience firsthand what it's like to receive bids and what impresses you about the bidders.

✔ Put up a portfolio with samples of your work. What a photographer or graphic or Web designer uses as samples is fairly obvious, but if you're a consultant, it's still worthwhile. To provide examples of projects you've managed successfully, if you have testimonials from customers, use them as text or audio files.

✔ Demonstrate that you have the skills and tools needed to do the job, so if you're seeking virtual-assistant–type work, and you're certified in Microsoft Office Certification, say so. Don't be shy — show the buyer what you've got to offer.

✔ Don't place your bids automatically or based on guesswork Ask good questions of the company or person seeking bids. Often, work descriptions are too sketchy or leave gaps.

✔ You are competing against bidders from all over the world, many of whom can and will underbid the prices most North Americans can charge. Do some market research; check to see what your competitors are bidding for the kind of work you want to do. Keep in mind wary buyers are apt to be just as suspicious of extremely low bids as they are turned off by a high one.

✔ Propose payment schedules that will show you're motivated to get the work done in a timely manner, such as asking for a relatively low initial down payment of 20 or 25 percent and with progress payments based on agreed-upon milestones.

✔ Go into more depth on your own Web site than you can with your portfolio. Portfolios can be too long, taxing buyers with too much to look at. Remember: They're reviewing other bidders' profiles and portfolios. If you interest them, they'll want to know more about you.

✔ If you're using Elance, consider becoming a Select Service provider. This helps the positioning of your bid and assures your prospects that your credentials have been verified.

✔ If at first you don't succeed . . . learn from your experience, and try again!

Keys to keeping clients and building your business with them

The best business relationships are long-term business relationships. Believe us: A bird in hand is definitely worth two or three in the bush. Whenever possible, work to build strong relationships with your current clients and customers that will keep them bringing business your way far into the future.

Here are some tips for keeping your clients happy and building long-term business relationships:

✔ **Be on time and on budget.** No client likes to hire someone who delivers his products or services late or wants more money to do the work than originally quoted.

✔ **Do great work.** Great work speaks for itself, and it will separate you from the home-based business wannabes.

✔ **Be flexible.** Business today is faster than ever, and companies must be able to change direction at moment's notice to keep up. So should you.

✔ **Be dependable and reliable.** Be someone your client can rely on — if you are, you've already got most of your competition beat.

✔ **No surprises!** Don't surprise your client with bad news — keep her informed if you anticipate problems or delays.

Getting Listed in Directories

Back in the good old pre-Internet days, if you were a small business and you wanted to attract customers or clients — especially if you ran your business out of your home or some other nonstorefront location — one of the first things you would do would be run an ad in the Yellow Pages. Having a listing in the Yellow Pages was essential for many kinds of businesses, especially service businesses such as plumbers, building contractors, tree trimmers, and many others.

Although the Yellow Pages are nowhere near obsolete yet, there's a new directory on the block: the *online directory*. In this section, we'll explore some of the most common versions of this new business tool.

Online business directories

There are more online business directories on the Internet today than you can shake a stick at. These electronic Yellow Pages are all over the Internet. Some are — like anything else in life — better than others. Here are a few of the best:

- www.directory.google.com
- www.yahoo.com
- www.dmoz.org
- www.business.com
- www.bizweb.com
- www.abusinessresource.com
- www.industrialquicksearch.com
- www.businesspatrol.com
- www.b2btoday.com

You can get your site placed on any number of online directories, but our advice is to stick to the top ones — that is, the ones that get the most traffic and the ones specifically targeted to your kind of business (for example, a directory of landscape architects). Seek out these directories, and apply to have your site listed. You may have to follow up to ensure that it is indeed listed and that the listing information is correct. Be persistent if you need to be — it's your business we're talking about here.

Association memberships

Do you belong to an association? For example, if you're a graphic artist, you might belong to the Graphic Artists Guild or the Society of American Graphic Artists. Or you might belong to your local chamber of commerce or a community-based business association. Whatever your affiliation, one of the fringe benefits of belonging to many associations is the opportunity to be listed in their online member directories.

Go to the Graphic Artists Guild Web site, for example (www.gag.org), and you can look at not just a listing of association members, but samples of their work as well, organized by practice: cartooning, graphic design, package design, and so forth. Associations do this to showcase the work of their members — all the better for a potential client who is looking for a certain style of artwork.

If you don't yet belong to an association, consider joining one and getting listed in its online directory. If you already belong, make sure to take advantage of all the promotional and networking activities your association has to offer, including being listed in their online directories. One more thing: If there are changes in your business, such as a new phone number or Web site, remember to keep your directory listings current.

Going local: SmartPage listings and search-engine local listings

The problem with many online search engines and directories is that they include the whole wide world when you just want to attract customers in your small town in Saskatchewan. Some search engines and directories are getting wise to this desire and are creating services that focus on local offerings. When someone does a search for a specific kind of business — say, an aquarium or bookkeeping service — she can specify a city and state in which to search, providing results that are much more relevant and useful than what she'd get if the entire world was included in the search.

Here's a sampling of some of the most popular:

- ✔ www.smartpages.com
- ✔ www.local.google.com
- ✔ www.citysearch.com
- ✔ www.local.yahoo.com
- ✔ www.dogpile.com
- ✔ www.411web.com
- ✔ www.jumptoyourcity.com
- ✔ www.yell.com (Great Britain)

Again, just as in other online directories, be sure your business is listed. If it's not, submit it to the listing service, using whatever process they require. As soon as your listing goes live, be sure to check the information — business name, address, phone number, e-mail address, Web site URL — for accuracy.

Networking the Internet Way

There's more to getting noticed on the Net than just putting up a Web site and waiting for the crowds to arrive. You can also make a splash — while driving traffic to your own site — by personally getting noticed on *other people's* Web sites. If you've got a particularly lively personality, or if you're knowledgeable and enjoy giving advice to others, and if you're polite and not prone to *flaming* (publicly insulting your online colleagues), you may soon find yourself a very popular fixture on many different Web sites — not just your own.

Online forums

There are online forums devoted to just about every conceivable hobby, business, activity, and avocation imaginable: parenting; steam trains; Tivo digital video recorders; vintage Jeeps; politics; personal finance and investing; math; freedom; writing children's books; and much, much more. If you can imagine it, someone probably has a forum on it.

Here's how one home-based business owner networks with potential customers through an online forum:

Doug Roccaforte is the founder and owner of Roccaforte Amps (`www. roccaforteamps.com`), a Brea, California-based manufacturer of high-end electric guitar amplifiers used by professional musicians such as Marc Ford, Ben Harper, Cesar Rosas, and many others. Sure, Doug could be content attending trade shows, developing his dealer network, and placing advertisements in guitar magazines, but he also spends time at the Amps discussion forum at `www.harmony-central.com`, which is most likely the most popular guitar-amplifier forum on the Internet. Doug is a very well-known and popular regular there. Not only is he a colorful personality — with strong opinions and a wry sense of humor — but he is also respected by forum members as one of today's greatest guitar-amplifier designers and manufacturers. The fact that he spends time on the site and is willing to give his advice and opinions about topics of interest to forum members keeps his products front and center in their minds and develops a buzz that no amount of advertising alone could buy, leading to lots of additional sales — sales that wouldn't have occurred without Doug's presence on the site.

What sites are devoted to topics that relate to your products or services? Seek them out, become a member, and begin contributing. For a relatively small investment of your time, you'll definitely see a positive impact on *your* bottom line.

You can find lists of forums and newsgroups on Google's Group directory site (`http://groups.google.com`) and the Yahoo! Groups site (`http://groups.yahoo.com`), as well as at sites like Jump City (`www.jumpcity.com`) and Tile.net (`www.tile.net`). You can search for listserv groups on the software company's Web site at `www.lsoft.com`. Joining is easy, but remember to learn and honor the unique etiquette for each group you join.

Many trade and professional associations have forums; some associations open them up to nonmembers. You can find many of these at the American Society of Association Executives' site (`www.asaenet.org`), where the group provides a "Gateway to Associations" as a service to the public.

Social networking sites

Social networking sites are a relatively recent phenomenon: Web sites devoted to creating networks and communities of new friends and acquaintances. As members are added, they bring along their own network of family and friends, quickly creating large online social networks, some linked by common interests (such as business) and some not. Here are a few examples:

- `www.ecademy.com`
- `www.friendster.com`
- `www.i-neighbors.org`
- `www.linkedin.com`
- `www.mobile.match.com`
- `www.ryze.com`
- `www.tribe.net`
- `www.fastcompany.com/cof`

Although the chances of developing serious business from your participation in a social networking site are more remote than by participating in forums specific to your expertise or business, if you've got the extra time available to make your presence known, it might be worth a try.

Online etiquette for making winning relationships

Just as in your offline life, there are rules and norms for behavior while participating in online forums and networks. Here are some basic rules to follow so that you'll find yourself a welcome participant rather than someone to be avoided.

Do . . .

- ✔ **Stay on topic.** Make a point of posting only messages that are relevant to the subject of the forum or network in which you are participating.

- ✔ **Include the necessary information.** If you're asking a question of forum members, be sure to give them a complete description of what your problem or issue is. This will help other readers of the forum in determining a resolution to your issue.

- ✔ **Indicate whether you've asked your question elsewhere.** If you pose your question through other channels, such as a third-party mailing list and so forth, indicate in your message all the places you're posting the question so your question gets answered only once. This saves effort and enables forum members to answer your question and other people's questions faster.

- ✔ **Be nice.** If you want the welcome mat to be out for you, refrain from inappropriate language and personal attacks. Remember the first rule of karma: What goes around, comes around.

- ✔ **Choose a descriptive title.** This will help subsequent visitors to the forum successfully identify your topic.

Don't . . .

- ✔ **Don't cross-post.** Posting a message to more than one forum is unnecessary and creates extra traffic for you and others to read through.

- ✔ **Don't quote previous messages.** Quote only when absolutely necessary. Readers can easily view previous messages in their newsreader when needed, so you're just wasting space — and risking the ire of your forum mates — by quoting previous messages.

- ✔ **Don't spam the site!** Although most forums and online social networks will tolerate a small amount of plugging your business, blatant and ongoing plugs will incur the wrath of your forum mates. The best bet is to put a brief plug about your business (along with a link to your Web site) in your *signature,* the identifying line or lines tacked to the bottom of your messages.

- ✔ **Don't include graphics or other files in the forum posts.** Don't post attachments. Most users don't want to download a file when reading your post, for time and security reasons. For those who have high connect costs, your post can be quite expensive. Please explain your point in writing, and include the URL of the file in your post so others can view it only if they wish to.

> ✓ **Don't duplicate threads.** Before posting messages, be sure to familiarize yourself with the forum. If possible, check to make sure your topic has not already been addressed in a recent thread so that you're not simply duplicating another recent post.
>
> ✓ **Don't get too personal.** Remember, all messages are public and will be viewed by others.
>
> ✓ **Don't perpetuate off-topic threads.** If someone makes an inappropriate or *spam* post, don't add more noise by replying to the forum. Criticize in private e-mail if you must.

Be polite, helpful, and friendly — you'll attract far more business with honey than vinegar.

Using Your Web Site to Attract Customers and Clients

Well, you've got a Web site; now what? Now you've got to figure out how to attract attention in the vast, open space that is the Internet. As of this writing, there were more than 43 million active *domain names* (Web site names such as `dummies.com` and `workingfromhome.com`), many of which have their own functioning Web sites attached to them. That's a lot of competition for customer eyeballs.

In the sections that follow, we take a close look at how to attract potential customers and get them to buy once they find their way to your site.

What it takes to get traffic

Traffic — that is, visitors to your Web site — is perhaps the key element that can make or break your online business. Generally, the more traffic, the better, assuming that it consists of people who might be interested in buying what you've got for sale.

Just because you have a Web site doesn't mean anyone is going to show up. You may think *if you build it, they will come,* but although that might work in a Hollywood baseball fantasy, it's not necessarily the case for your new Web site. If you hope to be successful, you'll need to get more — and the right kind — of traffic to your site. Here are a few ideas for making that happen:

✔ **Register with the most-visited search engines.** There are hundreds of search engines available, but you shouldn't waste your time with 99.9 percent of them. Our advice is to stick with the top ten:

- Google (`www.google.com`)
- Yahoo! (`www.yahoo.com`)
- MSN (`www.msn.com`)
- America Online (`www.aol.com`)
- Ask Jeeves (`www.askjeeves.com`)
- Overture (`www.overture.com`)
- MyWay.com (`www.myway.com`)
- Information.com (`www.information.com`)
- Lycos Networks (`www.lycos.com`)
- WebSearch.com (`www.websearch.com`)

✔ **Register with pay-per-click search engines.** The Google and Overture search engines offer an additional service (Google's is known as Google AdWords: `www.adwords.google.com`), where you can pay to have your company's site show up in a prominent location when someone searches a specific keyword or keywords. Let's say your home-based business is wedding consulting. Using Google AdWords, for a price you could have a small ad with a link show up any time someone searches the keywords *wedding consultant.* You pay only when someone does a search using your keywords, and the amount you pay depends on how popular the keywords are — more keyword competition means higher prices.

✔ **Create unique content.** Don't make your Web site just a place to buy things; make it a place people want to visit to learn something new or participate in a unique experience. Take time to create unique content for your site that will attract busy Web surfers and then make them want to stick around awhile. Maybe you're a dog breeder specializing in French bulldogs. Why not create a Web site that is *the* best source of information on the breed in the entire world? By doing so, you'll drive all kinds of traffic to your site.

✔ **Start an affiliate program.** Offer other Web site owners a commission on sales they send your way. The big sites, like Amazon, make affiliate programs a central part of their selling model — driving more traffic to their sites and increasing their sales. You can, too. Check out a variety of affiliate programs to see how commissions are structured and how to set up your own program.

✔ **Exchange links.** Are there sites out there that are somehow related to what you do but are not in direct competition? If so, ask the Webmaster to place a link to your site on the site in exchange for putting a link to the other site on yours. For example, say you provide fishing-guide services in the Yellowstone area. Why not exchange links with fishing Web sites or Web sites devoted to Yellowstone National Park?

Making it easy for visitors to become customers

The points of having a Web site for your home-based business are to (1) attract potential customers to your offer and then (2) make it easy for them to buy. Although many Web sites do a fine job getting people to visit, they drop the ball when it comes to converting visits to sales, often simply because they are too confusing, too slow, or just too much trouble to use.

So your job is to make it easy for customers to buy what they want directly through your Web site, assuming you've got a product or service that lends itself to buying online. Here are some tips for doing just that:

✔ Have a well-organized, professional-looking site. Nothing's worse than trying to buy something from an amateurish, disorganized site.

✔ If you're selling products, put up lots of high-quality photos and detailed descriptions. Many people want to see what they're getting before they order it.

✔ Make sure your Web hosting service has ample bandwidth to load your pages quickly. Slow servers mean your visitors will quickly get bored and leave.

✔ Give your customers plenty of payment options. Use a prepackaged e-commerce site, such as Yahoo! Small Business Merchant Solutions, that allows customers to use charge cards. Or consider signing up for a payment service, such as PayPal, that also allows customers to use their charge cards to pay.

✔ Provide ample contact information for customers who have questions. If you can quickly address questions — via phone or e-mail — there's a much greater chance of converting the contact into a sale.

Not sure if your site is welcoming or not? Give it a try yourself. Is it easy to get around? Does it load quickly? Is it easy to place an order? Have friends and family try it out, too. Use their feedback to fine-tune your site and make it as user-friendly as possible.

Building and Maintaining Your Web Site

Okay, so you've decided to start your own Web site — congratulations! Now what? Well, the first step is to build it. You can hire someone to do it for you or do it yourself (Peter built his Web site at `www.petereconomy.com` years ago using Microsoft FrontPage and maintains it himself to this day).

Each approach, of course, has its pluses and minuses. Hiring someone to create and maintain your Web site will likely get you the most professional-looking site, but it may cost a lot of money, and you may have to wait for your Webmaster to make site updates for you. When building your own site, you'll have ultimate control over the site, and you'll likely pay less than hiring someone to do it for you, but the results may look amateurish at best, and — while you're playing with the software and troubleshooting the inevitable issues that arise during the site-building process — you'll be distracted from doing the things you normally do to make money.

Hire someone to create and maintain your Web site

If you have no interest in creating and maintaining your own Web site, plenty of Web-site design companies (many of them home-based businesses, by the way) would love to design it for you. It probably won't be cheap — anywhere from a couple of hundred dollars for a simple site to thousands for a much more complex one — but if you have no interest in learning the ins and outs of Web sites yourself (and we can't blame you if you don't), this is clearly the best option.

Don't hire just *anyone*. Remember: Your site is going to be the first (and perhaps the last) thing that many potential customers and clients will see regarding your business. Make sure their first impression is a good one. Here are a few tips for finding a great Web-site designer:

- Interview Web-site designers just as you would a new employee. Get references, do an interview, check them out — the whole enchilada.
- Ask your business acquaintances if they know of anyone who is good at designing Web sites.
- After you locate some candidates, ask for a list of active Web sites that they have developed and actively maintain — and then visit them on your computer. How do they look? Are they attractive and well produced, or are they a turnoff? Are they current and up-to-date, or do they look like they haven't been touched for months?

✔ Ask how soon your site will be up and running, and how much it will cost — not just to set it up, but also to periodically maintain it and troubleshoot problems.

✔ Compare the work of several different designers before deciding.

Only after you have a chance to fully explore your candidates' work and compare it with the work of others should you select the Web-site designer who is right for you.

✔ If you see a Web site that knocks your socks off, find out who designed it. Sometimes the designer's name is posted on the site, often at the bottom of the home page, but sometimes you need to ask the site owner. It's a good idea to talk with prior clients anyway. That's how Paul and Sarah found the designer for their site www.workingfromhome.com. They had three earlier designs that for one reason or another fell short, but not only do they now have a site that hits all the bases, it also was designed so that they can update it themselves using Microsoft FrontPage.

Create a Web site yourself

If you have a basic knowledge of the Internet, you can create your own Web site and have a lot of fun in the process. Although it can be a lot of fun building your own site, make sure you don't have so much fun that you forget to sell your products and services, too.

1. **Select a Web hosting service.**

   A Web hosting service sets up your Web site address (or URL), something like yourname.com, and then hosts your site on its computers where anyone with access to the Web can access it. There are many, many Web hosting services, and they vary considerably in price and level of service. Most home-based businesses can get by with a barebones level of service, and you can figure on paying around $15 to 25 a month. It pays to shop around. Before you select a Web-hosting service, ask around for references, and be sure to visit some of the hosted sites to see how well they work. Peter's personal favorite is Dotster (www.dotster.com), but there are plenty of other ones around.

2. **Build your Web site.**

   Some Web site hosting services offer simple, built-in Web-site creation software as part of their hosting packages. This may be all you need to create the site you want, and it's probably the best option if you're new to all this Internet stuff. However, if your needs go beyond what your host provides, consider buying software specifically designed for creating Web sites. Microsoft FrontPage, Macromedia Dreamweaver, and NetObjects Fusion are powerful and simple to use. If you can use a basic word-processing program, such as Microsoft Word, you can create your own Web site. And here's a news flash: Microsoft Word even allows you to save regular text pages as HTML (Hypertext Markup Language, the language of the Web) documents. Woo-hoo!

Get free templates for Web sites at `http://freesitetemplates.com`. And you can learn about design standards at `www.webstyleguide.com`.

3. **Maintain your own Web site.**

   The great thing about creating and maintaining your own Web site is that you have full control over the content and when or how it is updated or modified. Need to add a new product to your listings? In five minutes, you're done. If you had to go through a hired third party, it could take days or even weeks for them to get around to making even this minor update. You'll also have direct access to your Web site's statistics: how many visitors your site has, who they are, and where they are coming from. Using these statistics, you can find out which of your Web pages are the most and least popular, and adjust accordingly.

For more information on this approach, be sure to take a look at *Marketing Online For Dummies,* by Bud Smith and Frank Catalano (Wiley).

Skip the Web site and create an e-commerce site

You can create an effective store on the Internet without having a Web site at all. How? An increasing number of established Web sites, including Yahoo! and Amazon.com, have gotten into the business of hosting e-commerce sites for other businesses.

Of the current e-commerce providers, by far the best is Yahoo! Small Business Merchant Solutions (`http://smallbusiness.yahoo.com/merchant`). For only $40 a month for a basic site (plus a nominal fee — currently 1.5 percent — for each transaction), you can get your own online storefront up and running within minutes. Your customers can view photos of your products, put them into a shopping cart, and pay for their purchases by credit card. You have access to an amazingly comprehensive statistics package (telling you what products are selling best, revenue by item, what sites shoppers are coming from, and much more), and you'll be in good company: the L.A. Lakers basketball team, Sanrio (you know, those Hello Kitty guys), Vermont Teddy Bear, Roadrunner Sports, and many more.

The ten best ways to promote your Web site

A Web site won't do you or your business much good if no one knows about it or visits it. What can you do to make sure people find out about your site and visit it?

- ✔ Send announcements for your Web site (including a picture of your home page) to all your customers and clients, as well as to the media and targeted mailing lists of potential clients.

- ✔ Include your Web-site address on all external materials, including letterhead, business cards, catalogs, invoices, newsletters, packaging, and so on.

- ✔ Incorporate your Web-site address into your standard fax cover sheet.

- ✔ Include your Web-site address in your voice-mail system and in your on-hold message.

- ✔ Include your Web-site address in all advertising.

- ✔ Visit Internet newsgroups and message boards, leave messages, and participate in relevant discussions.

- ✔ Seek out busy Web sites where you can volunteer to host online chats and conferences. Large sites, such as America Online and iVillage, are always looking for knowledgeable hosts who are willing to share their expertise with others.

- ✔ Register your site with the five most popular Internet search engines (Google, Yahoo!, MSN, America Online, and Ask Jeeves), and be sure it is optimized to rank high in the search results (by incorporating meta tags and other tricks of the trade).

- ✔ Trade links with your customers and clients and with other relevant Web sites.

- ✔ Create an e-mail signature for yourself and your employees that includes your Web-site address. A *signature* is a short paragraph that's automatically included at the bottom of every e-mail message you send out. It usually contains a plug for your business, along with your address, phone or fax number, and a Web-site address.

Regardless of who creates it, make your site good

There are a number of secrets to creating a Web site that attracts and holds your clients' interests and encourages them to send their money your way:

- ✔ **Be easy to find.** Don't make it difficult for your clients to find you. Your URL (www.yourname.com) should be intuitively obvious. If, for example, your company's name is Acme Computer, your URL could be www.acme computer.com. That way, clients (and clients-to-be) who don't have your address at their fingertips can easily guess it. Also, take the time to register your Web site with the four or five most-visited Internet search engines and directories. Referrals from these sites — including Yahoo!, Excite, and Google — are a critical link in helping people find you. Check out a site called The Art of Business Web Site Promotion (`www.dead lock.com/promote`) for free advice on how to work the search engines to your advantage.

Of course, many domains are taken, so you may have to settle for one that's longer (like AcmeofSacramento.com). Or, because many domain names are minimally used, you may be able to purchase a domain name you want from its current owner. If it's unused, and you are willing to wait for it to expire, you can back-order the name from a domain registration service. Whatever your approach, put on your thinking cap, and be creative!

✔ **Advertise your new address like crazy.** Everywhere, all the time. Include its address on your business cards, letterhead stationery, invoices, marketing brochures, and anyplace else you can possibly fit all those letters and dots.

You may be approached by firms that promise to increase the traffic to your Web site. Maybe they will, and maybe they won't. If you do decide to hire a firm to increase traffic, be sure to ask exactly what they plan to do to reach the people most likely to buy your products and services, and what sort of guarantee they offer. Chances are you can do the same things on your own and save a lot of money in the process.

✔ **Give your visitors a reason to visit — and to come back again and again.** The attention span of the average Web surfer can be measured in seconds. If your site is boring, or if it takes too long to load, your client or prospect will click out of the site just as quickly as he or she clicked in. Take a look at your competitors' sites to get an idea of what works and what doesn't. Use graphics, photographs, and attractive backgrounds to make your site look more appealing, but be careful that these byte-intensive files don't dramatically slow the speed at which your Web pages load. Above all, provide lots of fresh, value-added content in the form of news, reports, articles, surveys, industry trends, networking forums, and the like that will keep your clients and prospects coming back for more.

✔ **Capture contact information.** When people visit your site, they're probably not there by accident — they're there because they're interested in what you have to sell. Take advantage of this opportunity by encouraging your visitors to give you contact information that you can use in your organization's marketing and promotional efforts. For example, you can set up a guestbook where visitors can leave comments about your site, along with their name, title, address, and phone number. Or you can offer to mail a complementary copy of your client newsletter to prospects who are willing to give you their contact information. Contests, special offers, and surveys are all great ways of encouraging your visitors to give you their contact information.

✔ **Check Web stats, and visit your site regularly.** A good hosting service gives you access to vital statistics for your Web site: number of visitors each day; where they're from; how long they stayed; which pages they viewed; which search engine (if any) referred them to your site; and much, much more. By analyzing these statistics, you can quickly identify which parts of your site attract the most (and the least) visitors and test visitor response to site changes on a real-time basis. (Hint: Do more of what your visitors like and less of what they don't.)

Also, regularly visit your site to make sure that it's working the way it's supposed to. Perhaps you won't be surprised to hear that some Web hosting services are better than others, and it's in your interest to make sure that your site is on more often than it's off. The easiest way to make a habit of visiting your site is to set it as your browser's home page. This way, it pops up every time you log onto the Internet. And ask your friends and family to also check it frequently and let you know if they run into any problems. If you're not sure how to change your browser's home page settings, click the Help button.

Part II
Managing
Your Money

The 5th Wave   By Rich Tennant

"...and don't tell me I'm not being frugal
enough. I hired a man last week to do
nothing but clip coupons!"

In this part . . .

Money definitely makes the world go around, in life and in business. Home-based businesses are no exception. In this part, we talk about transitioning from a regular, 9-to-5 career into your own home-based business and we discuss the fundamentals of financial management. We consider how to price your products or services to maximize your return and then examine health insurance, retirement, and taxes.

Chapter 6

Making the Transition to Working for Yourself

*O*ne of the biggest obstacles that lie in the way of many prospective home-based business owners is a very simple but very important question: What are you going to live on while you get your new business off the ground? Money doesn't grow on trees, and to ensure the long-term success of your business, you've got to start out with sufficient income — from whatever source — to pay your bills.

Seven out of every ten Americans at some time in their lives decide that they want to start and own their own businesses. Yet most don't. Why not? Because they are afraid that they don't have enough money to do it. The fact is, while certain home businesses may require a significant investment in equipment and inventory, many home-based businesses require little or no money to start. But aside from startup costs, it does take a lot of work and careful planning to build a business that will pay the bills over the long run — years into the future. And that's why understanding the right ways (and the wrong ways) to transition into your own business is so very important.

In this chapter, we review the steps for transitioning to a home-based business — specifically, what you should do before you leave your day job behind (or before you're laid off, riffed, or retired). We also consider the importance of developing a business plan, as well as securing financing (and finding the best places to get the money you need). Finally, we take a close look at a variety of strategies for exiting your current job and making the move to your own home-based business.

Transitioning into Your Home-Based Business

It's exciting to start your own business. For those who have spent all their working lives employed by someone else, it's often the culmination of a dream that's lasted for years or even decades. Imagine the power and personal satisfaction you'll feel when you realize that you're the boss, that you call the shots — from setting your own work schedule, to deciding how to approach your work, to choosing your computer and office furniture.

Believe us, it's a feeling you'll not soon forget.

But there's a right way and a wrong way to make the move. Your goal is to ensure that you maintain a sufficient supply of cash to pay the startup costs of your business while paying for the rest of your life — the mortgage or rent, car loans, health insurance, gas and electric, and your daughter's piano lessons.

The fact is, few businesses — home based or otherwise — bring in all the money necessary to get them off the ground and keep them going for a prolonged period of time within the first six months of operation. In other words, you will need *a lot of cash* — income from a job, from your spouse or partner's job, savings, loans from friends or family or a bank — to keep both your business and your personal life going until the business generates enough revenue to take over.

While you have to decide for yourself exactly what schedule to follow while transitioning into a home-based business, unless you're unemployed or retired, we generally recommend that you start your business on a part-time basis while you're still holding down your regular full-time job. Why? For a number of reasons, including the following:

- ✔ You can develop and test your new business with virtually no risk — you still have your regular job to fall back on if your new business doesn't work out (and remember, no matter how great your business idea, there is a chance it won't work out).

- ✔ You won't be under the intense pressure to perform and show the results that you would have to show if your new business were your only source of income.

- ✔ You're able to keep your established health insurance, retirement plan, leave, and other benefits. Given the difficulty and expense of securing a decent health-care plan when you're on your own, and not under the umbrella of your employer, this alone may be reason enough to keep your day job while you start your own business.

✔ You have a steady source of income to pay your bills as you establish your new business.

✔ You may be able to take advantage of tax benefits, like the ability to write off early losses against income (see Chapter 10).

✔ You have a stronger basis for obtaining bank loans and other financing for your new business.

Of course, the decision is ultimately up to you. When starting a home-based business, you have to follow your heart and make sure the transition fits into your schedule and your life.

Although you can find good reasons to start your home-based business part-time, you may also find grounds to be cautious about such an approach. If you need the income of your day job to keep you and your business both afloat, you definitely don't want to jeopardize it.

✔ Your regular position may require you to be on the job during the hours that would also be the best for your new business. Spending time on your new business while working your day job is not only unethical, but also could put you at risk of being fired.

✔ You may need to spend more time than ever away from family and friends, usually the evenings and weekends that they are accustomed to spending with you.

✔ If you get too little sleep or too few days off, your performance at your job may suffer. Underperforming on the job you rely on to pay the bills is not the best way to hang onto your paycheck.

In the following sections, we take a close look at five steps to take before you leave your regular job to devote yourself fully to being your own boss. We also walk through the different steps involved in the process of establishing your home-based business.

Five steps to take before leaving your job

After you're consistently earning enough income from a part-time business to cover your bare-minimum living and business expenses, you're ready to make the jump to a full-time commitment of your time and attention. Before you turn in your resignation, however, take the five following steps:

✔ **Check when any company benefit plans you have will vest or increase in value.** If you have a 401(k) or other retirement plan to which your employer has been contributing, it may not be fully available to you until you have served a particular number of years of service. The idea is to give you an incentive to stay with the company for some minimum amount of time. Checking this information may help you determine the best time to resign. It would truly be a shame, for example, if you quit two weeks before the value of your retirement benefits was set to jump from 80 to 100 percent.

✔ **Find out when you can expect to receive any bonus money or profit sharing.** You may, for example, be slated to receive an annual performance bonus or profit sharing a month after the end of the company fiscal year. This information can help with the financial planning for your business.

✔ **Get all annual health exams and routine procedures done, and fill all prescriptions, while you and your family are still covered by your medical/dental/vision insurance.** Check to see if your group coverage can be converted to an individual policy at favorable rates (some can be, although be very careful about changes in coverage, co-pays, and deductibles that may actually end up costing you much more money in the long run) or what other health coverage options are open to you.

Don't forget that if you work in the United States, you're likely covered by COBRA (the Consolidated Omnibus Budget Reconciliation Act of 1985), which requires your employer to allow you to continue your identical group health coverage for a period of 18 months or more at the same rate (probably subsidized by the company) as all other employees for comparable coverage.

✔ **If you own a house, take out a home equity line of credit before leaving your current job.** Having a line of credit to draw upon is invaluable during the first two years of your new business, and your chances of getting approved for it are much greater while you're employed in a regular job. That's right — after you leave your job, you probably won't qualify for a line of credit or other loans for your business until your business has been successful for two or more years.

✔ **Pay off or pay down the balance on your credit cards while you still have a steady job.** This helps your credit rating (always a good thing) and provides you with another source of potential funds to help you to finance various startup costs (and depending on the nature of your business, you may have plenty of those!).

Don't make your announcement or submit your resignation until you're really, actually, for sure ready to go. Some companies are (sometimes justifiably) paranoid about soon-to-be former employees stealing ideas, proprietary data, or clients. This can make for a very hasty exit, with a personal escort, when you do resign.

And you don't want to quit and then have to back out of it because you weren't *really* ready to make the move to full-time status with your own company. If you have made other announcements that have fizzled for one reason or another, your credibility will surely take a dive (ever heard the story about the boy who cried wolf?), which can have a negative impact on your working relationships.

Your odds are better than you think

There's been a lot of bad information out there about how long businesses (including home-based businesses) can be expected to survive after founding. Most everyone has heard this one: that 95 percent of the businesses started in any given year will be gone within five years.

Guess what? It's not true.

In reality, most home-based businesses survive for five years or more after their founding. According to surveys conducted by IDC/LINK, an average of only five percent of home-based businesses drop out each year. So after five years have gone by, only 25 percent of home-based businesses have dropped out — far less than the average for all businesses, which can be over 50 percent! How, then, can you ensure that your home-based business will thrive and not become an unfortunate statistic?

The Small Business Administration (SBA) has uncovered four key indicators of business success. They are as follows:

✔ Sound management practices, including an ability to manage projects, handle finances, and communicate effectively with customers

✔ Industry experience, including the number of years you have worked in the same kind of business you intend to start and familiarity with suppliers and potential customers

✔ Technical support, including your ability to seek out and find help in the technical aspects of your business

✔ Planning ability, including an ability to set appropriate business goals and targets and then create plans and strategies for achieving them

If you, or the combination of you and a partner, possess all four traits, the probability of your business succeeding is much higher than if one or more of these traits are missing.

After completing these steps, you're ready to take what may well be one of the most significant steps forward you'll ever take in your entire life: starting your own home-based business. For those about to embark on this path, we salute you!

Overview of starting a home-based business

In the sections that follow, we go through exactly how to start up your own home-based business. We cover these topics in much greater detail in Chapters 4, 7, 11, and 12.

Develop a business plan

Let's be honest: Many home-based business owners can get by without drafting a business plan. Indeed, though many believe it would be crazy to start a business — any business — without sitting down and putting together a comprehensive, 50-page-plus business plan to go along with it, business plans today are used mostly to obtain financing from third parties such as banks or investors. That said, the process of drafting a business plan can be very beneficial — both to you as a business owner and to your business. It helps you do the right things at the right time to get your business off the ground and soaring on a path to success.

A good business plan:

- ✔ Clearly establishes your goals for the business
- ✔ Assists in analyzing the feasibility of a new business and its likelihood of being profitable over the long haul
- ✔ Explores the expansion of an existing business
- ✔ Defines your customers and competitors (very important things to know!), and points out your strengths and weaknesses
- ✔ Details your plans for the future

Even if you think your business is too small for a business plan, it's really worth your time to see what it's all about — the process of developing the plan for your business will produce a clarity of thought that can't be equaled in any other way. See the section "Putting Together a Business Plan," later in this chapter, for details on business plan development.

Consult outside professionals

As a new home-based businessperson, you want to consider establishing relationships with a number of outside professionals — trained and experienced people who can help you with those aspects of your business in which you may have little or no experience. By no means do you have to hire someone from each one of the different categories that follow. But if you run into questions that you can't easily answer yourself, don't hesitate to call on outside professionals as you go through the business startup process (and be sure to check out Chapter 12 for detailed information on this topic).

Any professional advice you get at the beginning of your business may well save you heartache and potentially expensive extra work down the road.

- ✔ **Lawyer:** An attorney's services are an asset not only in the planning stages of your business, but also throughout its life. An attorney can help you choose your legal structure, draw up incorporation or partnership paperwork, draft and review agreements and contracts, and provide information on your legal rights and obligations. Look for an attorney who specializes in working with small businesses and startups.

✔ **Accountant:** Consult an accountant to set up a good bookkeeping system for your business. Inadequate recordkeeping is a principal contributor to the failure of small businesses. Regardless of how boring or intimidating it may seem, make sure that you understand basic accounting and the bookkeeping system or software you're using and that you receive and closely review regularly produced financial reports. The business you save may be your own!

✔ **Banker:** The capital requirements of a small business make it essential to establish a good working relationship with a local banker. Bankers can approve immediate deposit of a check that would normally be put on a 10-day hold, for example. They are good sources of financial information — and for obtaining cash to tide you over when times are tough or financing expansion of your business when times are good.

We recommend establishing a relationship with your banker *prior* to applying for a loan, not after you decide to initiate the loan process. This relationship may make the difference between getting approved for the loan you need and being turned down.

✔ **Business consultants:** Every person has talents in many areas, but no one can be a master of everything. Consultants are available to assist in those areas where you need expert help. You can use business, management, and marketing consultants; promotion experts; financial planners; and a host of other specialists to help make your business more successful. Don't hesitate to draw on their expertise when you need it.

✔ **Insurance agent/broker:** Many kinds of insurance options are available for business owners, and some are more necessary than others. An insurance agent or broker can advise you about the type and amount of coverage that's best for your business. The agent may also be able to tailor a package that meets your specific needs at reasonable rates. If you're starting a new business, the insurance company will need in-depth information about your business in order to provide the insurance coverage necessary. Insurance for new businesses can be expensive, but the price can be well worth it in the event of a covered loss — especially if it's your health or that of a loved one. Check out Chapter 9 for more information on health insurance.

The relationships you establish with outside professionals during the startup phase of your business can last for years and can be of tremendous benefit to your firm. Be sure to choose your relationships wisely. This is a case where you often get what you pay for — be penny-wise, but don't suffer a poor-quality outside professional simply to save a dollar or two.

Choose the best legal structure for your business

Because they are the easiest kinds and the least expensive, most home-based businesses begin as either sole proprietorships or partnerships. But as these businesses grow, many explore the transition to another kind of legal entity altogether.

✔ **Sole proprietorship:** A sole proprietorship is the simplest and least regulated form of organization. It also has minimal legal startup costs, making it the most popular choice for new home-based businesses. In a sole proprietorship, one person owns and operates the business and is responsible for seeking and obtaining financing. The sole proprietor has total control and receives all profits, which are taxed as personal income. The major disadvantages include unlimited personal liability for the owner (if the business is sued for some reason, the owner is personally liable to pay any judgments against the company) and potential dissolution of the business upon the owner's death.

✔ **Partnership:** A partnership is relatively easy to form and can provide additional financial resources. Each partner is an *agent* for the partnership and can borrow money, hire employees, and operate the business. Profits are taxed as personal income, and the partners are still personally liable for debts and taxes. Personal assets can be attached if the partnership can't satisfy creditors' claims. A special arrangement called a *limited partnership* allows partners to avoid unlimited personal liability. Limited partnerships must be registered and must also pay a tax to the appropriate authorities in their jurisdiction. On the plus side, partnerships allow people to combine their unique talents and assets to create a whole greater than the sum of its parts. On the other hand, partnerships can become sheer living hell when partners fail to see eye to eye or when relationships sour.

When entering into any partnership, consult a lawyer, and insist on a written agreement that clearly describes a process for dissolving the partnership as cleanly and fairly as possible.

✔ **Limited liability company:** The limited liability company (LLC) is treated as a partnership for U.S. income tax purposes and also provides the limited liability of a corporation. This option may be the preferred choice for certain new operations and joint ventures. Owners of limited liability companies, called *members,* are comparable to stockholders in a corporation or limited partners in a limited partnership. To create a limited liability company, articles of organization are filed with the secretary of state. The members must also execute an operating agreement that defines the relationship between the company and its members. Not all states have this option available.

✔ **Corporation:** As the most complex of business organizations, the corporation (also known as a *C corporation*) acts as a legal entity that exists separately from its owners. While limiting the owners from personal liability, this separation creates a double taxation on earnings (corporate tax and personal tax). A corporate structure may be advantageous because it allows capital to be raised more easily through the sale of stocks or bonds, and it can continue to function even without key individuals. It also enables future employees to participate in various types of insurance and profit-sharing plans. Costs to incorporate vary from state to state — contact your secretary of state for more information.

A special type of corporation, an *S corporation,* allows owners to overcome the double tax and shareholders to offset business losses with personal income; however, if you offset losses for an S corporation against regular income, you assure yourself of being audited.

With C corporations, you need to be certain you aren't classified as a professional service corporation, which is treated much less advantageously than other C corporations.

As you're setting up your new home-based business, take time to carefully think through the ramifications of your business's legal structure. Each has many potential advantages and disadvantages for your firm, and each can make a big difference in how you run your business. If you have any questions about which kind of legal structure is right for your business, talk to an accountant or seek advice from an attorney who specializes in small businesses. Chapters 10 and 11 can also help you sort through the options.

Decide on a name

Naming your business may well be one of the most enjoyable steps in the process of starting up your own home-based business. Everyone can get in the act: your friends, family, and especially your clients-to-be.

Consider your business name carefully — you have to live with it for a long time. Your business name should give people some idea of the nature of your business, it should project the image you want to have, and it should be easy to visualize. Names can be simple, sophisticated, or even silly. Try to pick one that will grow with your business and not limit you in the future.

Along with a name, many businesses develop a logo, which provides a graphic symbol of the business (see Chapter 14 for more ideas). As with the name, your logo should be carefully developed to project the image you want. Spend a few extra dollars to have a professional graphic artist design your logo for you.

After you come up with a name, make sure it isn't already in use by registering it with your local government. (See Chapter 11 for further details.) If you don't check first, you may very well have to throw out your stationery and business cards and redesign your logo and Web site when you eventually find out that another company has your name — and registered it 15 years before you did!

Take care of the red tape (and it will take care of you)

Taking care of all the local, state, and federal government legal requirements of starting up a business is something that too many budding home-based entrepreneurs put off or ignore. Unfortunately, ignoring the many and sundry legal requirements of going into business may put you at risk.

Getting through the maze of government regulations can certainly be one of the most confusing aspects of doing business. But though this process may be intimidating, it is important to do it — and do it correctly — because non-compliance can result in costly penalties and perhaps even the loss of your business. Consider this step as one that fortifies the professionalism of your business at the same time that it helps you rest easy at night, knowing that you're following the rules. Do you want people to take you seriously? Then you need to establish your business in a professional way.

Even very small or part-time businesses have certain requirements. It is your responsibility to adhere to any and all regulations that apply to your business. Fortunately, a lot of people are willing and eager to answer questions and help you with this task. For your sake — and the sake of your business — don't hesitate to ask.

What kinds of red tape do you need to address? The answer is different for every different kind of business, and it's different in every city, county, and state. Chapter 11 can help you get started.

Get the insurance you need

In today's expensive, litigious world of business, insurance isn't really an option anymore — it's an essential. Without it, all your years of hard work can be lost in a minute due to a catastrophic loss.

So what kinds of insurance are needed for your business? Our advice is to talk to an insurance agent, and discuss your business and its needs with him or her. Some of the most common kinds of business insurance include the following:

- **Basic fire insurance:** Covers property losses due to fire. Sometimes covers loss of business as well.

- **Extended coverage:** Protects against conditions not covered by fire insurance, including storms, explosions, smoke damage, and various other disasters.

- **Liability insurance:** Covers claims against the business for bodily injury incurred on the business's premises.

- **Product liability coverage:** Insurance against liability for products manufactured or sold.

- **Professional liability and/or errors-and-omissions insurance:** Protects the business against claims for damages incurred by customers as a result of providing them with professional advice or recommendations.

- **Vandalism and malicious mischief coverage:** Covers against property losses resulting from vandalism and related activities.

✔ **Theft coverage:** Protection from burglary and robbery.

✔ **Vehicle insurance:** Covers collision, liability, and property damage for vehicles used for business.

✔ **Business interruption insurance:** Payment of business earnings if the business is closed for an insurable cause such as fire, flood, or other natural disaster.

✔ **Workers' compensation:** Disability and death benefits to employees and others who work for you, as defined by your state law, who are injured on the job.

✔ **Health insurance:** We've saved the best (and, for many home-based business owners, the most important) for last. Health insurance includes medical, dental, vision, and other coverage designed to maintain and promote employee health and wellness and to protect employees against catastrophic loss in case of injury or illness.

A homeowner's policy is usually not enough insurance. First, a typical homeowner's policy provides only $2,500 of coverage for business equipment and does not insure you against risks of liability or lost income.

Insurance is the kind of thing that you don't think about until you need it. And in the case of insurance, when you need it, chances are you *really* need it! Take time to set up proper coverage now, before it's too late.

Decide on an accounting system

Accounting is one of those topics that makes people nervous (with visions of IRS audits dancing in their heads), but keeping books doesn't need to be complicated. In fact, simplicity is the key to a good system for home-based businesses. Keep in mind that your records need to be complete and up-to-date so that you have the information you need for business decisions and taxes.

When establishing an accounting system, our advice is to pick up one of the excellent computer software programs dedicated to this purpose. Programs such as Microsoft Money, Quicken, QuickBooks, and Peachtree Complete Accounting do everything your home-based business will ever need — and more.

There are two basic bookkeeping methods: *single entry* and *double entry*. Single entry is simpler, with only one entry required per transaction. This is our preferred method for most home-based businesses, and the vast majority can operate very well with this system. If you go this route, we recommend that you use either Microsoft Money or Quicken. Double entry requires two entries per transaction, which provides cross-checks and decreases errors. Consider going with a double-entry system if someone else manages your books, if you use your accounting system for inventory management, or if you want more sophisticated reporting for analyzing your business. If you decide that double entry is for you, we recommend either QuickBooks or Peachtree Complete Accounting.

You can also use two methods to keep track of the money coming in and going out of your business: *cash* or *accrual*. Most small businesses use the cash method, in which income is reported in the year it is received and expenses are deducted in the year they are paid. Under the accrual method, income is reported when it is earned, and expenses are deducted when incurred, whether money has changed hands yet or not.

The accounting methods you use will depend on your business. You may want to talk to an accountant for help in setting up your system. Even with the support of a professional, you should understand your own system thoroughly.

Many home-based businesses can get by without detailed financial reporting or analysis — after all, if you can keep up with your bills and perhaps have a little bit of money to sock away in your savings account, you must be making money, right? If you really want to understand your business's financial situation, though, you need some basic financial reports. The following financial statements are the minimum necessary to understand where your business stands financially. With them in hand, you'll be able to review your business's financial strengths and weaknesses, and make accurate plans for the future.

- ✔ **Balance sheets:** A balance sheet shows the worth of the business — the difference between its assets and liabilities. If you shut down your business today, paying off all your bills and loans and liquidating your assets, would you have any cash left over?

- ✔ **Profit-and-loss statements:** Profit-and-loss (P&L) statements show you the difference between how much money your business is bringing in *(revenue)* and how much money it is spending *(expenses)*. If you're bringing in more money than you spend, you have a profit. If you're spending more money than you bring in, you have a loss.

- ✔ **Cash-flow projection:** Cash-flow projections tell you where your money is going and if you're likely to have sufficient money each month to pay your bills and operate the business. For many startup companies — especially those with employees, rent, and other significant recurring expenses — a cash-flow projection is the most important financial statement of all.

Years after starting his home-based business, Peter still keeps a detailed cash-flow projection that shows expected revenues — by client — on a monthly basis for an entire year. Shortfalls that can be dangerous to his personal financial health can be seen far in advance, and Peter can address them before they become major problems.

For much more detailed information about these and other financial matters, including the use of financial ratios to gauge the financial health of your business and a much more in-depth look at accounting software packages, be sure to check out Chapter 7.

Develop a marketing plan

It's not enough to start a business and then patiently wait for customers to walk in your door; you need to let potential customers know about your new business, get them in to have a look, and then encourage them to buy your product or service. Marketing is all of this and more. Your specific approach to marketing depends on your business, your finances, whom you're trying to reach, and your goals.

Marketing sells your products and services, which brings in the cash you need to run your business. Marketing is so important that it deserves a plan of its own. A *marketing plan* helps evaluate where your business currently is, where you want it to go, and how to get there. Your marketing plan should also spell out the specific strategies and costs involved, and it can be integrated into your business plan as one comprehensive section. As with the business plan, it should be referred to regularly and updated as necessary.

Successful marketing for a small or home-based business doesn't happen all by itself. It requires a lot of work and careful analysis and is a terrific opportunity to use your creativity and hone your business sense. For lots of information on marketing your home-based business, be sure to check out Chapter 4. For even more information on the topic, pick up a copy of Paul and Sarah's book *Getting Business to Come to You . . . A Complete Do-It-Yourself Marketing Guide for Attracting All the Business You Can Enjoy* (co-authored by Laura Clampitt Douglas, Putnam Publishing Group) and *Small Business Marketing For Dummies,* by Barbara Findlay Schenck (Wiley).

Seek out assistance when you need it

An almost unlimited number of organizations and agencies — private, public, and not-for-profit — are ready, willing, and able to help you work through the process of starting up your home-based business. The following list is just the beginning.

Check out the Web sites of each of these organizations for an incredible amount of free information and help:

- Small Business Development Centers: www.sbaonline.sba.gov/sbdc
- SCORE (Service Corps of Retired Executives): www.score.org
- Chambers of Commerce: http://chamber-of-commerce.com
- Minority Business Development Agency: www.mbda.gov
- Federal Business Opportunities: www.fedbizopps.gov

✔ Small Business Incubation Association: `www.nbia.org`

✔ Small Business Administration (SBA), Starting a Business Site: `http://sba.gov/starting_business/index.html`

✔ Small Business Innovative Resource Center: `www.darpa.mil/sbir`

✔ SBA Small Business Training Network: `www.sba.gov/training`

✔ Business plans: `www.sbaonline.sba.gov/starting_business/planning/basic.html`

✔ Information on choosing a form of business: `www.toolkit.cch.com/text/P12_4210.asp`

✔ Business names: `www.toolkit.cch.com/text/P01_4800.asp`

✔ U.S. Patent and Trademark Office: `www.uspto.gov`

Six Ways to Get the Cash Flowing

Every new business starts at the beginning. No matter how much experience you have in your current job or how many other businesses you may have started in the past, when you create a new home-based business, you're starting from scratch. In the beginning, every sale counts, and building financial momentum quickly is the primary goal. The faster you get cash coming into your business, the sooner you're able to leave your 9-to-5 job behind and dedicate yourself fully to your own business.

Beginning part-time with your new business

When you start your own business, you will usually have a choice to make: Keep your day job or quit. As we mentioned earlier in this chapter, it's our recommendation that you keep your regular job for as long as you can while building your own business part-time. At some point — after your own business has built up a sufficient clientele — you can leave your regular job and devote yourself fully to your home-based business. And if your own business fails for whatever reason in its early stages, you still have your regular job to fall back on.

Working part-time at your old job

If you have enough work in your home-based business, but not enough to make it your full-time vocation, consider working part-time in your regular job. Depending on your particular situation, your current employer may be willing to be flexible with your schedule. It's often better to keep a good employee part-time than lose her or him altogether.

Turning your employer into your first client

If you're really good at what you do, what better way to get your business off the ground than to do work for your current employer on a contract basis? Not only will your employer have the benefit of your expertise while contracting with a known entity, but you can also develop your business while working with people you already know, using systems and procedures you're already familiar with.

Take care, however, to clearly separate yourself from your former employer as an independent contractor rather than continuing to work in the role of employee. If you don't make this distinction clear, any tax deductions you have taken for your home-based business may be disallowed by the IRS. See Chapter 10 for a discussion on how to ensure that you're on the right side of this fine line.

Taking business with you (ethically!)

Although it's unethical to steal clients away from a previous employer (not only that, but it also may very well land you in court, forcing you to pay an attorney a lot of money to get you out of trouble), you may be able to get your employer's blessing if you let them know what you would like to do. The advantage of taking clients with you to your new business is that you already have a strong working relationship in place. This is of great benefit to your new business and to your clients.

Financing your business with startup funds

It takes money to start a business — any business. By lining up sources of startup funds, you're able to ease the financial entry into owning your own home-based business. There are probably more potential sources of startup funds than you can ever imagine. In the section "Sixteen Sources of Startup Funds" later in this chapter, we let you in on the best sources.

ASK PAUL & SARAH

Bringing a partner into your business

Q: I am looking for a business partner for my company. I wondered if you had any suggestions on how to find one.

A: The best business partner is someone with whom you have a long track record of working well — someone with whom you share common goals and philosophies and compatible work styles. The more experience you've had working together, the better. But don't despair if you can't find anyone from your existing pool of contacts to team up with. You can find partners by networking through professional and trade organizations or by getting referrals from others whose judgment you value and respect. Here's what we suggest:

✔ Don't go directly from stranger to business partner. That's like getting married on the first date. Instead of telling people you're looking for a business partner, put the word out that you're looking for an associate to run a joint venture with. This initial joint venture should be a short-term or discreet project that gives you a chance to get to know a prospective partner and see if you have the chemistry to work well together.

✔ Ask for referrals from those in a position to know people who will meet your criteria: the officers of a trade association, the president of the chamber of commerce, the editor of the trade journal, or a valued supplier or client. You can network with such individuals online as well as in person. These days, you need not limit yourself to teaming only with colleagues in your locale. Many people are successfully using e-mail, fax, and the telephone to team up with associates anywhere in the country or even internationally.

As you talk with people about the possibility of collaborating on an initial venture, look for compatibility in the following areas:

✔ Strengths that are complementary

✔ Honesty

✔ Fairness

✔ Aesthetics and etiquette

✔ Personal integrity

✔ Attitudes about family/work priorities

✔ Money and financial matters

✔ Timeliness and punctuality

✔ Quality and educational level

✔ Manners and treatment of others

✔ Attitudes about your profession or business

Take note of any red flags. If anything like the following comes up in initial conversations, watch out!

✔ A history of financial problems

✔ A history of combative relationships or lawsuits

✔ Soap opera tales of woe with previous partners or joint ventures

✔ Here-and-now behavior, such as being late to meetings or frequently putting down others

✔ Unwillingness to put plans and agreements in writing

When you find someone you click with, do several short-term projects or joint ventures together before committing to a formal, legal partnership. Make sure that your initial assessment is accurate and that you can, in fact, trust your partner and work well together.

Piggybacking with your spouse or significant other

If you're married or live with a significant other, he or she can continue to work his or her regular job, providing a steady paycheck, benefits, and more, while you start your own home-based business. Although your overall income will be reduced until such time as you're able to crank up your sales, this way you have the shelter of a secure job and benefits. Such a shelter can save you a lot of sleepless nights, allowing you to focus your attention where it's most needed — on building your business.

Sixteen Sources of Startup Funds

The number-one concern of most people who are planning to start their own home-based businesses isn't what kind of business they are going to start, where they are going to start it, or how they are going to market their products and services. It's not who their customer is going to be, who their competition is, or whether or not to involve a spouse in the business. It's money. More specifically, it's where to get the money needed to start up a home-based businesses.

It takes money to make money, and this is especially true when starting up a new home-based business. With cash, you can buy the things your business needs to operate and stock up on the inventory of products that you will sell to your customers and clients.

But where does this money come from, and what are the best ways to pull together the cash you need to start up your home-based business? Here are 16 of our best suggestions:

- **Personal savings:** Savings accounts are probably the first place that most home-based business owners turn to when looking for cash to start up their new businesses. And why not? You get instant loan approval — no matter how good or bad your credit report may be — and you can't beat the interest rate of 0 percent!

- **Credit cards:** More and more often, home-based business owners are turning to credit cards as a source of cash for business startup. A word of caution: Beware of extremely high interest rates and extra fees for cash advances. If you do decide to use a credit card for your business, try to get one dedicated solely for business expenses. You'll have an easier time figuring your taxes for the year.

- **Retirement funds:** If you're currently working a full-time job, you probably have some sort of retirement fund established. This fund is as good as gold, and you can apply the cash within it to help you start up your new business. There are a couple of problems, though, with early distributions of retirement funds. First, Uncle Sam is probably going to penalize you for doing so (check the rules for your particular kind of retirement account) and will then add insult to injury by taxing you on the income you pull out of your fund. Second, if you wipe out your retirement account, you have nothing to fall back on if your business fails (not to mention nothing to fall back on when you're ready to retire).

- **Barter:** Okay, while not strictly a source of cash, bartering with others — trading your products or services for theirs — can be a terrific way of getting the things you need to get your business off the ground. Need a computer? If you are starting a massage business in your home, for example, we'll bet you can find someone who would love some massages in trade for a computer that they're no longer using.

  Craig's List (www.craigslist.org) is a great place to give bartering a try.

- **Disability grants:** If you've been granted a disability payment because of an on-the-job injury that prevents you from pursuing your former vocation, the cash you receive may be useful for beginning a new career — a career at home.

- **Inheritances:** Although inheritances may be subject to taxation depending on exactly how much you inherited and in what way (check with a tax adviser for all the details), you may still be left with a substantial amount of funds that can be applied to starting up your new business.

- **Credit unions:** Because credit unions are member-owned, they often offer better interest rates than do regular banks or other financial institutions. If you belong to a credit union, be sure to try there for a loan first. Keep in mind, however, that credit unions are generally even more adverse to risk than regular banks, so your credit will have to be very strong for you to have a chance of getting the money you'll need.

- **Funds from investors:** Many new companies rely on cash from investors to fund their startup and initial operations. Be aware, however, that when you accept money from investors, you probably have to give them something in exchange. That something is usually equity in the company. And with equity goes the power to have a say in how the business is run. If you don't want anyone telling you how to run your business, this may not be the best way for you to pull together funding for your business.

- **Life insurance policies:** Depending on the kind of life insurance policy you have (term, cash value, and so on), you may be able to cash it in or take out a loan against it. Read the fine print of your policy or consult your insurance agent to see if you have this option. If you've had a cash-value policy for a long time, you may be pleasantly surprised at how much money is available to you for your new business.

✔ **Home equity line of credit:** If you have a home and have built up equity in it (the value of the home over and above what you owe for it), you may be eligible for an equity line of credit. These have several great advantages: You don't pay any interest or payments unless you actually borrow against your line of credit (you may have to pay some sort of loan origination fee, however, to set up the line of credit); loan terms are often much longer than standard loans — up to 15 years or more; and the interest you pay is tax deductible. On the downside, you have to put your home up as collateral — if you default on your loan, you may lose your house. All in all, however, it is a smart way to finance your new business.

✔ **Loans from friends and family:** When aspiring home-based entrepreneurs don't personally have the resources to finance their new business, friends and family are often the first potential source of funding they turn to. As long as your request for a loan doesn't cause your relationships to sour, loans from friends and family can be a great way to put together the financing you need. Be sure to treat relatives and friends as you would any business relationship, using signed, written documents with clear terms and conditions.

✔ **Loans from suppliers or colleagues:** You believe in yourself, right? If your idea's a good one, chances are others will believe in you, too. Drop the hint that you're looking for money to finance your new business, and you may well find yourself with the cash you need to get started.

✔ **Local seed-money funds such as one sponsored by the Amarillo Economic Development Center:** Many local governments offer seed money to help finance new businesses in their communities. Check with your local small business office to see what's available in your community.

✔ **Selling personal assets such as a boat, extra vehicle, camper, and so on:** Think: big yard sale, eBay, www.craigslist.org, or your local classified ads.

✔ **Microloan programs:** The government and a number of foundations offer a variety of microloan programs, particularly targeted to women and minorities. Check with your local Small Business Administration office to find out what's available and whether you qualify.

✔ **Reduced tax withholdings:** If you aren't taking any exemptions on your income tax withholding at work, you can unlock an instant stream of cash by increasing your exemptions in line with the deductions that you expect to have available when you file your annual income taxes. Simply follow the instructions on the IRS form or consult your accountant for more information.

Finding money on the Web

A number of places on the Web offer cash to finance your home-based business. Garage. com (www.garage.com), for example, matches investors who have the cash with home-based businesses that need it. And not only does it match up investors with home-based businesses, but it also schedules conferences (often called *boot camps*) on how to start a home-based business and how to attract financing. Has this unique source of business financing attracted any interest? In a word, yes. According to the company president, Bill Reichert, the initial expectations in terms of the number of business plans they would receive was off by a factor of ten. They were overwhelmed by the number of entrepreneurs who came to them.

Here are some other good places to look:

✔ www.americanexpress.com

✔ www.quicken.com/banking_and_ credit

✔ www.nvca.org

✔ www.nvst.com

You can find all kinds of different ways to put together the money you need to start up your home-based business. One thing to keep in mind: Keep your borrowing as low as you possibly can. And when you do borrow money, borrow only for items that will pay you right back. For example, if you start a home-based gardening business, a $500 investment in a professional-grade lawn mower will no doubt be quickly recouped — perhaps in only a month or two of work. A $500 investment in an office desk, however, may take years to recoup. The best approach is to minimize the amount of money you need to come up with to start up your business. If you already have a computer, and you already have some sort of office set aside, you may have all the tools you need to get your desktop-publishing business off the ground.

Before you run out and buy that snazzy new company car, computer, or modular furniture unit, ask yourself if the old one won't serve you just as well for another year or two. It may not be as exciting as shopping for something new, but the money you save can be put to better use generating income for the business. And in a home-based business, generating income for the business means generating income for you.

For much more information on raising money for your new business, be sure to check out Peter's book (with co-author Joseph Bartlett) *Raising Capital For Dummies* (Wiley).

Putting Together a Business Plan

Every great business begins with a plan. Whether it's written on the back of a napkin or fills hundreds of pages with full-color charts and photos of happy customers, a plan helps prioritize and direct the actions you take to start up and run your business. And while formal business plans are used less often nowadays than they were in the past (today, business plans are usually put together for the benefit of loan officers at banks and potential investors), the process of putting together a business plan for your home-based business is an education in itself — one you'll get nowhere else.

Though you have some flexibility in determining the exact format of your business plan (especially if it's an informal one that's strictly for your own use), if the intent is to use the plan for securing financing from a bank or investors, they expect to see certain information presented in specific ways. This allows them to make informed judgments on the viability of your business and its potential for growth and profitability.

A formal business plan should contain, at minimum, the following elements:

- ✔ **Mission statement:** The company's mission statement sets the tone for the business, relating it to its values and goals. Mission statements are inspiring and serve to galvanize the actions of employees toward attaining the company's goals. Paul and Sarah's mission statement fulfills all of these criteria: "We're authors, broadcasters, and facilitators. Our mission is to explore new and better ways of living and working through the interface of nature and technology." Peter's mission statement is "The best books, on time, and on dollar."

- ✔ **Description of the company's products and services:** This is a complete description of all the products and services that the company presently offers and plans to offer in the future. If your home-based business specializes in producing the best wedding cakes in the tri-state area, using the latest in confectionery technology, this is the place to lay it all out. Be complete — leave nothing to the imagination.

- ✔ **Market analysis:** If you have already put together a marketing plan for your business, you already have the material you need to fill out this part of your business plan. The market analysis takes a close look at the markets in which you intend to sell your products and services, and details the number of potential customers, the potential growth rate of the market, information about your competition, and particulars of your marketing strategies. See Chapter 4 for a complete analysis of a marketing plan.

- ✔ **Financial projections:** Do you plan to go from $100 a month in revenues to $100,000 a month? This is where you present your financial projections, including revenues, expenses, and profit or loss. Plan to include the three basic financial statements — a balance sheet, a profit-and-loss (P&L) statement, and a cash-flow projection — and be ready to back up your guesses and prognostications with hard data.

- ✔ **Management strategies for achieving company goals:** You have your products and services, your marketing strategies, and your financial projections. Now, exactly how do you intend to achieve your goals? This section presents the details of the strategies you select to achieve your company's goals and lays out when and how you go about achieving them.

ASK PAUL & SARAH

Farming out your business plan

Q: I want to start a business, but the bank needs a business plan before I can get a loan. I don't know how to write a business plan and am not good at writing. Is there a service that can write one for me?

A: Absolutely. You can hire a professional business plan writer. Your bank loan officer may be able to recommend one to you or you can find one online. Many business plan writers now have their own Web sites. You can also look for business planning consultants at www.bplans. com/pc — look for someone who has general business background in the areas of accounting,

bookkeeping, and marketing, and familiarity with financial statements, business jargon, and your local business community. Definitely ask for samples of their work, and if possible, have your bank loan officer review the samples to be sure they are of the type and quality the bank is seeking.

Professionals can generally prepare a business plan in two to four weeks. Fees range from $2,500 to $5,000, depending on the time needed to research needed financial data, analyze the competition, develop sample marketing plans, and so forth.

Although space doesn't allow us to present a sample of a formal business plan within these pages, you can view several at www.businessplans.org. Also check out *Business Plans For Dummies,* by Paul Tiffany and Steven Peterson (Wiley), for details on writing a successful business plan.

Knowing When to Move On

Every great businessperson — whether he or she owns a one-person, home-based business or is the CEO of a Fortune 500 company — knows when it's time to dig in and fight the good fight and when it's time to move on or change direction. Despite all your careful planning, product development, marketing and business strategies, and the time you devote to making your business the best it can be, sometimes it's just not the right time or place for your business. (Where, for example, have all the Y2K consultants gone?) Other times, the business isn't right for you.

The need to move on and try something different can be motivated by a couple of different elements:

> ✔ **Are you ready to be in this particular business?** Starting a business is quite a bit more complicated than simply quitting your day job, moving into your new business, and making lots of money. Are you ready for the long hours and sacrifice that are required to be successful? Chances

are you'll work far more hours than you ever worked when you were employed by somebody else. Did you choose the right business? Your choice of a business should be the result of extensive research and soul searching, not just what seems to be a nice idea at the time. If, for whatever reason, you're not ready to be in this particular business, you may need to move on to the kind of business you're ready for.

✔ **Is the market ready for your product or service?** You may well have the greatest product or service since the invention of the hot glazed doughnut. Unfortunately, if the market isn't yet ready for it, or if the market is ready but isn't large enough to generate the sales you need to stay afloat, it may be time to move on. The key is to recognize this problem quickly so that you can take action before your personal finances are depleted and you're left with nothing.

How to patent your ideas

Q: I would like to sell patented ideas to companies that manufacture similar products. But because I don't have a lot of disposable income or collateral, how do I finance my patent searches and applications? Also, when I write to companies about my ideas, I get rejection letters or no response. How do I get into companies to sell them my ideas?

A: Patent attorney and author David Pressman recommends waiting before sending letters to manufacturers until you have completed a thorough patent search and submitted your patent application. You can hire a professional searcher for under $1,000, but if you're a conscientious worker and have the time, you can do your own search. Pressman outlines this in his book *Patent It Yourself.* Another book focused entirely on patent searching is David Hitchcock's *Patent Searching Made Easy.* You can begin your search on the Internet at www.uspto.gov/patft or at a Patent and Trademark Depository Library in your state. A list of Patent and Trademark Depository Library sites can be found at the Patent and Trademark Depository Library Program (PTDLP) page on the US Patent and Trademark Office Web site at www.uspto.gov. For patents issued before 1971, you will need to go to a depository library.

You still have some expense, however, because after you've completed your search, each patent application fee costs $385. After an application is filed, Pressman recommends finding and writing to suitable companies. Most, he says, respond with a form letter requesting that you sign an enclosed waiver form. Some people do offer to sell their patented ideas for a lump sum, but he finds that most seek instead to license their ideas, usually for around 5 percent of sales.

Pressman urges that you not get involved with an invention development company. These companies offer to review your ideas and then charge an inflated price to complete a search for you. If you'd rather be just the idea man and leave the financing, model building, searching, and filing to others, we suggest putting together your own development team. Ideally, you have contacts to draw upon for such a team from your experience in the fields related to whatever ideas you're developing. If not, you can begin making such contacts by networking through professional organizations either face-to-face or online.

For additional information on obtaining a patent, contact the U.S. Patent and Trademark Office, Washington, DC 20231, (703) 308-HELP or www.uspto.gov.

Whatever you do, when you recognize that it's time to move on, do just that. You can find plenty of other opportunities, and you're far better off looking sooner rather than later.

Chapter 7

Keeping Track of Your Money

. . . .

In This Chapter

▶ Separating your business and personal finances

▶ Setting up a business bank account

▶ Deciding on a bookkeeping system

▶ Watching your finances

▶ Understanding invoicing, collections, and cash flow

▶ Establishing credit

. . . .

*T*hey say that money makes the world go around, and nowhere is this truer than when you own and operate your own home-based business. As you quickly learn, if you have cash, you can get almost anything done. Unfortunately, the opposite is also true; if you are constantly short of cash, you may find keeping your business afloat to be a major challenge.

Financial management is therefore one of the key points of focus for any home-based business, and proper financial management requires a good system of bookkeeping, as well as constant attention to the numbers. Your business's finances are not something you should leave to chance. In this chapter, we take a look at how to manage your finances so that your finances don't manage you.

Organizing Your Finances

In most large organizations, tracking cash — where it comes from, where it goes, and how it is used — is one of the most important administrative functions. Cash serves many functions in a business: It's a way to keep score, a way to measure the profit generated by different products and services, and a way to reflect the equity built by the company's investors and owners. And not only does cash serve as a yardstick for performance, but it also is the way that companies pay employees and purchase supplies and services.

Will you need an accountant?

Will you need an accountant to help you keep track of your business's finances? The answer to this question depends on how capable you personally are in handling your own bookkeeping, accounting, taxes, and financial strategies, and on how complicated your business is. Some business owners love to take care of the administrative tasks involved in running their own businesses; others hate it. And some home-based businesspeople are naturally skilled at doing financial tasks, while the talents of others are better suited to delivering products and services to their customers. In addition, doing your own bookkeeping and accounting takes time and discipline — records need to be updated regularly and periodically checked for errors.

If, for example, your finances are fairly simple, you're computer savvy, and you have sufficient time and interest to keep your records up-to-date by yourself, you can use a software package such as Quicken, Money, or QuickBooks to do your bookkeeping. Simply input your receipts and expenses, and the program performs every accounting function and trick you could ever imagine. You'll be able to generate all kinds of financial reports and graphs (something your lenders will want to see, should you need to borrow money to grow), write checks, and collect the information you'll need to do your taxes.

If, however, your business isn't simple, or if you've got a unique business setup (for example, if your home-based business is a C corporation instead of the more common sole proprietorship), getting the help of a professional bookkeeper or accountant may be worth your time and money. When looking for professional assistance, avoid choosing someone out of the Yellow Pages — you just never know what you're going to get. Ask your home-based business friends in the area for referrals to a good accountant or bookkeeping service — preferably one that specializes in handling businesses like yours.

Indeed, cash is the focal point of most organizations — both large and small. When you have a small home-based business, cash — or the lack thereof — can quickly make or break you.

Why should you worry about keeping your business finances organized anyway? Isn't that shoebox that you keep your receipts in sufficient for your home-based business, as long as you have enough money to pay your bills and yourself? Not quite. There are four main reasons for keeping your finances organized and accurate:

✔ You need adequate financial information to know where your business stands — whether it is profitable or losing money and whether expenses are out of line with income.

✔ You need adequate financial information about your business to apply for loans and receive credit from vendors and suppliers.

✔ You need adequate financial information to prepare your federal and state income taxes.

✔ You need adequate financial information to provide to interested buyers in the event that you decide to sell your business.

Can your shoebox do all that?

Setting Up a Business Account

When setting up your company's finances, the first step is to establish a separate bank account for your home-based business. While the Internal Revenue Service doesn't require that you separate your business finances from your personal finances, take our word for it: It sure makes things a lot easier when you prepare your taxes. Without this separation, you can spend hours and hours trying to first identify the business expenses in your personal checking account or credit card receipts and then pulling them out and classifying them.

At minimum, you need a checking account, although a savings account and even a retirement account may be a good idea, too. Setting up a new checking account is easy, particularly if you've already established a personal account at the bank or other financial institution that you select. Drop by your friendly local bank, fill out a form or two, deposit a bit of money (or transfer it from an existing account), and pick out your check design. In minutes, you'll be all set.

If you set up a new account in the name of your business (not in your own name) — particularly if the account is not with the institution where you do your personal banking — you may find that the bank will place holds on checks you deposit over a certain amount of money, say $500 or $1,000, making your funds inaccessible until they clear the originating bank. These holds can remain in place for a couple of days to a week or more, and needless to say, they can cause you and your business major problems if you need your cash right *now*. The good news is that after your business establishes a record of stability (a process that may take anywhere from a few months to a year or more), the requirement to put holds on deposits to your business account will probably be lifted. If not, be sure to ask your bank manager to lift it.

One more thing: Consider applying for a credit or debit card that you use only for your business. Visa, MasterCard, Discover, and American Express all offer cards that are specifically geared to the unique needs of small business users. They can provide quarterly spending reports by employee — breaking down your charges into specific categories such as retail, restaurant, lodging, and telecommunications — and give discounts on business services, extended warranties on equipment purchased with the card, and many other benefits. Debit cards issued with a VISA or MasterCard insignia are particularly flexible because they can be used as either debit (or, often, ATM) cards or as credit cards, depending on the situation and on your personal preferences. The choice is yours.

Accepting Credit Card Sales

If you sell products, you probably also want to be able to accept credit card payments. In fact, as a way to improve your cash flow, you may want to require that your clients pay you by credit card before you deliver their product orders or services.

While many home-based businesses don't need to be able to accept credit card payments, others — particularly home-based businesses that sell products — do. If you have the kind of business that's suitable for taking credit card sales — perhaps you sell dollhouses, computers, or rare records through your Web site — you'll have many of the following advantages when accepting credit cards:

- ✔ Accepting credit cards is a convenience for your customers — particularly those customers who would rather not wait to send a check or payment through the mail before you ship their orders.

- ✔ People who use credit cards to purchase items tend to spend more money per transaction (250 percent more on average, according to some sources) than non-credit card customers.

- ✔ You get your cash from the transaction much more quickly than if you invoice your customers and let them pay later, improving the cash flow of your business. A credit card payment is immediately directly deposited into your bank account.

- ✔ Internal paperwork due to invoicing customers and following up on delinquent payments is reduced or eliminated.

- ✔ Accepting credit cards makes your business appear more established and credible than businesses that don't accept credit cards.

Being able to accept credit cards is definitely a good thing. As with many other good things in life, however, accepting credit cards isn't free. In fact, you have to pay for the privilege.

How much? The answer depends on who processes your transactions and on the overall dollar amount of the transactions that you submit for processing.

Here are typical costs to expect:

✔ Setup charges including application fees: around $300, plus software licensing fees and equipment purchases if you need a point-of-service terminal instead of just using your computer's Internet access.

✔ Transaction fee: a flat fee charged for each transaction that may range from $0.20 to $0.50 per transaction.

✔ Discounts: a percentage taken from each order, ranging from less than 2 percent to 5 percent or more.

✔ Monthly charges: including a statement fee, a monthly minimum if the discount and transaction fees don't equal a monthly minimum, and leasing fees if you lease instead of buy equipment.

Accepting credit cards is definitely not a free service, but if the level of your sales justifies it, it's a small price to pay — and could be offset by the price of just one or two bad checks.

Establishing a merchant account

Before you can accept credit cards, you have to find a bank, credit card company, or other financial institution that will grant you *merchant status* or allow you to open a *merchant account* — that is, authorization to accept credit card payments. This process is not quite as easy as you may think; in fact, for a new business or one that's considered to be risky by credit card companies, it can be downright difficult. Here is a list of the kinds of businesses that are considered particularly risky by credit card companies (and that may make getting approval more difficult):

✔ Adult Web sites

✔ Dating services

✔ Limousine/taxi services (independents)

✔ Online casinos

✔ Massage services

✔ Mall kiosks (seasonal/independent)

✔ Ticket brokers

If you've been in business for some time (at least two or more years), you're not involved in a particularly risky business, and you have a good credit history, you should have no problem getting merchant status. Of course, until you apply, you'll never know.

Finding a way to accept customers' credit cards

Q: I own a home-based mail-order company that sells computer and electronic equipment, and uses manufacturers that ship directly to my customers. To increase business, I tried to get a merchant account so I can take MasterCard, Visa, Discover, and American Express. My average ticket will be about $3,000 and monthly should be $20,000. The problem is, the banks want to hold 50 percent of each credit card payment for a month. That would put me out of business. Is there a way around this?

A: Yes. First, recognize that there are different requirements for accepting payments with a credit card online than for traditional merchant account sales. If you can't find a bank that will work with you, consider finding a broker. Brokers call themselves such terms as *independent sales organization* (ISO) and *merchant account provider* (MAP). A broker acts as an intermediary between small businesses and banks. You will most likely pay more using an ISO, because these companies derive their income from fees and surcharges added to what you would normally pay if you were able to deal directly with a bank. Add-on costs include such things as application fees, leasing costs for card swipe machines, transaction charges, statement fees, voice verification fees, and so on. But ISO fees vary considerably, so be a shopper. Just be sure to read any contracts carefully for hidden charges and requirements.

They are becoming increasingly popular and competitive with banks.

You may also be able to get better terms going through a membership organization or company, such as Costco, that provides access to merchant accounts.

A third way to go is to use a third-party processor, which links directly from your Web site's order page to the third-party processor. The third party makes you an agent, with the third-party processor actually being the legal entity that makes the sales. Some third-party processors also provide fulfillment functions such as providing live telephone operators and packing and shipping the goods.

Also consider trying the credit card companies directly. Both Discover/Novus (www.discovercard.com) and American Express (www.americanexpress.com) accept applications for merchant status through the mail or online.

One caution: Some companies are falsely representing themselves as ISOs, and eager merchants have been scammed. To determine whether the ISO you're talking with is legitimate, ask for the bank the ISO is affiliated with, and contact it to verify the status of the ISO. You can also check with your local Better Business Bureau.

Different companies charge vastly different prices to create and maintain a merchant account for you. Do your research thoroughly, and compare prices. And carefully read any contract or agreement you're asked to sign. If you have any questions, it may be worth your time and money to have a lawyer review it for you.

ASK PAUL & SARAH

Encouraging customers to make online purchases

Q: Could you tell me the best way to instill confidence in the purchaser's mind in order to make a sale online? I run a small business, and I don't accept credit cards. What would make the customer comfortable in sending their money to an online business that they don't know?

A: The key issue, of course, is the credibility of your product and you as a provider. So anything you can provide to convey the integrity of your company and your product is important. Prominently displaying your company name, street address, e-mail address, and phone number reassures visitors that you're an accessible business and aren't trying to hide who or where you are. Testimonial letters or quotes signed by real people that include their names, locations and businesses are also helpful. A satisfaction or money-back guarantee is most reassuring, as is anything that you can add to

your site to convey your positive reputation, experience, expertise, and track record. Positive, personal, and forthright communication without a lot of hype is important, too.

Consider these other ways beside credit cards:

- Checks online (called e-checks) through services like XpressChexOnline (`www.xpresschex.com`)

- Debit cards, which you arrange with your merchant account provider

- Digital wallets or e-wallets, such as Microsoft's Passport

- Person-to-person e-mail payments (P2P) that the customer arranges through his or her bank or through services offered by Yahoo!, the U.S. Postal Service, and Citibank

Open Accounts

If a customer asks you to give it a line of credit, it's always wise to check out the customer's creditworthiness. You can get credit reports on businesses from firms like Dun & Bradstreet Business (`www.dnbcreditreport.com`) and Credit.Net (`www.credit.net`). For credit checks on consumers, the major credit reporting agencies — Equifax, Experian, and TransUnion — provide this service to businesses. Visit their Web sites or give them a call for more information.

Using the PayPal option

As a direct result of the explosion of the eBay online auction service, PayPal (`www.paypal.com`) and a number of similar financial services companies have sprung up to facilitate the resultant transactions. In addition to offering the ability to accept cash transfers from customers with their own PayPal accounts, PayPal allows your customers to pay you by using their credit cards. You can then either keep the funds in your PayPal account or electronically transfer it to your business's bank account.

Using PayPal to accept your customers' credit cards can result in some compelling advantages over the more traditional process of qualifying for and establishing a merchant account, including the following:

- You do not have to fill out a lengthy application or jump a bunch of hurdles to be able to accept credit cards for your business. Simply establish a PayPal account (which takes at most a few minutes), and you're ready to go.

- Although not free, the fees that you'll pay to accept credit cards may be significantly less than what you would pay a bank for running charges through a merchant account (currently 2.2–2.9 percent, depending on average number of transactions each month, plus $0.30). If you're processing a lot of credit card payments, these savings can really add up.

- Unlike merchant accounts, there are no monthly fees for leasing credit card software or generating transaction records.

Our advice? Give the PayPal option serious consideration when you're starting out. It's far easier than establishing a merchant account, and the cash is just as green when it hits your bank account.

Choosing the Best Bookkeeping System for Your Business

Keeping track of your business's financial transactions is a must — there are simply too many good reasons for doing so to ignore it. Your business's finances aren't going to get less complicated as your business grows; in fact, the opposite is likely to be true. Start your business off on the right foot, and make accounting for your financial transactions a regular part of doing business.

Although you may enjoy playing with Microsoft Excel, instead of creating your own spreadsheets from scratch, our advice is to pick up one of the many excellent accounting software programs available on the market today. Programs such as Quicken, QuickBooks, Microsoft Money, and Peachtree Accounting can take care of your business's every financial need — now and into the future.

Here is a listing of some of the many features in QuickBooks: Basic — a capable and easy-to-use software program for most home-based businesses.

- Print checks, pay bills, and track expenses
- Invoice customers, and track payments and sales taxes

✔ Generate reports, including profit and loss, statement of cash flows, balance sheet, sales reports, and more

✔ Manage payroll and payroll taxes

✔ Track information for taxes and share information with an accountant

✔ Extensive tutorials and help functions

The accounting method you decide to use ultimately depends on the nature of your business and on the amount and complexity of the financial transactions that you incur. If you're at all in doubt as to how to proceed with your bookkeeping or accounting system, talk to an accountant for help in getting set up the right way.

You'll have a great feeling when you get your business off the ground and receive your first payments for your products or services. After all your hard work and planning, this is what you've been waiting for. Chances are you'll be busier than you ever imagined and may easily get so caught up in taking care of customers that you forget to take care of your business.

However, successful businesses don't just happen — they require constant attention. Like a wonderfully productive vegetable garden, businesses need to be carefully tended and watched for signs of trouble. In business, one of the best ways to keep your eye on the health of your business is to review the wide variety of financial reports available to you. Make a regular habit of generating the reports you need and reviewing them. Don't just assume that everything is fine — prove it to yourself regularly.

Check registers and bank statements

The most basic form of financial analysis is done once a month, when you balance your check registers against your bank statements. Most bank statements summarize the total dollar amount of the deposits you made during the month, as well as the total dollar amount of the money you disbursed from your account. After you have double-checked to make sure that the bank statements are in agreement with your check register, subtract the amount of your checks from your deposits to give yourself a quick-and-dirty idea of what direction your business is heading financially — north or south.

Spending far more than you're taking in? Then you know that you have to find ways to bring in more money while controlling expenses. Bringing in far more money than you're spending? Terrific! Figure out how to do more of what you're doing.

Financial statements

Financial statements take the data you've entered into your accounting system and organize it in a way that can allow you to quickly gauge the financial health of your company. While financial statements may seem a bit intimidating to many — especially for new home-based businesspeople — accounting and bookkeeping software make the process easier than ever before. It's really as simple as one or two clicks of your computer's mouse.

Two of the most popular and useful financial statements are the income statement and the balance sheet. Each has its own unique role to play in your financial analysis and, ultimately, in the way you run your business.

The income statement

The *income statement* (also known as a *profit-and-loss statement,* or P&L) measures the *profitability* of your business: how much money is left over after you add up all your business revenues and subtract all your business expenses.

Income statements reveal three key pieces of information:

✔ A business's sales volume during a specified period

✔ The business's expenses during a specified period

✔ The difference between the business's sales and its expenses — its profit (or loss) — during a specified period

Table 7-1 shows what a typical income statement looks like.

Table 7-1	Susan's Antiques
Income Statement — Twelve Months Ended December 31, 20XX	
Revenues	
Gross sales	50,000
Less: Returns	(1,000)
Net sales	**49,000**
Cost of Goods Sold	
Beginning inventory	50,000
Purchases	10,000
Less: Purchase discounts	(2,000)

Income Statement — Twelve Months Ended December 31, 20XX	
Net purchases	8,000
Cost of goods available for sale	58,000
Less: Ending inventory	(48,000)
Cost of goods sold	**10,000**
Gross profit	**39,000**
Operating Expenses	
Total selling expenses	(5,000)
Total general expenses	(10,000)
Total operating expenses	(15,000)
Operating income	24,000
Other income and expenses	5,000
Total other income and expenses	5,000
Income before taxes	**19,000**
Less: income taxes	(10,000)
Net income	9,000

In the example in Table 7-1, Susan's Antiques had $49,000 of net sales revenue and a cost of goods sold of $10,000, leaving the company with a gross profit of $39,000. However, this gross profit was further reduced by the expenses of selling products and running the company (advertising, printing, rent, salaries, bonuses, and so forth) and by income taxes. The result is net income of $9,000.

The balance sheet

The entire world of accounting hinges on a simple mathematical truth, the accounting equation:

Assets = liabilities + owners' equity

Assets include cash and things that can be converted to cash. *Liabilities* are obligations — debt, loans, mortgages, and the like — owed to other organizations or people. *Owners' equity* is the net worth of the company after all liabilities have been subtracted from the organization's assets.

Table 7-2 shows a sample of a typical balance sheet.

Table 7-2	Susan's Antiques
Consolidated Balance Sheet — as of December 31, 20XX	
Assets	
Current Assets	
Cash and cash equivalents (checks, money orders)	12,000
Accounts receivable	25,000
Inventory	30,000
Total current assets	**67,000**
Fixed Assets	
Equipment	20,000
Furniture, fixtures, and improvements	15,000
Allowance for depreciation and amortization	(2,000)
Total fixed assets	**33,000**
Total assets	**100,000**
Liabilities and Owners' Equity	
Liabilities	
Current Liabilities	
Notes payable to bank	10,000
Accounts payable	5,000
Accrued compensation and benefits	19,000
Income taxes payable	6,000
Deferred income taxes	3,000
Current portion of long-term debt	1,000
Total current liabilities	**$44,000**
Long-term debt	10,000
Deferred income taxes	10,000
Total liabilities	**64,000**

Consolidated Balance Sheet — as of December 31, 20XX	
Owners' Equity	
Common stock	20,000
Additional paid-in capital	10,000
Retained earnings	6,000
Total owners' equity	**36,000**
Total liabilities and owners' equity	**100,000**

The value of the assets of Susan's Antiques is exactly balanced by its liabilities and owners' equity. Because of the accounting equation, there is no other option. The balance sheet demonstrates the fact that assets are paid for by a company's liabilities and owners' equity. Conversely, the assets are used to generate cash to pay off the company's liabilities. Any excess cash after liabilities are paid off is added to owners' equity as profit.

Key financial ratios

Want to quickly assess the financial health of your organization? *Financial ratios* provide the tools you need to do the job quickly and accurately. Most of the numbers are readily available from your accounting reports, including the income statement and balance sheet. The following sections discuss the most commonly used financial ratios.

Current ratio

The *current ratio* gives you an indication of your ability to pay your company's current liabilities out of your current assets. Generally, a ratio of 2 or more is considered favorable.

Current ratio = Current assets ÷ Current liabilities

$$= \$67,000 \div \$34,000$$

$$= 1.97$$

Quick ratio

The *quick ratio* (also known as the *acid-test ratio*) is used to measure your ability to pay your current liabilities out of your current assets. It is the same as the current ratio, except for one thing: Inventory is subtracted from current assets before the ratio is computed. A ratio of 1 or more is generally considered good.

Quick ratio = (Current assets – Inventory) ÷ Current liabilities

= (67,000 – 48,000) ÷ 34,000

= 0.558

Debt-to-equity ratio

The *debt-to-equity ratio* reflects the amount of debt an organization has accumulated to outside creditors versus the amount of money invested by owners or shareholders. Banks are particularly interested in assessing your debt-to-equity ratio as part of the loan decision process. In general, debt-to-equity ratios in excess of 1 are considered too high and indicative of too much debt.

Debt-to-equity ratio = Total liabilities ÷ Owners' equity

= $54,000 ÷ $46,000

= 1.17

Return on investment

Return on investment (ROI) tells you how effective you are at earning a profit from the money that its owners invest in the company. The higher the ROI, the better.

Return on investment = Net income ÷ Owners' equity

= $9,000 ÷ $46,000

= 0.195 or 20 percent

Finding Happiness in Positive Cash Flow

For a new business — especially a new, home-based business that you depend on to generate income in both your work and your personal lives — generating a positive cash flow as quickly as possible after startup of the business is absolutely critical. Every new business goes through an initial period during which expenses exceed revenues (thus generating a negative cash flow), but the sooner this can be reversed, the better for the short- and the long-term financial health of the business (and the easier you'll sleep at night).

Happiness in business truly is a positive cash flow. The following sections help you put your company into the black and out of the red.

Treating cash as king!

For most home-based businesspeople who have chosen the sole-proprietorship form of business (see Chapter 11 for more on the most common forms of business), money is used to pay not only business expenses, but also personal expenses if you're the primary wage earner. The money from your business enables you to fulfill your obligations, such as rent and car payments.

Should you lease or buy?

Q: I'm thinking about acquiring a new van for my business and upgrading my computer system. Should I lease or buy?

A: The choice to rent, lease, or buy has many important business considerations. For example, leasing may enable you to get a better van or computer than you could otherwise afford. Because leasing is normally equivalent to 100 percent financing, it may allow you to keep more working capital on hand. Leasing may allow you to pay for the items out of your earnings instead of having to use your savings or get a home-equity loan.

But of course, you need to qualify for a lease, which means you must have good credit, although probably not as flawless for leasing office equipment and furniture as for leasing a van. As a general rule, if you're leasing under your business name, you can expect to be required to have been in business for at least a year. But computer companies like Dell and Gateway all have consumer leasing programs based on credit history.

Leasing has a cash advantage over a purchase on credit because a lease usually requires little or no down payment, whereas a credit purchase may require 20 to 30 percent down. However, a disadvantage of leasing is that it's more expensive than buying because it includes charges to cover overhead and profit. If dealers are offering

zero-interest financing, leasing is decidedly more expensive. Technological obsolescence is another reason often cited for leasing, though some leases include annual automatic upgrades. At the end of a lease period, you can give back what may be obsolete equipment that may have little market value. You may also get additional tax benefits from leasing, but because tax laws are continually changing and have many exceptions to exceptions, consult with your tax specialist before deciding about leasing.

Taking all this into account, you can see there is no stock answer as to whether renting, leasing, or buying is best. If you do decide to lease, consider

- ✔ The exact nature of the financing agreement: Does it have liens or restrictions?

- ✔ The amount of each payment: Look for add-on and document-processing fees or termination penalties.

- ✔ The person responsible for insurance, maintenance, and taxes (usually, the lessee).

- ✔ What happens to the leased item at the end of the lease.

- ✔ Renewal options.

- ✔ Cancellation penalties, if any.

- ✔ Disadvantageous terms and conditions.

- ✔ Length of the lease period.

(continued)

(continued)

Generally, it's cheaper if you arrange your own vehicle financing instead of going through a dealer, which marks up the loan rate. You can determine the cost of a loan in advance by using sites like Bankrate.com (www.bankrate.com), E-Loan (www.eloan.com), CapitolOne Auto Finance (www.capitalone.com), or LowerMyBills.com (www.lowermybills.com). For information and to calculate leasing costs, you can get a lease quote at www.leasesource.com, as well as purchase their pricing services.

Whether you buy or lease, but particularly if you lease, consider getting *gap insurance* included in your lease. This protects you if you find yourself in a situation where a week or two after you've gotten your vehicle, it's stolen or totaled, and the insurance company will pay you only $18,000 on a $26,000 vehicle. Gap insurance will cover the difference.

Something to consider about leasing computers is that you may be restrained to add memory or make other changes, because you will have to restore each computer to its original condition at the end of the lease period.

There are, however, many different forms of money available to you, including cash, checks, money orders, and credit cards — and some are better than others. For most businesses, being paid in cash — either before delivering a product or service, or at latest upon delivery — is by far the top preference, followed by checks. Here are the different ways you can be paid, in order from the most to the least preferred:

- ✔ **Cash:** Assuming it's not counterfeit, being paid in cash is ideal. It's 100 percent liquid, you can spend it immediately if you like, and you can be sure it's not going to bounce or have a one-week hold placed on it when you deposit it to your business bank account.

- ✔ **Checks:** In many cases — particularly for large payments of many thousands of dollars — being paid in cash is just not practical, so using checks makes the most sense. However, checks aren't as liquid as cash; you have to take them to the originating bank or deposit them in your bank account (where they may be held until they clear) to be able to obtain cash. This takes time. Not only that, but checks also introduce the possibility that the customer's account may not have sufficient funds available to pay the obligation or that the checks are bogus.

- ✔ **Credit cards:** Credit cards are another step down the ladder of preference for receiving money. Credit card companies take a piece of every transaction that you give to them to process. But if a card turns out to be stolen or bogus, or if your customer decides to dispute the charge because she is unhappy with the product or service you delivered, you may be out the amount of the entire transaction.

✔ **Online payment:** This includes services such as PayPal, Western Union's MoneyZap, and PayByCash.com for customers who don't have credit cards or who may be credit-adverse (who account for about 10 percent of online sales).

✔ **Credit:** When you sell someone a product or service and let him pay for it later, you're extending credit to your customer. Although this practice is quite common in business, it is by far the least preferred way to be paid. It may be weeks or even months before you finally get your money — perhaps well after you have sold and delivered your products or services — and you run the risk of never being paid at all. If you do decide to bill your clients for your products and services, be sure to first check out their credit history. If in doubt, require your clients to pay you in cash, by check, or with a credit card.

Creating a positive cash flow starts with bringing cash into your business. The longer you take to convert whatever form of payment you decide to accept into cash, the more time goes by before your cash flow is positive. And don't forget: *Happiness is a positive cash flow.*

Finding seven ways to kick-start your cash flow

Do you always seems to be a day late and a dollar short? Although you're bringing in good money, it's already spent as soon as it arrives? These are all warning signs that you have a problem with cash flow. Assuming you're charging enough for your products and services, either you're not collecting your money quickly enough or you're spending too much money too quickly.

Here are some ways to put your cash flow on the right track:

✔ **Get your money up front.** If at all possible, ask for payment before you deliver your products or services. Have you noticed how most businesses that sell their products on the Internet require that payment be made by credit card when an order is placed? Or how fast-food restaurants want you to pay your money before they hand you a bag of fries or a soda? There's a reason for this: cash flow. And there's no better way to get your cash flowing in the right direction than being paid sooner rather than later.

✔ **Don't pay your bills any sooner than you have to.** Many people feel that they should pay their bills as soon as they receive them. This is a mistake. Your cash flow will thank you if you wait to pay your bills until you're required to do so. If, for example, your utility bill requires payment 30 days after you receive it, wait until day 25 before you write out your check and drop it into the mail. This doesn't mean that you should hold your payments longer than the date that payment is required to be made. Late payments may, at best, create ill will between you and your vendor or supplier and, at worst, damage your credit.

✔ **Make sure your invoices are timely — and accurate!** Send out invoices as soon as you deliver a product or service — preferably with the delivery itself. And make sure they are accurate. Many payments are delayed or rejected because of honest but preventable mistakes in invoicing.

✔ **Bill more often.** The more often you bill your clients or customers, the more often you'll be paid. And the more often you're paid, the better for your cash flow. Instead of billing your clients quarterly, why not bill them monthly? If you're supplying products, try breaking your deliveries into smaller chunks that you can bill sooner and more often.

✔ **Give prompt payment discounts.** Everyone loves price discounts, and if you offer discounts to clients who pay their bills quickly, you're sure to have many takers. You may get a little less money as a result, but this is offset by the fact that you get your money sooner rather than later.

✔ **Manage your expenses.** The flip side of bringing cash into your company is sending it out. The less cash you spend, the better your cash flow will be. Spend money on your company only when necessary. Instead of buying the latest and greatest computer every year, for example, try to make the one you have last as long as you can — replacing it only when necessary.

✔ **Manage your accounts receivable.** This means nothing more than being sure to keep track of what's owed you and taking action to collect late payments. There are plenty of reasons why you haven't been paid the money that is due you, however, and you'll never find out why if you aren't keeping track of your clients' payments. Accounting software programs such as QuickBooks can easily generate a *receivables aging report,* which tells you the status on all of your payments. If payments are even a day late, take immediate action to get paid.

Understanding collections

There comes a time in the life of every home-based business owner when a client either forgets to pay you for the products or services that you sell her or outright refuses to do so. It's one thing if the products and services that you sold your client were never delivered, were supplied late, or were poor in quality. Most customers are going to have a problem paying you in those kinds of situations, and they may express their displeasure by holding on to the cash that they owe you. It's another thing altogether, however, if you did what you agreed to do when your client placed his or her order.

But why wouldn't your clients pay you the money they owe you? Or why would they drag the process out so long that it becomes almost more trouble getting your money than it's worth? There are a number of possibilities, including:

 ✔ The check may be in the mail — really.

 ✔ Your client may have forgotten to pay you.

 ✔ A mistake in your invoice may prevent your client from paying you.

 ✔ Your client may not be satisfied with the product or service that you provided.

 ✔ Your client may be trying to improve his own cash flow or make a last-ditch effort to save his business before declaring bankruptcy or going out of business.

Each of these issues can be addressed, but you have to find out why you haven't been paid before you can address them. Collecting money owed you isn't the best part of having your own business, but it is necessary.

Peter sometimes thinks he leads a charmed life. In the 15-plus years that he has been writing professionally, on only one or two occasions has he had to lean on a client to make payment, and never once has a client not eventually made good on his or her obligations. In the handful of situations where payment was slow, it didn't take more than a phone call or two to get the client to stick a check in the mail. One time, Peter had to write a two-page letter explaining his position in detail to get the client to see the error of his ways and secure payment.

Here is a six-step plan that should get even the balkiest client or customer to pay up:

1. **Personally call your client.**

   Before you do anything else, get on the phone with your client to find out what the problem is. If it's minor, you can take care of it right then and there, over the phone. In the vast majority of cases, this is all it will take to nudge your clients into paying you. By calling first, you extend your clients the courtesy of allowing them to rectify any problems themselves or to explain why they have decided to withhold payment (perhaps they are unhappy with the products or services they received). If, however, calling your client doesn't get payment to you right away, you need to take further action.

2. **Send out a past-due notice immediately.**

   Don't wait after a payment is due to send out a past-due notice. If payment is due 15 days after you invoice, and you don't receive it, send out a past-due statement on day 16. If payment is due 30 days after you invoice, send out a past-due statement on day 31. This is no time to be shy — it's your money, so go after it. In addition to sticking the past-due statement in the mail, try faxing and e-mailing copies. You can use software to tickle or remind you when to act on a payment. For example, QuickBooks has a reminder feature.

3. **Stop work.**

If your client or customer drags things out longer than is acceptable to you, you may have to stop work to get their attention. If you sell products, this means suspending deliveries of any further orders until your client pays his bill. If you deliver services, this means putting any current projects on hold until payment is made. Stopping work shows your client or customer that you're serious about getting paid, and it is sure to solicit some sort of response. Before you undertake this step, however, be sure to give your client fair warning that you plan to take this action if you don't receive payment by a particular date.

4. **Enlist the services of a collections agency.**

If you've gone through all of the previous steps and still haven't been paid, it's probably time to assign the tardy account to a collections agency. A *collections agency* specializes in motivating customers to pay their financial obligations. Subject to federal, state, and local regulation, collections agencies use a variety of tactics to get your clients' attention — including phone calls, letters, and even lawsuits — and to get them to pay. You pay a price for this service, however. Expect to pay anywhere from 10 to 50 percent of any monies collected by the agency. Although an agency takes a healthy cut, the probability of getting some payment will likely increase with an agency in your corner.

5. **Mediate.**

Taking a client or customer to court isn't our idea of fun. Before you're forced to take that last, most drastic step, you have one more way to get out of your impasse: mediation. A *mediator* is an impartial third party whose job it is to help you and your customer work through your problems and reach a reasonable solution — one that is a win for both parties. If your client has simply decided not to pay you, mediation may not be fruitful. However, if your client is upset because of some perceived shortcoming in your performance, you may have a chance of resolution through mediation. You can find mediators in the Yellow Pages, listed under *Mediation Services*.

6. **Take them to court!**

Taking your clients to court is always the last resort. It not only takes up a lot of your precious time (and, if you need a lawyer, your money), but also, suing a client will surely put the last nail in the coffin that was your business relationship. If, however, despite all your efforts, you still haven't been paid, and you decide that it's in your interest to do everything in your power to get the money that is owed you, by all means take your client to court. In many cases — for relatively small amounts of money owed — taking your client to court means going to *small-claims court,* which, by design, offers a simple and inexpensive way for you to have your case heard by a judge. The amount of money that qualifies as a small-claims action differs from state to state, and from country to country. In Alaska and Colorado, for example, a small-claims action can't exceed $7,500, whereas $1,500 is the limit in Kentucky and Rhode Island. And although you can sue a client for up to $10,000 in small-claims court in the Canadian province of Ontario, you'll find a limit of £5,000 in England and Wales.

The extent to which you pursue your money is up to you. In some cases, you may decide that it's easier to write off the money (and the business relationship) than to pursue it to its ultimate conclusion. In other cases, you may decide to do whatever is necessary to get paid.

Getting a Loan

Studies show that one of the primary reasons so many businesses fail in their first year of existence is because they are undercapitalized — in other words, they don't have sufficient cash to meet their ongoing obligations over the long haul. Depending on what kind of business you have, putting enough money aside to allow you to make it through your first year can be a daunting proposition. But it shouldn't stop you from starting a successful home-based business — because you can always apply for a loan.

For many home-based businesspeople, the first choice in lenders is a time-honored one: F&F (friends and family). If friends and family aren't able to meet your business needs, though, you need to look elsewhere for the cash you need to sustain your business as you get established and build sales.

In the following sections, we explain some of the most commonly used sources of loans for home-based businesses.

Discovering different kinds of credit

Banks, credit unions, savings and loans, and other financial institutions are always coming up with new-and-improved loan products. Keep in mind, though, that you may have trouble obtaining a loan in the name of your business until it has established a track record of success over some extended period of time.

Here are some of the most common forms of credit for home-based businesses, along with their pluses and minuses:

- ✔ **Credit card:** Many a home-based business has been financed with credit cards. In fact, a recent survey showed that more than one-third of all small business owners use credit cards to at least partly finance their business operations. Not only are credit cards incredibly easy for most people to get (perhaps *too* easy; many people receive at least one or two credit card offers a month), but they are also convenient and easy to manage. All this convenience comes at a price, however. Credit card interest rates can be obscenely high — up to 25 percent, in some cases — and they are so easy to use that you can quickly find yourself bumping up against your credit limit. Although you'll likely be able to write this interest expense off when you do your taxes, you can quickly find yourself in over your head if you aren't careful. Used judiciously, credit cards can be a terrific business tool — and may be all the credit you ever need.

- ✔ **Personal loan:** Personal loans are made to individuals based on their own personal income and creditworthiness. Assuming you have sufficient income and a good credit rating, there's a good chance that you qualify for the loan you need. After you have your loan, you're free to spend the money as you please, making personal loans quite flexible. If you decide to apply for a personal loan, be sure to do so while you're working at your regular job — *before* you leave to start your own business. Your income is likely to be higher, at least initially, improving the chances of approval as well as increasing the amount of money your bank will be willing to loan to you.

- ✔ **Business loan:** Banks and other financial institutions make business loans to finance business startups, cover ongoing operational needs, or finance business expansion. New businesses are inherently risky — they often have little or no *equity* (value) built up, usually lack a sufficiently long track record of success, and have a statistically high rate of failure within the first few years after founding. So business loans can be difficult for home-based businesses to obtain. Although rates can be reasonable — usually only a few points over the prime rate established by the Federal Reserve — the hoops you have to jump through, as well as the ongoing reporting and bank reviews, may be enough to send you looking elsewhere for funding. You may even have to pledge your personal assets as collateral in the event of a loan default. To get a business loan, at a minimum you need a business plan, and you need to establish a good working relationship with your banker. If you and your business have what it takes, business loans can be your best solution.

✔ **Line of credit:** A line of credit is a business loan with a unique twist: Instead of a lump sum for the full amount of the loan, you're given approval to borrow funds up to a certain limit in whatever amounts or as often as you like. Costco, the large nationwide warehouse retailer, in cooperation with American Express, offers unsecured (no-collateral) lines of credit of up to $100,000 to its executive-level members. It charges an annual fee of $99, and the current interest rate is prime plus 0 percent — a rate that's hard to beat. For information, check out the Costco Web site at www.costco.com.

✔ **Home equity loan:** A home equity loan is similar to a personal loan, with one major difference: You're required to pledge your home or other real property as collateral in the event that you default on your loan obligations. Because your equity bears the burden of risk — a fact that can weigh heavily on your mind if your business gets into financial trouble — home-equity loans for substantial amounts of money can be obtained relatively easily. Loan terms can run 15 years or more. You likely have a choice of a lump sum or setting up a line of credit that you can draw on — and pay back — as necessary.

✔ **SBA loan:** SBA loans are business loans that are backed by the U.S. Small Business Administration. Because the lending bank has less of a risk in the event of default, home-based business owners can obtain them more easily than a standard business loan. Interested? Talk to your friendly local banker or visit the SBA at www.sba.gov.

So what kind of loan should you get? The answer depends on your particular situation, financial goals, how much money you plan to borrow, and your own personal credit history. Remember, however, that you should always minimize how much you borrow and be diligent about paying back your loans as soon as you can.

Getting the loan you want

The best way to get the loan you want is to first understand what factors go into a decision to extend or deny credit to an applicant. The standard rule used by banks, credit unions, savings and loans, and other financial institutions is called the *Five Cs:*

✔ **Capacity:** Will your business have the financial wherewithal to make loan payments — in full and on time — as required by your agreement with the bank? Will your cash flow support this additional burden of debt on your business? If the answers to these questions are no, you need to figure out how to improve revenues while tightening up on expenses. Do this before you apply for your loan, not after.

✔ **Capital:** Capital represents the ratio of your company's debt to assets or equity. Unfortunately, most business startups — including home-based businesses — have a relatively high debt load versus equity or assets. This is normal. You can, however, improve your chances of getting the loan you want by minimizing the debt you carry and maximizing equity and your own investment in the business.

✔ **Character:** Are you personally a good credit risk? Do you have a history of meeting your own financial obligations, including repaying loans on time and avoiding defaults or bankruptcies? If your own credit is shaky, this is an indication to a lender that your character is less than sterling. If this is the case, be sure to do whatever you can to repair your own credit before you apply for a loan. Obtain a credit report from one of the major credit reporting agencies — Equifax at (800) 525-6285, Experian at (888) 397-3742, or TransUnion at (800) 888-4213 — and take action on any problems that may show up. We discuss exactly how to do this in more detail in the "Fixing your bad credit history" section that follows.

✔ **Collateral:** What kind of property can you pledge in case you default? Car loans require your car to be pledged as collateral. Home mortgages require that your house be pledged as collateral. What are your options? In many cases, lenders may require that you pledge your assets or property to secure your loan. Your ability to provide sufficient collateral will greatly enhance your chances of getting the loan you seek.

✔ **Conditions:** Conditions include the health and growth potential of the markets within which you operate, the demographics of the typical buyers of your products and services, and many other economic factors external to your business. Although you can do little to influence or control the behavior of your markets or your customers, you can influence exactly which markets and customers you plan to target.

As you prepare to apply for a loan, review each of the Five Cs, and make an honest assessment of how you measure up. Are there areas you can improve in? Do so — before you apply for your loan. There's no reason why — if you do your homework — you can't get the loan you want for your business.

Fixing your bad credit history

It would be terrific if we all had great credit histories, but this isn't always the case. Unfortunately, a bad credit history can prevent you from getting the loan you want and the money you need. The good news is that bad credit histories can be turned into good credit histories. It takes time and patience, but the rewards can be well worth the effort.

In her book *Money Troubles: Legal Strategies to Cope with Your Debts,* Robin Leonard presents an eight-point plan for repairing your credit and improving your chances of getting a loan:

1. Secure a stable source of income.
2. Create a budget you can and will live within.
3. Open a passbook savings account (and add money to your account on a regular basis).
4. Apply for a savings passbook loan.
5. Pay back this loan over a six- to nine-month period.
6. Obtain a secured credit card.
7. Use this credit card sparingly (and pay off balances quickly to avoid potentially high interest charges).
8. Apply selectively for other cards (including gasoline companies, department stores, and other nonfinancial institutions).

If your credit is seriously damaged, and this plan isn't enough to solve the problem, consider working with a credit counselor or credit repair agency. For more information, contact the National Foundation on Consumer Credit at www.nfcc.org.

Chapter 8

The Price Is Right: Deciding How Much to Charge

* *

In This Chapter

▶ Understanding what your prices must cover

▶ Sizing up your potential customers and how much they will pay

▶ Researching your competition

▶ Applying pricing strategies that lead to sales

▶ Deciding whether to discount

* *

*P*ricing plays an extremely important role in the ultimate success of your business. Do it right, and your business will flourish; do it wrong, and your business will likely die a slow and miserable death. Because your business will live or die as a result of your pricing, this topic deserves your undivided attention.

Here's how it works: If you set your prices too high, your clients will seek out less expensive sources for the products and services you provide, and you'll soon find yourself going out of business from lack of sales. Set them too low, however, and although you'll be swamped with customers — everyone loves a bargain, after all — your profit margins will be too small to sustain your business as it grows. The key is to find a compromise between these two extremes that pays you what you're worth while generating sufficient business to keep you working as many hours as you want.

You can set prices for your products and services in a variety of ways. In many cases, though, finding the right price comes down to good old-fashioned trial and error: Do some research, check the competition, set a price, and see what happens. If sales aren't high enough, you can decide whether to lower your prices as an incentive for potential buyers to part with their cash. If sales are too high, but the resulting profits too low, you can choose to raise your prices to improve your margins (see the section "Changing your prices" near the end of this chapter).

The best pricing strategies are ones that strike a balance of generating the sales you need to survive while earning a reasonable profit that will allow your business to grow in the future. This chapter helps you understand how to develop a pricing strategy that is best for you, your business, and your customers and clients. In the sections that follow, we help you sort out the costs that you must cover when you set your prices and help you get a feel for what your customers will be willing to pay. We give you ideas for how to research your competition and review a number of different approaches to pricing that will aid your sales efforts. Finally, we consider the reasons why you should (or shouldn't) consider discounting your prices.

Figuring Out What Your Prices Must Cover

Whereas the motivation behind your business might be to help others get things done or to provide them with the products that they need to run their own businesses successfully, you can't have a business — at least for very long — if you don't charge your customers some amount of money for your trouble. Yet you shouldn't just charge them any old price; your price has to be low enough to attract the attention of prospective customers but high enough to allow you to generate a profit.

From time immemorial, the whole idea of pricing products and services has been to pay for all expenses in running a business while leaving a reasonable profit. Unfortunately, many home-based businesspeople don't fully understand the expenses they actually incur in running their businesses. Not only that, but they also sometimes forget that their home-based businesses should pay a decent salary and generate a reasonable profit — just like non-home-based businesses.

Imagine that the finances of your home-based business are a house. Just like any other sturdily built house anywhere in the world, it has a roof, a foundation, walls, doors, and windows. This house also has a first and second floor. Figure 8-1 shows this money house.

The following lists the major components of this money house and how they relate to the finances of your home-based business:

- ✔ **The foundation — your salary:** Whenever your company sells a product or service, a portion of the cash you take in is set aside to pay you and any employees a regular salary.

✔ **The first floor — your overhead:** The cash you take in also pays for your overhead, including all the expenses that your business requires to operate, whether or not you're selling any products. Insurance, rent, and telephones are examples of overhead expenses.

✔ **The second floor — your direct costs:** Direct costs are expenses that you incur on behalf of specific projects or products. If you drive to another town for a meeting, for example, that's a direct expense.

✔ **The roof — your profit:** Profit is what you're in business to try to make; it's what's left over when you've brought in all your cash for selling a product or service and subtracted out your salary, overhead, and direct expenses. Profit is your reward for taking a risk (yes, starting your own business does involve taking a risk, even if you've signed up for a "proven" system), and it plays an important role in building your business.

Just like a large business like General Motors, IBM, or Pfizer, your home-based business can make a profit or incur a loss. Home-based businesses are real businesses, and the profit you make is just as real as it is for any other business. Profit can be viewed as many things. Some people may identify the revenue beyond what they expect to pay themselves as a higher salary. For others, it's having the money to spend on extra things, such as investing in one's business without borrowing (usually a better idea than taking out loans to grow your business) or taking a long-deserved trip to a ski resort or the beach. But for most, it's additional earnings.

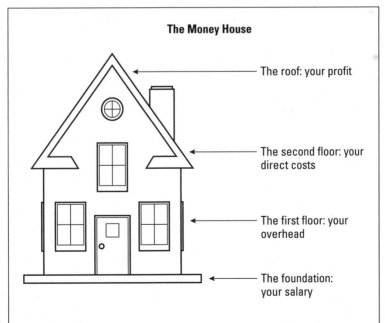

Figure 8-1:
The money
house.

The Money House

The roof: your profit

The second floor: your
direct costs

The first floor: your
overhead

The foundation:
your salary

In the following sections, we take a closer look at the kinds of financial elements that make up each part of your money house and how they all work together to determine the prices you charge for your company's products and services.

Salary

When you are set up as a sole proprietorship, it's unlikely that you will pay yourself a salary. Why not? Because under a sole proprietorship, the money you make in your business is automatically counted as income to you for tax purposes. If you've set up your business as a partnership or corporation, however, you may find that paying yourself a salary makes a lot of sense. But how much should you pay yourself? When deciding how much salary to draw from your business, first you have to decide what level of lifestyle you want your business to support. There are three major options:

- **Survival:** In this mode, your business is just getting by, and there is little or no extra money to set aside to pay yourself. Ideally, you're still working your regular job or have a spouse or significant other to help support you while you're working to build your sales.

- **Comfortable:** Comfortable means things are going pretty well — well enough to allow you to quit your regular job and work at your home-based business on a full-time basis. You can choose to continue with the status quo — and be quite comfortable where you are — or work to increase your sales and see your business really takes off.

- **Much better than average:** At this salary point, you're making more money than most people in your community or even nationwide. Attaining this level of income requires a lot of hard work and perhaps no small amount of luck. But for many, the rewards are worth the extra effort.

Overhead

Overhead consists of all of your home-based business's nondirect costs and nonsalary expenses. These are the costs of doing business — the expenses that your business incurs even when you aren't creating products or delivering services to customers. Here are some examples of common overhead expenses:

- Computer, copier, telephone, fax, and other office equipment
- Office furniture
- Internet and e-mail connection

- Web-site hosting fees
- Other marketing costs
- Letterhead and business cards
- Office supplies
- Travel for business operations, marketing, or other nonproject purposes
- Phone line(s)
- Water, electricity, and other utilities
- Newspaper, journal, and magazine subscriptions
- Insurance
- Licenses
- Rent or mortgage
- Repairs and maintenance

Because overhead doesn't directly produce revenue (or, ultimately, profit), smart business owners work hard to minimize overhead expenses, keeping them to the lowest possible level while still providing the highest-quality service and products. Before you spend a dime on any overhead item (see the preceding list for examples), take a moment to decide whether the expense is critical to your business or if you can live without it — at least for a while. And don't forget: Your overhead (and direct) expenses are tax deductible! Check out Chapter 10 for more details.

Direct costs

Direct costs are the expenses that you incur as you create products or deliver services; if you aren't making products or delivering services, you have no direct costs. Generally, the more direct costs, the merrier, because they directly become part of the products and services that you deliver to your clients, increasing the overall amount of money that you bring into your business (and ideally increasing your clients' satisfaction at the same time). Here are some examples of direct costs:

- Materials and supplies consumed in the manufacturing process
- Travel at your client's request
- Time spent in client meetings
- Postage and phone calls for specific projects

> ✔ Fees to consultants contracted to assist on specific projects
>
> ✔ Equipment dedicated to producing a specific product or delivering a service to a particular client

If you aren't creating products or working on client projects, you don't incur direct costs. (But you do still have to pay for your overhead — whether or not you're producing and selling your products and services.)

Profit

While *profit* might seem like a mysterious concept if you're new to owning your own business, it really boils down to a fairly simple idea:

> *The difference between a company's revenues and its costs.*

When you take all the cash that your company brings in from selling products and services, along with income from other sources such as interest-bearing bank accounts and investments, and then subtract your salary, overhead, and direct costs, you're left with the company's profit. If the profit is negative (because your costs exceed your revenues), this is called a *loss*.

ASK PAUL & SARAH

Starting a training business

Q: I've been teaching various aspects of computer applications for several years. I've developed one-day seminars on topics like the Internet that I give at local colleges. The classes are popular — they close out immediately. Many of my students follow me to different colleges to take all of the different seminars I give. They also bring their friends. In other words, the seminars are well received and popular. I was wondering if I could give these seminars at business conferences. I also do in-house corporate training, and I'm hoping that I will make contacts for future contracts for training. Generally, I get paid $200 for the day. Would I get paid more to do a business seminar? How would I go about getting such jobs?

A: Yes, you can speak at business conferences and do in-house training. I understand, however, that one of the major seminar producers in the United States is now paying only $200 a day, and this involves lots of travel. But the conference and corporate pay rates are typically better. To make a go of it, you need to develop marketing materials (a video and a media kit) and individually solicit meeting planners. You will be able to fortify this with great testimonials, perhaps on tape. The book *Speak and Grow Rich*, by Dottie and Lilly Walters, may help.

Although we suspect you might already know this, remember this about profits and losses: Profits are good; losses are bad.

Profit is the roof on the money house that we built earlier in this chapter, and it's the motivation that drives many businesses to ever-greater heights. In the case of a home-based business, profit is the reward to the owner who risks his or her capital in the marketplace. If allowed to accumulate within the business, it becomes the *equity* — the money put aside in savings — that gives the company real value.

Sizing Up Your Potential Customers and What They Will Pay

Pricing your products and services is more than simply sticking a price tag on them — pricing is an integral part of the overall strategy for your home-based business. In fact, it may well be one of the most important components (one reason we devote an entire chapter to the topic). Not only is pricing important because it determines to some extent exactly how much cash your business brings in, but it is also important from a marketing perspective and from the perspective of the overall health of your business.

Set your prices too high, for example, and your sales will be few and far between. The result? Little or no cash into the business, and an overall financial loss for the business as you continue to expend money that isn't being offset by income. Not only that, but you'll also spend an awful lot of time twiddling your thumbs as you wait for your phone to ring. Set your prices too low, on the other hand, and you're setting yourself up for a going-out-of-business scenario as you expend far too much time and money for too little return on your investment.

Before you launch headlong into your new home-based business, you should take a close look at your prospective customers — who they are and how much they're willing to pay. What if your targeted customers don't seem willing to pay the price that you need to turn a reasonable profit? Then you've got little choice but to rethink your entire business strategy, either by creating more value for your clients-to-be to justify a higher price or by moving to an entirely different product or service that you *can* sell at the right price.

Take a moment or two to picture the kind of person who would buy your products or services. As you imagine your typical client or customer, ask yourself the following questions:

> ✔ **What is your product or service worth to your prospective customers and clients?** Will your customers and clients see what you're selling as high value, low value, or something in between? Have you targeted the

right market for your products and services? If not, what is the right market? Are you providing the right products and services to your target market? If not, what are the right products and services?

✔ **What price are your prospective customers and clients willing to pay?** Is the price low, high, or somewhere in between?

✔ **Are you charging enough for your products and services to establish and grow a healthy business?** Will the price your customers and clients are willing to pay allow you to cover your business expenses — including the value of your time — while leaving some money left over as profit? Will these prices enable you to grow your business, or will they cause your business to shrink?

✔ **Do you have the right mix of price versus hours worked?** Are your prices set high enough to make a reasonable return on your investment of time and money, or are they so low that you have to work around the clock to make enough money just to keep your business afloat?

Pricing can play an important role in your business's success or its failure and deserves your focus and attention — both in initially setting prices for your products and services and then in monitoring them over time to ensure that they are creating the return you desire. Find the right pricing, and you ease the way to increased sales at a high return — something that every home-based business owner is happy to have.

Researching Your Competition

As you've noticed, we've been making a big deal about of pricing in this chapter. It really is important. But if you're new to your home-based business and have little or no previous experience selling the products and services you now offer, what is the best way to decide what prices to charge?

By far the quickest and easiest way to determine whether your prices make sense is to research your competition and see what they are charging. Once you understand what other businesses like yours are charging, you'll have a much better idea of the prices that you should charge. Want to attract more business than the competition? Then just charge a little less than they do. Want to position your company as a premium brand? Then charge a little more than the competition.

Here's some good news: The Internet has made researching your competition much easier than it has ever been. Researching competition used to mean spending a lot of time leafing through the Yellow Pages and making phone calls. No more. Today, with a few clicks of your mouse, you can find all kinds of free information about the companies you compete against — information that you can use to structure your own competitive strategies and tactics.

The best business media

Q: Before I start work each morning, I like to read the newspaper over breakfast. I find this routine both relaxing and motivating, as I am able to scan the articles for ideas, leads, general inspiration, or information. Unfortunately, I only have time to read one paper before work beckons. Which do you think offers more relevant information for a home-based business owner: a local newspaper or a national newspaper such as *USA Today* or *The Wall Street Journal*?

A: The answer depends on the nature of your business and your clientele. If your customers are businesses, your best bet is *The Wall Street Journal*. This is the newspaper that even owners of small businesses most often read. However, if your business serves only local customers, your local newspaper is, in almost all cases, your best bet. Another alternative, if you live in a city large enough to have one, is a local business journal that blends both local and business news. If your business addresses a broad consumer market on the Internet, through mail order or through wholesalers, a national paper like *The New York Times* or *USA Today* may better help you keep your finger on the pulse of popular consumer issues and tastes.

After making your choice of the one paper to read every morning, use the following time-saving techniques:

✔ **Read industry-specific newspapers online.** Most newspapers provide a significant portion of their content online. You can periodically peruse relevant topics in newspapers that you don't subscribe to. This is also a great way to keep up with the newspaper in an industry-specific town. If you're in the computer industry, for example, you could peruse the *San Jose Mercury Times* site periodically (www.sjmercury.com). If you deal with government, you can pop over to www.washingtonpost.com. In the entertainment business, try www.latimes.com. Such Web visits can be a great way to take a work break!

✔ **Create your own custom newspaper using a site like** www.crayon.net.

✔ **Subscribe to a weekly business news magazine, such as** *Business Week*, **instead of reading a daily paper.**

Here are some places to start your online search for information:

✔ **Hoover's Online:** www.hoovers.com

✔ **CanadaOne Directory:** www.canadaone.com

✔ **Big Book:** www.bigbook.com

✔ **Google:** www.google.com

✔ **Public Register's Annual Report Service:** www.prars.com

✔ **U.S. Chamber of Commerce:** www.uschamber.com

✔ **Business Wire:** www.businesswire.com

Fuld & Company is an international leader in obtaining competitive intelligence on businesses for a variety of clients. The company has developed the I3 Internet Intelligence Index, available for free on its Web site at www.fuld.com. The Internet Intelligence Index contains links to more than 600 competitive-intelligence Internet Web sites, covering an incredibly wide variety of information.

Pricing Strategies That Deliver Sales

In an ideal world, the prices you apply to your products and services should enhance — not hinder — your ability to sell them. Pricing is a fine art (some would say a mystical art), and much of the way that your clients-to-be react to them is determined by the psychology of marketing and how you present your products and your prices.

If, for example, your products and services are desirable and in short supply, people are willing to pay far more for them than if they are undesirable and available in overwhelming amounts. This is the basic law of supply and demand that many of us learned about in school. Think for a moment what happens when a few toys end up on the top of every child's list of wants during the holiday season. As a surge of parents hits the stores, the toys inevitably become hard to find, and people are willing to pay top dollar to get them — often, whatever it takes to ensure the happiness of their children. And for the toys that don't make the top of the list? They are plentiful and often on sale.

What does this mean for you? It means determining the best price points for your products and services. In the following sections, we explore different ways to develop pricing strategies that ease the way to sales.

Creating value for your clients

Above all, your clients and customers want to feel that they are getting the best value for their money. This is true whether the prices you charge are high or low. By increasing the *perceived value* of your products and services, for example (value is a subjective judgment, after all), you can increase the prices you charge for them and increase your profit at the same time!

Here are some of the best ways to create and increase the perceived value of your organization's products and services:

- **Go above and beyond:** Exceeding your customers' routine expectations dramatically increases the perceived value that you deliver to them. Think for a moment about how you feel when someone goes out of his way to give you the best possible service. Wouldn't you be willing to pay a little more to get more of that particular kind of service in the future? The better work you do, the higher your perceived value and the higher the prices you can charge.

✔ **Be different:** Many markets are crowded with competitors, each offering products and services that seem to differ little from the competition. If you can differentiate yourself from the rest of the pack — whether through novel packaging, a unique sales approach, or by the product or service itself — you increase your value to your clients and customers.

✔ **Focus on customer service:** The bad news is that every industry has more than its share of businesses that don't provide good customer service. The good news is that this shortfall is a terrific opportunity to provide the service that is lacking. Take advantage of it, and you greatly enhance the perceived value of your organization's products and services. Believe us — most people vastly prefer buying their products and services from companies that provide good service than from ones that don't.

✔ **Add value:** If you and a competitor offer the same item for the same price, why would a customer decide to buy exclusively from you? Because you add value to the transaction. Perhaps you provide better after-sales support, or maybe you're willing to take returned items for 30 days after an item is sold rather than the 10 days that your competitor allows. By adding value to the items you sell — value as perceived in the eyes of the buyer — you create value for your clients (and they will value you for it).

✔ **Build long-term relationships:** All business is about relationships, and your customers and clients value the long-term relationships that they develop with you and other trusted vendors. You become more than a place to buy something — you become a trusted friend and adviser, someone to turn to when your customer has questions or needs help. Help a few times, and you'll have a customer for life!

Always keep your customers' perceived value of your products and services in mind when you develop and set your prices. Adding value in your customers' eyes gives you much greater flexibility in the prices you ultimately choose.

Setting your prices: five approaches

Pricing is integral to the marketing process, and it can have a dramatic impact on whether potential customers choose to buy from you or from someone else. The right price can generate more sales, as we have seen, while the wrong price can send potential customers and clients looking elsewhere for companies to fulfill their needs.

Online auctions set the price for Sandy's finds

Auctions have long been a popular way for savvy buyers to purchase unique and valuable (okay, sometimes not-so-valuable) items. Until recently, however, auctions were generally the purview of a small subset of the general population. With the advent of online bidding at Web sites, such as eBay (www.ebay.com), anyone can participate in auctions 24 hours a day, seven days a week, in the comfort of their own homes. On eBay alone, more than 3 million unique items are for sale at any time. For home-based business owner Sandy Kleppinger of Leesburg, Virginia, this new way of doing business has been a godsend.

Sandy's business — Sandy's Finds — brings in well over $100,000 a year. Not bad for a woman who, just over a year ago, was home-schooling her 12-year-old son and trying to figure out how she could make a little extra money working part time. Now Sandy works 12-hour days, 6 days a week, fulfilling more than 75 software orders a day. And because Sandy sells all of her products through online auctions, Sandy doesn't set the price of her products — her customers do.

Sandy had no startup capital, no investors, no business experience — not even a Web site, let alone an e-commerce site. What she did have was a fast computer (which she purchased for $1,100), an Internet connection, and an irrepressible drive to succeed. She started her business with 100 boxes of closed-out software that she bought from a remainder bin at a local CompUSA store — for only 94 cents each. She listed the software on eBay and sold every box for an average of $10 each — a markup of more than 1,000 percent! When a software wholesaler then offered her $6,000 worth of software, she jumped — and she hasn't looked back.

Although Sandy doesn't control the price of the products she sells online, she does control the products she offers, and she has come to realize that she'd rather sell one piece of software for $35 than ten pieces of software for $3.50 each. Although the margin (the difference between what she pays for the item and what she sells it for) may be the same, selling ten pieces requires ten times the administrative work — pulling and packaging the software, generating mailing labels, updating her database, applying postage, and taking everything to the post office. So Sandy has pushed her auctions upscale, selling better-quality packages at higher prices. An example: She recently purchased a quantity of Broderbund 3-D Home Design Suite — complete with Wal-Mart price tags of $79.99 — from a software wholesaler for only $8.50 each. She promptly turned around and auctioned them off on eBay for about $35 each.

(Source: Margaret Webb Pressler, "Micro-businesses Bloom on eBay," *Washington Post*, August 29, 1999)

The following are five of the most common approaches that home-based businesses use to set their prices. As a part of determining your pricing strategy, carefully consider which approach (or combination of approaches) makes the most sense for your business.

- ✔ **Startup pricing:** If you're just getting started in your business, offer your customers an introductory rate that's set at a point somewhere between what other, established businesses charge and the amount you would be paid if you were doing the work on salary for an employer. Just don't forget to increase your pricing to bring it in line with the rest of the market after you get past the startup phase of the business and establish a track record. And to avoid unpleasant surprises, don't forget to let your early customers know that prices *will* rise in the future. Otherwise, they may not be very happy when your prices go up.

✔ **The going rate:** In some businesses, there may be a *going rate* that most every company charges for particular products or services. For example, the typical carpet-cleaning business in your community might charge $100 to clean three rooms and a hallway. You can choose to set your price at the going rate and differentiate your business through things other than price, such as better customer service or extra service that your competition doesn't provide. As some business owners have discovered, finding something that differentiates you from the competition can be as simple as a flashily painted van that advertises your business everywhere you go or an easy-to-remember phone number (for example, 1-800-CARPETS — of course, that's already been taken, but use your imagination).

✔ **Splitting the difference:** If you survey your competition, you may find that they offer a range of prices for the same products or services: some high, some low, and some in between. By splitting the difference between the top and the bottom of the range, you can be sure that your price is neither too high nor too low. After seeing how your customers react, you can make further adjustments later (see the section "Changing your prices" that follows).

✔ **Bargain basement:** If you really want to generate a lot of business quickly, you can dramatically undercut your competitors' prices. Before you try this approach, understand that some potential clients may be wary of buying products and services that are priced substantially below the competition — you'll need to find some way to make them feel that they aren't taking a risk by hiring you (great references from previous clients can do wonders here). Understand, too, that you may not be able to keep this approach up for long without doing serious financial damage to your company.

✔ **Premium:** At the other end of the spectrum from bargain-basement pricing is pricing at a premium, *above* your competition. This approach works well when the product or service you sell can be differentiated from those offered by your competition and you can add value that your clients and customers can see and appreciate. Consider a fancy dog-washing service that doesn't just come to your home, but that arrives in a brand-new, stainless-steel trailer, customized with all the latest tools of the trade, hot water, and big fluffy towels for Spot. For the dog owner who wants only the very best for her pet, paying a few extra dollars for first-class service like this is a no-brainer.

After you set your prices, keep close tabs on what your competition is doing. Are they raising their prices? Lowering them? When your competition moves, be prepared to adjust your prices accordingly.

Changing your prices

After you decide on a specific price for a product or service, your clients will expect to pay that price for the foreseeable future. No one likes buying things from a company that changes its prices every other week (or, in the case of gasoline, every other hour). You may, however, need to change your prices at some time, either up or down. If the changes translate into a price increase, you may have to overcome the resistance of your clients and customers. If the changes are price decreases, it's unlikely anyone will object to that!

In the following sections, we look at price increases, decreases, and stability — and how each impacts your business.

Price increases

Price increases are not usually a pleasant event for the company that makes them — no one wants to tell their clients that they are going to have to pay more money for their products — but they are often necessary. Here are some of the most common reasons for them:

- ✔ **You've underpriced your products:** After you set a price and begin to sell your products and services, you may discover that the money you're bringing in isn't enough to cover the expenses of the business and generate a reasonable profit. In this case, when you can't or don't want to reduce your expenses to bring your costs in line with the money you're bringing into your business, you have no other choice (assuming you want to stay in business) than to increase your prices.

- ✔ **Your expenses have increased:** If your costs of production increase, you can either reduce your profit or increase your price. The choice is up to you (although if your expenses have dramatically increased, you may have to do both).

- ✔ **You need to cover a client's hidden expenses:** If you're performing services for a client and discover costs due to working with that client that you didn't anticipate (for example, your client requires you to attend meetings twice a week instead of just once a month as you planned), you have to find a way to recoup them without reducing your profit. The easiest way is to increase your price.

- ✔ **You want to test the marketplace:** Sometimes you simply want to test the marketplace with a higher price, to see if the quantity of units that you sell increases, decreases, or stays the same. Airlines, food manufacturers, and others do this all the time. Who knows? You may discover that your customers are more willing to pay a higher price for your products and services than you ever imagined.

✔ **You don't want the work:** What if you don't want to do work for certain clients at the low prices you have agreed to? The best way to get out of this kind of situation is to raise the prices far beyond your normal rates. If the customer decides to pay more, great — you've just won the lottery! If not, you won't miss it. Peter has been known to do this when he's booked up with a lot of projects. If someone is willing to pay the (much) higher fare for a new project, he'll make room in his schedule to accommodate it.

There is no reason to be embarrassed by your prices, and you shouldn't hesitate for a moment to raise or lower them when it makes sense for your business. If you decide to increase your prices, however, be as forthcoming as you can possibly be when you do it, and give your customers plenty of notice so they can adjust.

Price decreases

In some cases, you find that there's good reason for decreasing your prices. Though this may not happen as often increasing your prices, it's bound to happen from time to time. The following are the main reasons for decreasing your prices:

✔ **You've overpriced your services:** If you've overpriced your services, you can choose to keep the extra money as profit (making for a very nice windfall, thank you very much), or you can give it back to your customers in the form of lower prices, or even a refund or rebate.

✔ **Your expenses have decreased:** Decreasing expenses are another good reason for lowering your prices. Then again, you can always keep the fruit of your decreased expenses as profit and increase the amount of money you're able to put into savings. This will motivate you to continue to find new ways to cut expenses even further.

✔ **You want to reward long-term clients:** Long-term clients always like to know that they are appreciated. You can show your appreciation (and build their loyalty) by reducing prices for them, either on a one-time basis or permanently — perhaps in the form of a discount card, special gift, or other premium.

✔ **You want to get new work:** One way to get new business is to drop your prices for new customers as a way to introduce them to your company and your products and services. Two-for-one specials for new customers, percent-off coupons, and the like are all ways to get new customers to try out your company — and ideally stick around.

✔ **You want to extend a professional courtesy:** Doctors, lawyers, and other professionals are noted for extending lower prices to colleagues as a professional courtesy. Why not extend lower prices to your colleagues, too (how about other home-based business owners)?

As with any other price changes, make sure you lower your prices as part of an overall strategy, not just as a reaction to some momentary event. If in doubt, leave your prices where they are until the case for changing them is more compelling. Not sure if it's time yet? Then it probably isn't.

Holding the line

Many times, you simply want to maintain your prices exactly where they are and deny requests to lower or discount them. Here are some strategies to help you hold the line on your prices when you feel it's in your best interest to do so:

- **Understand your limits:** When you want to hold the line on your prices, you first need to have an understanding of the limitations within which you can work and the minimum prices you're willing to accept.

- **Learn to say no:** Far too many people cave in the moment their customers show even one iota of resistance to their prices, no matter how well thought out and reasonable they might be. But there is a very easy cure to this kind of reaction: Just say no! Know your limits, and when someone wants you to go beyond them, be ready, willing, and able to just say *no*.

- **Be ready to explain why:** When you tell people no to a request that they think is reasonable, you should be able to explain why. Most people like to hear some rationale when what they consider to be sensible requests are denied. Responses like "I'll lose money on the deal at that price" or "That's a going-out-of-business plan for me" may be sufficient. Responses like "Because I got up on the wrong side of the bed this morning" or "I always charge you more than the rest of my customers" may not leave the best impression with your customers.

- **It's not personal — it's business:** Separate your personal feelings from the necessity of conducting your business in a way that ensures its survival. While you may like the feeling of cutting your prices and giving away your products and services to anyone who asks, you'll quickly go out of business with that approach. Remember: You've got a business to run; it isn't a charity.

- **Be prepared with a counterproposal:** Whenever you tell a prospective client or customer no, be prepared with an alternative that you can say yes to. For example, if you don't want to agree to dropping your price from $100 to $75 a unit, as requested by your client, you may be able to say yes to $95 — a figure that may well seal the deal for you.

You're going to face times when you have to hold the line against dropping your prices. Although you may lose potential customers in the process, your business will be healthier for it. And a healthy business is a business that thrives and grows — building long-term income for you and an ongoing partner for your clients.

Deciding whether to discount

When you're starting out in your home-based business, you need to get the ball rolling. Your prices can help with this, or they can stop the ball dead in its tracks. In the beginning, getting work — regardless of price — may be more important than how much you get paid to work. After you build up experience and references, you'll be better able to call the shots regarding your pricing.

In the beginning, you want to get known. You want to develop a buzz about your company and its goods and services. You want people to start talking about you and your company. As they do, and as more and more clients seek you out, you have the leverage to charge them what you're worth. In other words, if you're going to discount your products and services, the time to do that is as you're getting your home-based business established — not after you have developed a solid reputation, base of experience, and prices people have begun to rely on.

By far the biggest mistake home-based businesspeople make is chronic undercharging. Chronic undercharging creates a downward spiral that slowly eats away at the foundations of your business — the longer it goes on, the weaker your business becomes. Eventually, the bottom falls out altogether, and you're left with nothing but unpaid bills.

Chronic undercharging creates the following problems in home-based businesses:

- **Low-ball clients:** You tend to attract customers who are much more interested in paying as little as they can than in buying the best product or service possible.

- **Low-margin work:** You spend far too much of your time on low-margin work, rather than on a few high-paid projects with the greatest return for your time and money. Because there are still only 24 hours in a day, you're working more hours for less pay — a going-out-of-business plan if we've ever seen one.

- **Burnout:** You force yourself into a situation in which you focus far more time on your business than you do on your relationships with friends and family or on keeping yourself healthy and happy. Burnout is not unique to home-based businesses, but it can be a very real problem — especially for people who are juggling the demands of kids and family or a job that they have not yet left behind.

Discounting is okay as long as it is done consciously and is in line with long-term strategy. It's not okay when it becomes a knee-jerk reaction to every potential client who hesitates for a moment when you quote a price. If you're going to discount your services, consider some of the following approaches:

- ✔ Offer every tenth pound of coffee for free.

- ✔ Give a 25 percent discount on your client's first order.

- ✔ Offer volume discounts.

- ✔ Discount for paying before a certain date.

- ✔ Offer a variety of products and services at a variety of price points — high, low, and in-between. When faced with a client or client-to-be wanting you to discount your prices, you're far better off cutting the products or services delivered than cutting your unit price for those services. So, for example, if a client balks at your quotation of $1,000 to develop a turnkey Web site, don't say:

  "What if I drop my price to $750? Do we have a deal?"

  Do say:

  "No problem. Here's a complete list of all the different features you'll get in my $1,000 plan. Which features would you like to delete to meet your budget?"

Chapter 9

Getting Health Insurance and Planning for Your Retirement

. . . .

. . . .

Most people in regular jobs take their benefits for granted. Sick leave, holidays, tuition assistance, health care, worker's compensation, 401(k) savings plans, and more are an expected part of being a full-time employee. However, when you start your own home-based business, you quickly discover that benefits are nothing to take for granted; some aren't available to the home-based businessperson, and those that are have a real and substantial cost.

If you were to ask many prospective home-based businesspeople what most concerns them about leaving their jobs behind to start their own businesses, it's likely you would hear the same answer: losing benefits, especially benefits related to health care. After years of having benefits provided by their employers — generally without even having to ask for them — when you start your own home-based business, you're taking a step into the great unknown:

✔ Do you qualify for medical coverage? And even if you do qualify, can you afford it?

✔ What if you're injured and can't work — what then?

✔ Will you be able to set up a retirement fund? Are there limits to what you can contribute?

Questions like these — and many, many more — are valid concerns for individuals planning to make the move into self-employment, and it's important to address these concerns sooner rather than later.

In this chapter, we take a look at the benefits available to the home-based businessperson. Because health insurance is the primary concern for most prospective owners of home-based businesses, we'll take an especially close look at that particular benefit: what to look for in a health care plan and how to get it.

Providing Your Own Benefits

When you leave a 9-to-5 job and start your own home-based business, you go from getting a variety of benefits to providing for yourself. When you're the boss, you have to find the best benefits you can get for your hard-earned money, recognizing that what's best for someone else may not be best for you. This generally requires a lot of research on your part — you have to do your homework. But the payoff is an enhanced quality of life, and a moderate expense to bring you this enhanced quality of life is usually well worth the effort.

The best solution for your benefits likely involves two key factors:

- ✔ Price your products and services high enough to make sure you cover the cost of health insurance. The self-employed are more frequently uninsured than other parts of the workforce.
- ✔ Don't let yourself get taken in by what appears to be inexpensive and adequate coverage but turns out to be inadequate.

Working for yourself doesn't necessarily mean fewer benefits: If you do your homework, and if your prices are high enough, working for yourself can mean more — and often better — benefits. Instead of being saddled with whatever benefit plans your employer decides are best for you, you get to pick and choose which benefit plans you want. You pay only for the plans you need and can tailor your benefit plans to your own unique wants and desires.

Is having income in the event you're disabled — and unable to work — particularly important to you? Then focus on getting good disability coverage. Do you want to ensure that you'll be able to retire comfortably? You can structure a retirement plan that meets your exact needs. Or perhaps you'd simply like to have the best medical plan you can buy — no problem; it's your choice.

As a home-based businessperson, you — not someone else — get to decide what the best solution is for you and for your loved ones. And you have the power to make it happen. Having the ability to decide such important issues yourself is one of the things that makes working for yourself such an attractive option.

Working benefits into the mix

Q: This is my fourth year as a freelance translator, and it's been a good experience so far. My problem is not being able to secure individual health insurance due to past health conditions. Another concern is how to set aside funds for retirement. My income is good at times, but some months are typically low. Taking a vacation also seems impossible, because I can't afford to have no income while I'm away, and I may lose clients when they discover I'm not available when they need me. Any advice?

A: You have lots of company in worrying about how to provide for benefits like vacations, health care, and retirement. These three concerns are among the most critical issues facing those who are or want to be self-employed. The hurdles in lining up such benefits keep too many people working in less-than-rewarding salaried jobs instead of pursuing their dreams to be their own bosses.

Although lining up these benefits is more difficult than it should be or needs to be, doing so is one of the roles you must play if you want to become your own employer. Try to develop a new attitude toward these responsibilities: Keep in mind that the cost of benefits such as vacation time, retirement funds, and health insurance are part of the cost of doing business, and you must build them into your fee structure and set aside the funds needed to cover them. If you can't afford to take vacations, for example, this suggests that you're either not charging

enough or need to develop a marketing campaign to bring in more business during the slow times you mention.

That said, here are some options for getting past the difficulties involved in lining up these benefits:

- ✔ **Health insurance:** Obtaining affordable health insurance is a national crisis, especially for the self-employed. One option is to go through a professional association, which may be able to negotiate coverage for their members. In addition, some states — such as California, Colorado, Connecticut, Maryland, and Texas — have a mandatory small-business insurance provision. If you have two people working in your company (which can include your spouse!), you can get health insurance. For more information about this option, contact an insurance agent.

- ✔ **Retirement:** The real solution lies in passing legislation that allows the self-employed to invest half of the Social Security tax that you pay (the self-employed pay both the employer and employee share) into a private retirement account. In the meantime, here's a suggestion: Take 10 percent (or as high a percentage as you can) off the top of everything that comes in, and put it into a SEP-IRA or other retirement account. Make this a habit.

Choosing Your Health Care Coverage

Of all the different kinds of benefits available to most workers today, one in particular creates the most concern for people considering a move to starting their own home-based businesses: health insurance. Why? Because health insurance has a (much-deserved) reputation for being hard to obtain for individuals, it's often expensive, and the consequences for not having sufficient coverage can be financially catastrophic — particularly in the event of a major or prolonged illness.

In fact, the fear of having inadequate health insurance — or, even worse, no coverage at all — keeps many people from making the move to starting their own businesses. Instead, they remain stuck in jobs they don't like, getting paid less than they feel they should, in order to ensure that their health needs are covered.

The simple fact is that you, as a home-based business owner today, have more options available to you than ever before — both in the kinds of coverage available to you and in the different approaches you can take to get the coverage you want. In some cases, the health care plan you select as a home-based business owner may provide better coverage for you and your family for a lower premium than you've been paying in your regular job.

The spectrum of health coverage

When starting your own home-based business, you have a number of health care choices, all of which boil down to either obtaining health insurance or going it on your own.

At one end of the spectrum, *fee-for-service* is the traditional form of medicine (some today would call it old-fashioned) that many people grew up with. Under a fee-for-service health care plan, you decide which doctor you want to see, schedule your own exam, get diagnosed and treated, and make your payment directly to the doctor on the way out the door.

At the other end of the spectrum is a particular kind of health insurance, the *health maintenance organization* — also commonly known as an HMO. In an HMO, you agree to have all your health care needs taken care of by the HMO and its administrators and physicians. The HMO hires and pays the doctors, nurses, and physician's assistants who diagnose your illnesses; the HMO builds or leases the facilities where you go for medical examinations; and the HMO decides whether or not to authorize and pay for your treatment. In many cases, you never even see a bill or invoice, although most HMOs today require at least a nominal payment at the time of service, known as a *co-payment,* and these are increasing.

Each of these extremes on the health care spectrum — and all the variations in between — has its good and bad points. By going on your own, you have maximum control and flexibility over your health care, but unless you're well off financially, a catastrophic injury or illness could not only put you out of business, but also potentially bankrupt you. At the other end of the spectrum, in exchange for the peace of mind that HMOs offer, you give up a large amount of control over the management of your health care, as well as the flexibility to use whatever doctor you like, whenever you want.

When seeking health insurance for your home-based business, you have a number of options available to you:

- ✔ If you start up your home-based business while you're still working in your regular job, you can simply keep your current health care plan as it is. This is likely to be a relatively inexpensive option for you and your business — particularly if your employer covers the cost of your health care plan.

- ✔ If your spouse has health insurance at work, you can decide to use his or her plan to meet your health care needs as you establish your own home-based business. This, too, can be a relatively inexpensive option for you and your business.

- ✔ If you decide to leave your regular job to start your own home-based business, and you live in the United States, COBRA — the Consolidated Omnibus Budget Reconciliation Act — requires your employer to extend health care benefits to you for a minimum of 18 months (and in some cases, even longer) at the same rate offered to all other company employees (a piece of which most companies pay as an employee benefit) for comparable coverage. After the 18-month period elapses, you can generally convert to an individual plan with little muss or fuss, but usually at a significantly higher cost. (When Peter's COBRA plan expired a year ago, the cost to cover his family of five jumped from $750 a month to more than $1,350 a month. He shopped around for and found a new plan within minutes after he got that particular bit of news.)

- ✔ Find coverage on your own. You can conduct your own search for health coverage (a growing number of Internet sites are dedicated to helping small business owners select and apply for health insurance — do a keyword search on a search engine). Alternatively, a good insurance agent or broker can find the best coverage for you while saving you precious time in the process.

As a home-based businessperson, you have the luxury (and the burden) of almost unlimited choices when dealing with your heath care. From fee-for-service to HMO — the choice is up to you. The right decision depends on what's best for you, your family, and your business.

Fee-for-service and indemnity health care plans

Under traditional fee-for-service medical care, what's good for the patient is also generally good for the doctor, because their goals are aligned. *Fee-for-service* is where a doctor is paid directly for her medical services — whether by the patient or by an insurance company or other entity. Assuming the patient has enough money for the procedure, he is free to go to any doctor or hospital he chooses. While this method of payment is fine for simple, relatively low-cost procedures, it leaves the patient at tremendous financial risk if he becomes seriously ill or injured and requires extensive testing, hospitalization, or treatment.

With the traditional fee-for-service, on-your-own payment method, patients have the greatest freedom to choose their doctors and hospitals. They can get their health care directly — at any point in the system — without externally imposed limits. However, they often pay a lot of money for this privilege. Fee-for-service is the least regulated form of health care, and fees can be unpredictable. It is this unpredictability and the generally high cost of fee-for-service medicine that are driving it toward extinction — despite the nostalgia that many people have for it. Today, this is sometimes called *going bare* — that is, without insurance.

A desire to limit patient financial risk within the traditional fee-for-service approach has led to the emergence of *indemnity insurance plans.* Under indemnity plans, insurance companies agree to reimburse — or indemnify — policyholders for a fixed percentage of their medical bills after payment of a pre-established deductible. It is common for patients with this form of medical insurance, for example, to pay 20 percent of a medical expense and for their insurance company to pick up the remaining 80 percent. Although indemnity plans still leave patients with some amount of financial risk, many patients like these plans because they are free to select most any doctor or hospital they desire.

Many home-based business owners have found that it makes sense to take advantage of a fairly recent wrinkle in the tax laws: *medical savings accounts* (MSAs). MSAs allow you to set aside pretax dollars to pay for routine (and relatively low-cost) medical procedures such as annual physicals, eye exams, dental checkups, and the like while reserving insurance coverage for high-cost, catastrophic health events such as major surgery or cancer treatments.

Managed care plans

Managed care is the overall term applied to a system of health care in which an individual pays a fixed premium for a guarantee of all-encompassing, preventive, and therapeutic health care with minimal additional out-of-pocket expenses. The entire universe of managed care systems covers an incredibly diverse range of programs — from managed indemnity insurance to HMOs. Although it is sometimes difficult to draw distinct lines separating one form of managed care from another, all managed care programs implement formal policies and procedures to control three common characteristics:

✔ Access

✔ Cost

✔ Quality

By placing strict limits and controls over these three areas, managed care providers are able to provide complete, quality medical care to their members at a lower cost than other forms of health care. For example, one way that certain kinds of managed care providers control costs is by hiring their own doctors and nurses. Costs are also controlled by making concerted efforts at providing preventive care to patients. It is generally far less expensive to prevent a serious illness than to cure it.

Health maintenance organizations (HMOs)

An HMO is a form of managed care that either operates its own health care facilities or contracts with hospitals and doctors to provide health care services at predetermined rates. The membership fees go into a pool of money that pays for doctors, nurses, equipment, facilities, and the other costs of providing health care services to members. Any money left over is profit. After the membership fee has been paid, the greatest risk to the HMO is providing too much care or care that is too expensive.

All HMOs rely on the primary care physician to control costs by controlling access to the services of the HMO. A *primary care physician* is a doctor whose job it is to assess a patient's medical condition and determine which services are required to bring him back to a state of good health at the minimum necessary cost. Primary care physicians are often under considerable pressure to keep costs down, so their jobs sometimes appear to be to find ways to deny care rather than provide it. Because of this perception, primary care physicians are often known as *gatekeepers*.

Comparison shopping among different HMOs can be frustratingly difficult. Sophisticated, often confusing issues require your consideration, including a wide array of different co-payments (both for services and for prescribed drugs), coverage limitations and exclusions, waiting periods, and more. At times, even the information sources you use may not permit easy comparison of one HMO to another. Here are some things to consider:

✔ **Your health care needs:** You and your family want high quality, low costs, and easy access to your health care provider and a broad range of covered services. But there are limits set by your employer, by the government, or by you in terms of the amount of dollars you're willing and able to put into your quest for quality health care. Further, it is unlikely that you will find a plan that meets all your needs at a price you can afford. Your final selection will, therefore, involve some compromise.

Unless you have unlimited resources to pour into purchasing your health care, selecting an HMO also forces you to face some limits. Finding the best HMO for you and your family involves striking a balance between your health care needs and wishes and the resources that you have available to purchase them.

✔ **Other deciding factors:** Although you have your own unique medical needs, every heath care consumer should consider several factors when shopping for an HMO. Depending on your personal situation, you may have several health plans to choose among, or you may have only one or two. Whatever the options available to you, you need to carefully weigh the advantages and disadvantages of each before you make your final decision.

After you have enrolled in a plan, it may not be easy for you to switch plans if you discover you made the wrong choice. Take your time to review each plan carefully, and consider the following in your decision:

- **Basic needs versus extras:** With medical care, keep in mind the difference between what you need and what you want. Does the HMO you have chosen provide all the basic health services that you need to maintain your health or return you from illness? Does it also provide the extras — such as a pleasant and relaxing environment, clean and modern hospitals, or free car seats for newborns — that you consider important to your health care experience?

- **Access:** When you consider an HMO, does it provide you with access to the full range of physicians and medical facilities that are required to maintain your good health? Does the HMO offer specialists who are trained and competent in orthopedics, pediatrics, surgery, and so on? Are appointments readily available, or will you be required to wait long periods of time to see a doctor? Will you have access to 24-hour-a-day emergency-room care at a reasonable price?

- **Choice:** A real hot button for many health care consumers is the right to see the doctor of their choice. Although some HMOs are restrictive and offer few care options, others offer a wide variety of doctors, clinics, and hospitals to choose among. When considering an HMO, be sure to find out how flexible your plan will be. Will the HMO assign you to a primary care doctor, or will you be able to make your own choice? If you don't like your doctor, can you easily switch to another? Will you have to go to a specific clinic or hospital, or will you have the option to select which one you want to go to? Ask an insurance agent what would happen under different hypothetical situations.

- **Cost:** The price of health care is always a major issue for health care consumers. Is the plan affordable? Will you receive a full range of services for an amount you can afford? If you're comparing plans, what do you get in the higher-priced plan that the lower-priced plan doesn't offer? Should you consider add-ons to the plan, such as point-of-service options?

- **Coverage:** Every HMO is different — some provide more extensive coverage than others. What does the plan cover? Does it include office visits and hospital stays? How about eye and dental care? Are certain procedures excluded from the plan? Do you understand how your HMO defines *experimental* or *unproven* cures? What about pre-existing conditions? If you have asthma when you join the plan, for example, will your new HMO cover it? If you're outside the plan area, will the plan pay for emergency care at another hospital?

- **Ease of use:** Every form of health care involves a certain amount of red tape and bureaucracy — HMOs are no exception. Are office hours convenient, and are facilities, clinics, and hospitals within a reasonable distance from your home or work? Does the plan offer evening or weekend appointments? Are special phone lines available to make appointments or ask questions that don't require a physician's intervention? What kinds of paperwork will you be required to fill out, and how much will there be?

- **Quality:** The old adage that you get what you pay for is often true. Are the doctors and nurses in the plan top-notch, or are they something less? Are the facilities modern, clean, and large enough to handle the needs of the plan's members? What's the overall quality of care dispensed by the HMO — is it excellent, good, or just adequate? How does the plan score on member satisfaction? Does the HMO have a history of extensive member complaints and grievances? Is the HMO National Committee on Quality Assurance (NCQA) or federally qualified?

As you research your health care options, you will quickly find significant differences among plans. It's your job to determine whether a specific plan meets your needs. While the HMO's glossy brochures and glowing advertisements may seem attractive, try to get beyond their sugar-coated exteriors to the real story. Ask your insurance broker pointed questions. Which plan did he pick, and why? Is he happy with his choice? Why or why not? Is he planning to switch to another plan when he gets the opportunity?

Ultimately, you're faced with a choice that balances your health care needs with the resources you have available to pay for those needs. The best choice for you is the choice that closely balances these two competing demands.

San Diego cares about its businesses

In most cities in the United States, small businesses are left to fend for themselves when it comes to finding affordable health care solutions, but the city of San Diego, California, has decided to change all that. Specifically designed for small businesses with two or more employees, the City Care Benefits Plan — sponsored by the Business Improvement District Council — offers comprehensive group health, dental, and vision plans at the kind of rates usually available only to very large businesses. A variety of procedures and services are fully covered under these plans, with small co-payments of $10 to $20 for office visits and drug co-payments also between $10 to $20.

With this progressive benefits plan, San Diego has addressed a very important need in the community. Says Scott Kessler, CEO of the Business Improvement District Council, "Many small business owners forgo health insurance due to cost, quality, and administrative obstacles. The City Care Benefits Plan is designed to meet the unique needs of small businesses." Considering that 85 percent of the uninsured population of San Diego works for small businesses, the City Cares Benefits Plan may have a major impact on many thousands of employees and their families. For more information, visit the Seaman & Company Web site at www.seaman andco.com.

Preferred provider organizations (PPOs)

Some years ago, in an effort to contain spiraling costs, indemnity insurers introduced a new form of health care — the *preferred provider organization* (PPO). In a PPO, the insurer strikes deals with selected physicians to provide care on a discounted fee-for-service basis. Patients are then given financial incentives to use physicians on a list provided to them by their insurance company. PPOs can be thought of as a transitional arrangement between fee-for-service and HMOs because they exhibit some elements of a loosely organized managed care network while maintaining a degree of physician choice and/or service locations for the patient. They're also like fee-for-service plans in the sense that the more doctors do for you, the more they get paid.

Typical PPOs provide some expense predictability for their enrollees by having maximum out-of-pocket limits, but they often have exclusions and waiting periods for pre-existing conditions, which could include pregnancy. Within a PPO, preventive services are minimal, but most have disease screening and usually provide smoking-cessation programs. If you go out of the network for your care, your out-of-pocket costs increase.

Other health care coverage

A number of other health-related benefits, besides your main health care plan, are available to you. Depending on your situation, they may or may not make sense for you and for your business. Be sure to study your options carefully before committing to a plan.

> ✔ **Dental:** You can find a variety of dental insurance plans to choose among. While many have high deductibles and rigid guidelines for what they'll pay for — and how much — a dental plan can be a godsend in the event of a catastrophic dental problem, accident, or illness, or if your teeth are simply falling apart.

> ✔ **Vision care:** Vision care plans generally pay for eye examinations and sometimes for glasses or contact lenses as well. Elective procedures such as surgery to permanently correct nearsightedness are usually not covered.

> ✔ **Gyms and health clubs:** Many large companies have their own on-site gyms and health clubs. While you may not have the room (or the money) to set up your own on-site gym, don't let this stop you from joining a local gym and working out regularly.

Ways to cut your health care costs

While health care plans are becoming easier to obtain and more flexible for their users because of increased competitive pressures within the industry, the cost of health care continues to rise. In his book *Human Resources Kit For Dummies* (Wiley Publishing), Max Messmer offers the following advice for cutting your health care costs:

✔ **Affiliate with the largest group possible.** Although you can find exceptions, the larger the group that's insured, the more competitive the rates tend to be. Instead of seeking coverage as a one-person, home-based business, check into health care plans offered by local chambers of commerce, industry associations, alumni associations, and professional organizations. Most offer health care plans with competitive rates.

✔ **Increase the deductible (co-pay).** You can save anywhere from 10 to 50 percent on your premiums simply by increasing your deductibles or, in the case of HMOs, your co-payment. This can be particularly effective if you aren't a big user of your health care plan. Check with your health plan provider to see what your options are.

✔ **Consider working with a benefits consultant.** It's just about impossible for anyone who isn't fully dedicated to studying all the different health care coverage options available to know if he or she is getting the plan that is the best for his or her business. A benefits consultant is fully dedicated to that task and can be a genuine asset — both in locating the right plan for you and in negotiating the best rates possible. Ask friends and business associates for a referral to a qualified consultant, or check the Yellow Pages.

And here's a tip from us: Pay for health insurance *above the line* taxwise (with pretax dollars) by incorporating as a C corporation (see Chapter 11 for more information on incorporating) and reimbursing all medical expenses or by getting a high-deductible plan with a Health Savings Account that enables you to have more control over how you spend your health care dollars.

Because many health care plans don't include dental, vision, or access to gyms or health clubs, you need to decide if they are important enough for you to pay for out of the proceeds of your business.

Considering the Need for Other Benefits

If you currently work — or have worked in the past — in a regular business, you know that you may want to provide yourself many other benefits besides health insurance. Although insuring yourself against a catastrophic loss in the event of a serious or protracted illness is critically important for most people, other benefits can help you protect your income, save for the future, and provide financial and psychic benefits.

In this section, we discuss the most common benefits besides health care.

Income protection

Imagine that you're a professional writer, as is Peter, one of the authors of this book. And imagine that you depend on your physical ability to use your computer keyboard to do your writing. Now imagine that you are diagnosed with carpal tunnel syndrome or a repetitive-motion injury that prevents you from using your computer for weeks or even months or years. What would you do, and how would you and your family survive the loss of income that such an injury would bring about?

Benefits in the income protection category protect workers and owners from just these kinds of potentially disastrous financial events.

- **Disability insurance** is a form of insurance that pays a percentage of income — generally less than 100 percent — in the event that injury or illness prevents a worker or owner from performing his or her job. Available to home-based businesses in either short- or long-term versions, they can be very expensive.

- **Workers' compensation** provides a fixed amount of income to workers who are injured on the job and is required of companies with three or more employees. Some states provide for the business owner's also being covered.

- **Unemployment insurance** provides a fixed amount of income to workers who lose their job through no fault of their own and is required by federal and state law of employers with one or more employees for at least 20 weeks in a calendar year.

For most home-based businesses, long-term disability insurance is the only form of income protection benefit to be seriously considered. If you eventually hire employees, workers' compensation and unemployment insurance may be a requirement for your home-based business.

Life insurance

Of course, no one likes to think about dying and leaving our loved ones without a source of income. But if you die without having established some sort of retirement fund or a life insurance policy, that's exactly what will happen. Life insurance pays whomever you designate as your beneficiary a lump sum of money if you die, thus providing some peace of mind that their financial needs will be taken care of in the event of your death.

- ✔ **Life insurance** policies are widely available, affordable, and easy to get. Find a good broker, and have him or her explain the advantages and disadvantages of the different kinds of life insurance, including term, universal, and whole life.

- ✔ **Dependent life insurance** provides coverage for the spouse of a home-based business owner and is often available for a small additional charge beyond your own policy.

Life insurance is an essential part of the benefits package of many home-based businesses. While the money paid out in the event of your death won't do you any good personally (remember: you can't take it with you!), the peace of mind that it provides knowing that your loved ones will have the financial wherewithal to continue without you is often well worth the price of admission.

Retirement and savings plans

Retirement and savings plans are a regular part of most businesses, and they can and should be a part of your home-based business. As we discuss in Chapter 4, the prices you charge for your products and services should be sufficiently high to provide you with a decent income and benefits.

Most home-based businesspeople are probably aware that Social Security is not the best option for ensuring a comfortable and worry-free retirement. Social Security alone simply can't fill the bill. Unless you have a retirement plan or pension from your previous employer, the only way you're going to have any sort of retirement plan for your home-based business is if you create one yourself. Be sure to do just that to provide a reliable source of income after you leave the world of work behind once and for all.

Here are a few different options available to you:

- **Simplified Employee Pension (SEP-IRA):** Any home-based businessperson with at least some self-employment income can set up a tax-deferred SEP-IRA account to provide steady income in retirement. SEP-IRAs are easy to open and can be maintained with minimal paperwork or red tape. The beauty of the SEP-IRA is that you're allowed to contribute up to $30,000 or 15 percent of your business's net income per year, whichever is less. This could be ten times higher than you could contribute to plain old IRAs.

- **Keogh:** Keogh plans offer the highest limits for tax-deferred contributions, but they are complicated to set up and maintain. They come in two types:

  - *Defined contribution plan,* which fixes the amount and the source of the contributions (contributions are limited to $30,000 or 25 percent of your earned income for the year, whichever is less)

  - *Defined benefit plan,* which attempts to pay out a particular sum of money each month in retirement (contributions are limited to the amount needed to eventually produce an annual pension payment of the lesser of $130,000 or 100 percent of your average compensation for your three highest years)

- **SIMPLE:** The Savings Incentive Match Plan for Employees (SIMPLE) allows employees to make elective contributions of up to $6,000 per year and requires employers to make matching contributions of up to 3 percent of each employee's pay. Alternatively, you can decide to make a blanket contribution of 2 percent of each participating employee's pay regardless of whether he or she makes any elective contributions.

Each of these options has its pluses and minuses, and one may be better for your business than another. Consult an accountant or professional tax expert before you decide on a particular plan. After you set your plan up, you're pretty much stuck with it. Changing plan types is generally not encouraged by the tax code, and Congress has built in a variety of disincentives to ensure that you get the message.

Time off

Most regular businesses provide a wide variety of different forms of time off, including holidays and vacations. As the owner of your own home-based business, you get to decide which days you take off. In a home-based business, however, time off works a bit differently than it does in a regular job. In a regular job, you're usually paid for holidays and vacation leave — even though you don't actually work while you're on leave. In a home-based business, if you don't work, you don't get paid.

Regardless, be sure to set aside time off to get out of the office and spend time recharging your batteries with family and friends.

- ✔ **Holidays:** A number of standardized holidays are available for you to choose among, including Memorial Day, Independence Day, Labor Day, Thanksgiving, and Christmas. You decide whether you're open for business on those days.

- ✔ **Vacations:** Many small business owners find themselves working far harder than they ever did working in a regular job. This makes setting aside vacation time away from your business even more important.

Make taking time off a regular part of your benefits package and an established part of the way you do business — your attitude, as will your relationships with friends and family, will benefit.

Child care

Working at home offers you a unique advantage that working outside the home can't — you can be at home with your young children every day of the week, if that's what you want. For parents who want to work but who don't want to sacrifice their family lives to do so, this is truly the best of both worlds. However, if you work at home and have young children, you need to figure out how to keep them out of your way (and out of the way of your clients and customers) during your normal working hours. This generally means obtaining some sort of child care.

You basically have two options:

- ✔ **On-site child care:** Hire a babysitter or nanny to take care of your child in your home on a regular schedule. If you have in-town relatives — perhaps a child's grandparent or aunt or uncle — even better! This is often an ideal situation, because you're nearby if needed, but you're still able to close your office door and leave your family life behind while you work.

- ✔ **Off-site child care:** Numerous off-site child care facilities are available to the home-based businessperson. From individual day-care providers to programs at schools and churches to neighborhood centers, you have plenty of options for ensuring quality care for your child.

Flip to Chapter 15 for information on developing your own thriving home-based business and still having the contact and relationship with your children that you desire.

Chapter 10

Getting a Grip on Taxes and Deductions

*T*here's an old saying about taxes, generally attributed to Benjamin Franklin, that sums up the opinion of just about every businessperson we know: "In this world, nothing is certain but death and taxes." And for some business owners who pay a lot of taxes, taxes may seem the most certain thing of all.

According to the General Accounting Office, small business owners (including most home-based businesses) face more than 200 different Internal Revenue Service forms and schedules to pick and choose among in any given tax year. These forms and schedules — with more than 8,000 lines, boxes, and blanks to be filled in with your business's unique set of numbers — are accompanied by more than 700 pages of instructions. And although no one business would ever have to use anything approaching all 200 of these IRS forms and schedules, the paperwork problem is so pervasive that it can easily threaten to bury the unwary home-based business owner.

Is it any wonder that the first thing many savvy home-based businesspeople do when they start their businesses is hire a tax lawyer, certified public accountant (CPA), or both to help them plan and file their taxes? For many home-based business owners, the investment in a good tax planner can pay off many times over as the business grows and evolves.

This chapter is all about taxes: who pays them, when to pay them, how much to pay, and how to handle sales tax. As famous smart guy Albert Einstein once said, "The hardest thing in the world to understand is income tax!" And while our intent is not to make you an expert on the subject of taxes (we don't want to put any home-based accountants out of business), we do want to provide you with a basic understanding of the topic — enough to get your business started and be able to talk intelligently with an accountant, tax planner, or friendly IRS agent. Check out *Taxes For Dummies,* by Eric Tyson (Wiley Publishing), for detailed tax information.

Understanding Which Taxes to Pay — and When to Pay Them

The tax code may well be the most complicated piece of legislation in any country, but during the course of our extensive research for this book, we were fortunate to find what have to be the clearest, most concise, straightforward instructions we have ever seen for determining how to figure out the amount of money you owe in taxes for your home-based business. In fact, they are so clear, concise, and straightforward that we are frankly surprised that the IRS has not already put them into effect. Read them and see what you think:

1. **Add up all the money you took in from your business during the course of the year.**

2. **Write that exact amount on a check made out to the Internal Revenue Service.**

3. **Drop it in the mail.**

Okay, so maybe things aren't quite that bad, but for many owners of home-based businesses, it sure does feel like a lot of their hard-earned money goes to pay taxes. By the time you pay self-employment tax (the government's way of collecting payments for Social Security and Medicare from people who are self-employed), state and federal income taxes, excise and property taxes, and miscellaneous local taxes or assessments, you can easily be writing checks to all sorts of government agencies for 30 to 50 percent or more of your business's revenues.

Just like any other business, home-based businesses are required to pay income tax to the federal government and, in most cases, to the state government in which the business is located. The forms you use to calculate and file your taxes and the kinds of expenses you're able to deduct depend on the form of business you select: sole proprietorship, partnership, limited liability company, subchapter S corporation, or regular corporation. And while home-based businesses are granted some special tax breaks by the government — unless you have some really good tax deductions or you're not making any money, you're still going to have to pay at least some tax.

And that's one thing you can count on.

Who has to pay?

Within the United States, all businesses (except for partnerships, which file an information return) are required to file an annual income tax return. It doesn't matter if you make money or lose money; you still need to file a return. This means you.

Of course, we're assuming that your business is really a business and not a hobby. Suppose, for example, that you're an avid collector of *Star Wars* figures, and you buy and sell them on a regular basis. Not only that, but you're also taking a home-office deduction and writing off other business expenses — but you aren't conducting this activity on a businesslike basis (that is, to make a profit). If this is the case, the IRS doesn't allow you to deduct any of your expenses as business expenses — including the all-important home-office deduction (more about that in the "Taking a Look at the Home-Office Deduction" section, later in this chapter). And if you have been taking these deductions for years, get audited by the IRS, and find that these deductions are disallowed, the financial impact on you and your "business" could be more than a simple inconvenience — it could be devastating.

The hobby loss rule

Aside from the freedom that having one's own home business can provide, one of the main reasons for starting a home-based business is for the financial benefits — including taxes. If you want to benefit from the tax deductions and other advantages that having your own home-based business affords you (which can be considerable), it's in your interest for the IRS to agree that indeed you're operating a business and not a hobby.

But how do you know whether your enterprise is a business or a hobby? We're glad you asked.

The place to start is a law established by Congress called the *hobby loss rule*. In essence, the hobby loss rule says that to be considered a business instead of a hobby, your activity must have made a profit in at least three of the preceding five years. If your business is a new one — without an established track record of profit — or if it is truly a business but not a profitable one (after all, Amazon.com, founded in 1995 and with a current market value in the billions of dollars, only recently showed a profit) — it may still qualify as a business instead of a hobby.

Web sites that can make your job less taxing

While Congress continues to mystify the tax codes, the Internet is doing just the opposite. In response to popular taxpayer demand, a number of Web sites have sprung up to dispense help and assistance. These work hard to take the mystery out of preparing your income taxes. Here are some of the best:

✔ **OPEN: American Express Small Business Network:** This site contains articles addressing a variety of income tax issues of particular interest to small and home-based businesses at `www.americanexpress.com/smallbusiness`.

✔ **CCH Business Owner's Toolkit:** This comprehensive guide to starting and building a successful business has an extensive tax section at `www.toolkit.cch.com`.

✔ **TurboTax:** Intuit offers support for its TurboTax software and tax help at its online tax center 24 hours a day, seven days a week, at `www.turbotax.com`.

✔ **IRS Online:** For home office startup information and online publications and forms, go to `www.irs.ustreas.gov/businesses/index.html`.

✔ **L.A. Times Online:** The Times' burgeoning Web site offers much helpful tax and business information at `www.latimes.com/taxes` (you'll need to register to read the articles).

✔ **State tax forms:** Too bushed to mount a search for your state income tax forms this year? Try `www.1040.com`.

The IRS has established nine factors to help decide on which side of the fence to place your business. You don't necessarily have to satisfy all of these criteria, but you can bet that the more you do meet, the better your position in the event that an IRS agent comes knocking.

Here they are:

✔ **The manner in which the taxpayer carries on the activity:** If your business is really a business, it should conduct itself like a business, not like a hobby. For example, a business establishes accounting records and develops business plans and strategies. It obtains a business license and adheres to any zoning or other legal requirements. It establishes financial goals, abandons strategies that don't help it achieve its goals, and constantly seeks out and executes new strategies that do help it achieve its goals. It strives to make a profit and avoids financial losses. The owner establishes systems and resources dedicated to the business, such as dedicated computers and phone lines, Internet connections, an office, office equipment and supplies, a business logo or trademark, stationery, and business cards.

✔ **The expertise of the taxpayer or his or her advisers:** The knowledge and expertise that a home-based businessperson has in running his or her particular line of business can be a significant factor in deciding whether a particular activity is a business or a hobby. In fact, a person's knowledge or effort in managing a successful enterprise has been considered by the courts in several cases. Similarly, if the home-based businessperson has retained an accountant, a lawyer, and other experts to provide business advice, this would tend to indicate that the activity is indeed a business and not a hobby.

✔ **The time and effort expended by the taxpayer in carrying on the activity:** Although the IRS doesn't expect you to spend your every waking hour working in your home-based business, it does expect you to show some sort of personal commitment of your own time and effort on behalf of the business. If, for example, you develop, create, and deliver all of your business's products or services, and this takes an average of 20 hours a week to accomplish, you clearly have a major commitment of time and effort. And if you quit another job or go to part-time status so that you can devote even more energies to your new venture, you're investing much time and effort to your activity.

✔ **Expectation that the assets used in activity will increase in value:** Every business has assets, some more valuable than others. And although some business assets — such as computers, printers, and vehicles — tend to decrease in value over time, other assets — such as real estate and intellectual property — tend to increase over time. Most businesses start out in a loss position, so even if the activity isn't making a profit at the time, a new home-based business owner can demonstrate that he or she expects the company's key assets to appreciate, indicating that the activity is a business, not a hobby.

✔ **The success of the taxpayer in other activities:** A home-based businessperson may have a personal history of establishing a number of businesses that are initially unprofitable, but which he or she then shepherds into operations that are both profitable and successful. A track record like this can go a long way to convincing an outside observer that a particular activity is truly a business, though one that is not yet profitable.

✔ **The taxpayer's history of income or losses in this activity:** If your activity is generating a profit, it's clearly a profit-making activity. The fact that an activity does not generate profits, however, doesn't necessarily mean that it's not engaged in for-profit activities. The first years of a business can be a time of building and securing assets that the business needs to operate effectively. After these expenses are paid and revenues begin to climb, the activity should begin to show a profit. In some cases, extraordinary situations, such as the loss of a major client or the death of a principal in the business, may push the business into unprofitability for a period of time. Such explanations may help show that the activity is a business. Years and years of activity with no profit to show for it, however, may indicate that the activity is indeed a hobby and not a business for tax purposes.

✔ **The amount of occasional profits, if any, that are earned:** It's not enough to simply make a dollar or two profit in three years out of five. The amount of the profit made has to be significant. So, for example, a home-based business that shows a profit of $10,000 in each of three years out of five will likely have no problem whatsoever establishing itself as a business. A home-based business that showed only $10 profit in each of three years out of five may have a serious problem defending its status as a business and not as a hobby.

✔ **The financial status of the taxpayer:** Are you earning most of your money from your home-based business or from another source, perhaps a regular full-time job? If most of your income comes from your home-based activity, your case that the activity is a business is greatly enhanced. If, however, most of your income comes from another source, you'll have a harder time proving that your home-based activity is a business and not a hobby.

✔ **Elements of personal pleasure or recreation:** Is the activity carried out purely for recreation or personal pleasure, or is it intended to generate a profit? Peter, for example, loves to write. As much as Peter loves to write, however, his overriding concern (aside from doing the best job of writing that he possibly can) is to make a good living doing it. So in Peter's case, making a profit overrides Peter's joy of writing. The IRS says that it's okay to enjoy what you're doing for a living, just as long as your primary focus is on making a profit doing it.

So if you're absolutely sure that your home-based business is really a business, take a close look at your business — and at your own personal motivations in creating your business — to see what needs to be changed to make it more a business and less a hobby.

Of course, you may decide to keep your activities at the level of a hobby and not be bothered with having a business at all. That's fine, but be sure that you don't try to write off your hobby expenses as business expenses — and don't even think about taking the home-office deduction. If you do that, you'll likely be in for a big surprise when you're eventually audited by the IRS (and chances are you someday will be).

Different forms for different forms of businesses

The forms you need to submit when you file your taxes are different depending on what form of business your home-based business takes (and how many people you employ). It's easy to get lost in all the many different forms and schedules that are available for you to use when calculating and filing your taxes (this is another reason you should give serious consideration to hiring an accountant or CPA to help out with your company's finances).

Table 10-1 gives you a summary of the kinds of tax you may have to pay and the forms you'll need to use to pay them.

Table 10-1	Taxes to Pay and Forms to File
Form of Your Business	*Forms to File and Taxes to Pay*
Sole Proprietor	
Income tax	Form 1040 and Schedule C or C-EZ
Self-employment tax	1040 and Schedule SE
Estimated tax	1040-ES
Employment taxes	Form 941 (943 for farm employees)
Social Security, Medicare taxes, and income tax withholding	
Federal unemployment (FUTA) tax	Form 940 or 940-EZ
Depositing employment taxes	Form 8109
Partnership	
Annual return of income	Form 1065
Employment taxes	Same as sole proprietor
Partner in a Partnership (Individual)	
Income tax	Form 1040 and Schedule E
Self-employment tax	Form 1040 and Schedule SE
Estimated tax	Form 1040-ES
Corporation or S Corporation	
Income tax	Form 1120 or 1120-A (corporation), Form 1120S (S corporation)
Estimated tax	Form 1120-W (corporation only) and Form 8109
Employment taxes	Same as sole proprietor
S Corporation Shareholder	
Income tax	Form 1040 and Schedule E
Estimated tax	Form 1040-ES

There is one more form of business you should be aware of that's not listed in Table 10-1: the limited liability company (LLC). Limited liability companies are created under state law. For tax purposes, LLCs default to general partnerships, and the rules and taxes for partnerships apply. However, you can elect to file as a C corporation, S corporation, or a sole proprietor, and once again, you will file the appropriate forms that apply. Remember that each state has its own rules for limited liability companies — be sure to check out your state's unique tax rules before filing your state income taxes.

When do you have to pay?

As the IRS loves to remind the self-employed, the federal income tax is a *pay-as-you-go* system — in other words, you should be paying your taxes at roughly the same time you're making your income.

When you're an employee working in a regular job, the process is relatively painless. Your employer deducts a fixed amount of money from your paychecks — before you even get them. When you start your own home-based business, however, you need to plan to pay estimated taxes — four times a year, on April 15, June 15, September 15, and January 15. (Corporate estimated taxes are due on the fifteenth day of the fourth, sixth, ninth, and twelfth month after the end of the company's fiscal year.) Keep in mind that these are due dates, not postmark dates, so plan to send tax payments several days in advance. And after you start making your estimated payments — and writing the big checks to the federal government that go along with them — you'll surely long for the time when your employer took a little out of each paycheck.

The rules for paying estimated taxes are different for the different forms of business. Here's a brief summary:

- ✔ **Sole proprietors, partners, and S corporation shareholders:** If you expect to owe taxes of $1,000 or more when you file your income tax return, you probably need to make estimated payments to the federal government. Use Form 1040-ES — Estimated Tax for Individuals — to determine how much to pay and then to submit your payment.

- ✔ **Corporations:** If you expect to owe taxes of $500 or more when you file your tax return, you probably need to make estimated payments to the federal government. Use Form 1120-W — Estimated Tax for Corporations — to determine how much to pay.

Of course, the day of reckoning for most home-based businesses comes each year on the same day as it does for individual taxpayers: April 15. (Corporations have a slightly different arrangement; corporate federal tax returns are due on the fifteenth day of the third month after the close of the company's fiscal year, or March 15 for a fiscal year that ends on December 31.) This is the day that you submit your tax return for the preceding calendar year and the day that you write out one more check to pay the IRS for tax shortfalls that weren't already covered in your estimated payments (and the day that you celebrate if you have money coming back because you overpaid your estimated payments).

How much do you have to pay?

This is really the $64 question (or, perhaps, more like the $6,400 or the $64,000 question, depending on your situation), isn't it? Every business is different, and every business has its own unique tax situation. One thing for certain, though, is that the kind of business entity your business is has a definite bearing on the amount of taxes you pay.

Is there a corporation in your future?

Corporations are nothing new in business. What's new is that an increasing number of home-based businesses are choosing to incorporate as regular C corporations instead of the more traditional routes of sole proprietorships and subchapter S corporations. Why is that? We discussed this trend with James Schneider, LL.M., a tax attorney located in San Diego, California, who specializes in this topic.

Home-Based Business For Dummies (HBBFD): Is it important to consider taxes when you set up your home-based business?

Schneider: Yes. Taxes have a major impact on cash flow because you have to pay your taxes, in many cases, in advance. To the extent that you can take advantage of tax savings in the home, you can improve your cash flow and create a more successful business.

HBBFD: Why haven't more home-based businesses set themselves up as regular C corporations?

Schneider: Most people have been told about the home-office deduction, and they focus on the rules to satisfy that deduction, but the home-office deduction doesn't apply to regular corporations. In addition, some home-based business owners feel a reluctance to set up a regular corporation because of the perceived

complexity in doing so. From my point of view, with the help of how-to books, I think incorporation is the way to go. It's not that expensive, and it's easier to set up than many people may think.

HBBFD: But what are the tax implications of incorporating your home-based business?

Schneider: The major issue that I find is self-employment tax — which I believe is currently as high as 15.6 percent — which doesn't apply to a regular corporation but must be paid on all income earned by an individual company, a sub-chapter S company, or a partnership. Suppose you have $50,000 in business income. Depending on your deductions, you may end up paying $20,000 in self-employment taxes and individual income taxes, leaving you with $30,000 to live off of.

HBBFD: How does incorporating your business change that?

Schneider: When you incorporate, your business can provide fringe benefits that are available for employees and deductible by the business. The person who had $50,000 of taxable income before incorporating may find out that his taxable income is only $12,000 after incorporating. I'm not suggesting abusing the system — this is just the way the system is.

If your home-based business is a sole proprietorship, a partnership, or a sub-chapter S corporation, your taxable business income will be combined with any other source of income and taxed at the individual level on your form 1040. At the time of this writing, the current individual tax rates range from 10 percent to 35 percent. C corporation tax rates range from 15 percent to 39 percent. The tax on the first $75,000 of taxable income is relatively the same for both individuals and corporations. Generally speaking, corporate tax will far exceed individual tax once income is above the $75,000 mark.

A corporation is a separate tax-paying entity unless it elects to take advantage of subchapter S of the tax code. C corporations pay taxes at corporate rates. Choosing to use subchapter S enables you to not pay separate (federal) taxes (California doesn't recognize S corporations), which means that you show the corporation's income on your 1040. However, in doing this, some tax deductions available to corporations are lost. Corporations can be started as S and changed to a C later or can have their S status revoked. A corporation is considered a C corporation unless subchapter S is elected.

Table 10-2 shows a comparison of the 2004 tax rates for various amounts of taxable income for C corporations versus individual taxpayers (which also apply to sole proprietorships, partnerships, and subchapter S corporations):

Table 10-2	2004 Tax Rates	
Taxable Income	*C Corporation*	*Individual*
$1 to $7,000	15 percent	10 percent
$7,001 to $28,400	15 percent	15 percent
$28,401 to $50,000	15 percent	25 percent
$50,001 to $68,800	25 percent	25 percent
$68,801 to $75,000	25 percent	28 percent
$75,001 to $100,000	34 percent	28 percent
$100,001 to $143,500	39 percent	28 percent
$143,501 to $311,950	39 percent	33 percent
$311,951 to $335,000	39 percent	35 percent
$335,001 to $10,000,000	34 percent	35 percent
$10,000,001 to $15,000,000	35 percent	35 percent
$15,000,001 to $18,333,333	38 percent	35 percent
$18,333,334+	35 percent	35 percent

Hiring yourself out

Q: I am a computer contractor working within a niche in a specific software package. There are few people in this locale who are qualified to work with this application and even fewer with experience with this package. So my competition is essentially the manufacturer of the software. They know who I am and would like to subcontract with me, if not hire me. Due to their business practices, however, I would prefer not to represent this company, even though I would actually make more money subbing out to them. My problem is finding potential clients and key contacts without their help. Do you have any suggestions?

A: You're wise not to become encumbered with a company with poor business practices. Life is too short and litigation too costly. Can you work out something other than a subcontracting relationship with this company — for example, a referral relationship through which you pay a referral fee? You can make clear to your clients that your relationship with the company is limited to their referring clients to you. Alternatively, can you rent the company's mailing list? From this, you can do mailings (snail or e-mail), a newsletter, a Web site, and so on. If a publication already exists for these users, can you contribute articles, a column, or letters to the editor? If the company is a poor one to work with, customers will gladly want to know about you as an alternative. Just be sure not to bad-mouth the company.

C corporations are not allowed to take a home office deduction because a corporation cannot have a home, only a business location. Ten percent shareholders cannot rent their home to the corporation, either. However, an employee and/or shareholder can submit a reimbursement request for use of their home. There are many ramifications in choosing the proper business entity and how it relates to deductible home offices and reimbursements to the owner.

When is an independent contractor not an independent contractor?

So let's say that you've started your own home-based business, and you're starting to deliver services — say, interior design — to a client. Chances are you consider yourself to be a business separate from your client's business — an independent contractor. But what if we told you that there's a possibility that the IRS might not agree with your particular view of your business and that the IRS might instead decide that you're performing your services as an employee?

"Okay, that's interesting," you might say to yourself, "but what's the big deal?" The big deal is, if you think you're a home-based business — and take advantage of all the deductions for business expenses that you're entitled to — you may be in for an unpleasant surprise if the IRS decides that you're really an employee. This unpleasant surprise includes disallowing all the deductions you've been taking for your home-based business and recalculating your taxes without them — possibly resulting in a substantial amount of money (plus penalties and interest) now owed to the IRS. Believe us, this is one surprise most of us could do without. The good news is that there are steps you can take right now to ensure that this does not happen to you.

In its ongoing quest to be helpful, the IRS has developed guidelines to help you determine whether you're an independent contractor or really an employee. These guidelines are categorized by how much behavioral and financial control a business has over the person doing the work and the exact nature of the relationship. Here are the IRS's independent-contractor guidelines, presented as they currently appear in *Publication 15-A: Employer's Supplemental Tax Guide* (revised January 2004):

✔ **Behavioral control.** Facts that show whether the business has a right to direct and control how the worker does the task for which the worker is hired include the type and degree of:

• **Instructions the business gives the worker:** An employee is generally subject to the business's instructions about when, where, and how to work. All of the following are examples of types of instructions about how to do work:

• When and where to do the work

• What tools or equipment to use

• What workers to hire or to assist with the work

• Where to purchase supplies and services

• What work must be performed by a specified individual

• What order or sequence to follow

The amount of instruction needed varies among different jobs. Even if no instructions are given, sufficient behavioral control may exist if the employer has the right to control how the work results are achieved. A business may lack the knowledge to instruct some highly specialized professionals; in other cases, the task may require little or no instruction. The *key consideration* is whether the business has retained the *right to control the details* of a worker's performance or instead has given up that right.

- **Training that the business gives the worker:** An employee may be trained to perform services in a particular manner. Independent contractors ordinarily use their own methods.

✔ **Financial control:** Facts that show whether the business has a right to control the business aspects of the worker's job include:

- **The extent to which the worker has unreimbursed business expenses.** Independent contractors are more likely to have unreimbursed expenses than are employees. Fixed, ongoing costs that are incurred regardless of whether work is currently being performed are especially important. However, employees may also incur unreimbursed expenses in connection with the services that they perform for their business.

- **The extent of the worker's investment:** An independent contractor often has a significant investment in the facilities he or she uses in performing services for someone else. However, a significant investment is not necessary for independent-contractor status.

- **The extent to which the worker makes his or her services available to the relevant market:** An independent contractor is generally free to seek out business opportunities. Independent contractors often advertise, maintain a visible business location, and are available to work in the relevant market.

- **How the business pays the worker:** An employee is generally guaranteed a regular wage amount for an hourly, weekly, or other period of time. This usually indicates that a worker is an employee, even when the wage or salary is supplemented by a commission. An independent contractor is usually paid a flat fee for the job. However, it is common in some professions, such as law, to pay independent contractors hourly.

- **The extent to which the worker can realize a profit or incur a loss:** An independent contractor can make a profit or loss.

✔ **Type of relationship:** Facts that show the parties' type of relationship include:

- **Written contracts describing the relationship the parties intend to create.**

- **Whether or not the business provides the worker with employee-type benefits, such as insurance, a pension plan, vacation pay, or sick pay.**

- **The permanence of the relationship:** If you engage a worker with the expectation that the relationship will continue indefinitely, rather than for a specific project or period, this is generally considered evidence that your intent was to create an employer–employee relationship.

> • **The extent to which services performed by the worker are a key aspect of the regular business of the company:** If a worker provides services that are a key aspect of your regular business activity, it is more likely that you will have the right to direct and control his or her activities. For example, if a law firm hires an attorney, it is likely that it will present the attorney's work as its own and would have the right to control or direct that work. This would indicate an employer–employee relationship.

The lines that separate independent contractors from employees can be blurry. Here are a couple of examples that the IRS itself uses to illustrate the problem. Review the following examples, and see who you think is an employee and who is an independent contractor:

- Steve Smith, a computer programmer, is laid off when Megabyte, Inc. downsizes. Megabyte agrees to pay Steve a flat amount to complete a one-time project to create a certain product. It is not clear how long it will take to complete the project, and Steve is not guaranteed any minimum payment for the hours spent on the program. Megabyte provides Steve with no instructions beyond the specifications for the product itself. Steve and Megabyte have a written contract, which provides that Steve is considered to be an independent contractor, is required to pay federal and state taxes, and receives no benefits from Megabyte. Megabyte will file a Form 1099-MISC. Steve does the work on a new high-end computer that cost him $7,000. Steve works at home and is not expected or allowed to attend meetings of the software development group. Employee or independent contractor?

- Jerry Jones has an agreement with Wilma White to supervise the remodeling of her house. She did not advance funds to help him carry on the work. She makes direct payments to the suppliers for all necessary materials. She carries liability and workers' compensation insurance covering Jerry and others that he engaged to assist him. She pays them an hourly rate and exercises almost constant supervision over the work. Jerry is not free to transfer his assistants to other jobs. He may not work on other jobs while working for Wilma. He assumes no responsibility to complete the work and will incur no contractual liability if he fails to do so. He and his assistants perform personal services for hourly wages. Employee or independent contractor?

What did you guess? According to the IRS, Steve Smith is an independent contractor, and Jerry Jones and his assistants are employees.

Be constantly aware of how you do business, and guard against conducting business in a way that would cause the IRS to believe that you're actually an employee instead of an independent contractor. The differences are often subtle, and the line between them is easy to cross. With a bit of forethought and planning, however, you can always make sure that you're on the right side of that line.

Taking a Look at the Home-Office Deduction

For many home-based businesspeople, taking the home-office deduction is a major financial incentive to start businesses in their home, and it can have a significant and positive effect on a home-based business's financial position (as well as the personal financial situation of the owner). For many home-based business owners, the ability to take the home-office deduction literally means the difference between success and failure.

The beauty of the home-office deduction is that it allows you to deduct the costs of operating and maintaining the part of your home that you use for business. And it doesn't matter what kind of home you live in. Whether you live in a single-family home, a condominium, a commercial building, or even a houseboat, if you meet the IRS's criteria for the home-office deduction, you're eligible to take it.

To qualify to claim expenses for the business use of your home, you must meet the following tests:

- ✔ **Your use of the business part of your home must be:**
  - • **Exclusive:** A specific area of your home must be used only for your business. (Note: there are two exceptions to this exclusive use test: (1) You use part of your home for the storage of inventory or product samples or (2) You use part of your home as a day-care facility.)
  - • **Regular:** The business part of your home must be used for business on a continuing, not just an occasional or incidental basis.
  - • **For your trade or business.**
- ✔ **The business part of your home must be one of the following:**
  - • **Your principal place of business.**
  - • **A place where you meet or deal with patients, clients, or customers in the normal course of your trade or business.**
  - • **A separate structure (not attached to your home) that you use in connection with your trade or business.**

So assuming you meet these criteria, you can take the home-office deduction. The benefits of doing so are immediate and extensive. Not only are you allowed to deduct your normal business expenses (paper, pencils, phone calls, and so on), but you're also able to deduct a portion of the indirect expenses related to your entire home! Here are some of the most common indirect expenses that may be at least partially deductible under the IRS's home-office rules:

- ✔ Rent
- ✔ Mortgage
- ✔ Security system
- ✔ Housekeeping
- ✔ Household supplies
- ✔ Condominium association fees
- ✔ Trash collection
- ✔ Utilities (gas, electric, and so on)

To determine the total amount of indirect expenses that you can deduct under the home-office deduction, you first have to calculate the percentage of your home devoted to your home office. So, for example, suppose you have a 240-square-foot spare bedroom (12×20 feet) that you've set aside as a home office and that the total square footage of your home is 1,200 square feet. Here's how to determine the portion that will determine the amount of your home-office deduction:

240 sq. ft. office ÷ 1,200 sq. ft. home = Percent of expenses deductible

240 ÷ 1,200 = 20 percent

You will, therefore, be able to deduct 20 percent of your home's indirect expenses — an amount that, depending on your situation, could be quite substantial. Keep in mind, though, that the tax rules don't allow you to deduct an amount greater than the amount of gross income that you've earned in your home-based business. The government doesn't mind if you make money from individuals and other companies, but it does not want you to make money off the IRS.

Be aware that if you take the home-office deduction, you will be required to depreciate the home office business square footage of your home. When you sell your home, you will need to reduce your cost basis by the amount of depreciation deducted. When you sell your home that you lived in for more than two years, you can exclude $250,000 (or $500,000 on a joint return) of your gain. The gain would be a capital gain eligible for reduced preferential rates, which will be taxed at a maximum rate of 15 percent. However, as a home-office deductor, you will have to do one more calculation: You will have to subtract from the capital gain the amount of depreciation taken and pay tax at a maximum rate of 25 percent. This calculation is known as *depreciation recapture*.

It is widely believed that taking the home-office deduction waves a red flag that can gain you extra scrutiny by the IRS — and perhaps an audit. While we don't know if this is really true, we do know that you should consult with an accountant, tax planner, or other tax professional before you first take the home-office deduction. The rules are complicated, and the penalties for doing the wrong thing can be significant. For more information on the allowability of deductions for your home-based business, check out *IRS Publication 587: Business Use of Your Home.*

Reviewing Other Important Tax Deductions

Aside from the important home-office deduction, home-based businesses are allowed to deduct a wide variety of other business expenses from their taxes. To be deductible, the Internal Revenue Code specifies that expenses must be *ordinary and necessary* for the operation of your business. So although the purchase of a vintage 1959 sunburst Gibson Les Paul electric guitar for $150,000 may be ordinary and necessary (and thus an allowable deduction) for a professional musician, it likely wouldn't fly for a home-based software designer — in fact, it would surely sink like a lead balloon.

As you may imagine, a home-based business owner can legally deduct lots of different things from his or her taxes. Here are examples of legal deductions:

- ✔ Rent
- ✔ Phones
- ✔ Utilities
- ✔ Postage
- ✔ Health insurance
- ✔ Auto expenses
- ✔ Internet access
- ✔ Business travel
- ✔ Business meals and entertainment
- ✔ Professional services and consultants
- ✔ Business cards and stationery
- ✔ Retirement plans
- ✔ Interest payments on business credit cards

> ✔ Education
>
> ✔ Office supplies
>
> ✔ Office furniture

And as you may also imagine, the federal government has determined that plenty of things aren't deductible. Too bad! Here are a number of deductions that may not be considered legal by the IRS:

> ✔ Anticipated liabilities
>
> ✔ Bribes and kickbacks
>
> ✔ Demolition expenses
>
> ✔ Personal expenses
>
> ✔ Social or recreational clubs
>
> ✔ Lobbying expenses
>
> ✔ Political contributions
>
> ✔ Federal income taxes
>
> ✔ Penalties and fines as a result of breaking the law

When in doubt, check it out. Consult with an accountant or tax advisor to see which expenses you're allowed to deduct and which ones you aren't. It's far better to be sure about your allowable deductions *before* you take them instead of years later, when your business expenses are disallowed by the IRS.

Discovering Sometimes-Overlooked Ways to Save On Your Taxes

As you're probably well aware, the rules that govern income taxes and the deductions you're allowed to take are complex. But despite appearances to the contrary, you're not required to pay any more tax than is necessary. In fact, you shouldn't pay any more tax than you're legally required to pay. Because of the complexity of the tax rules and the fact that they change — sometimes substantially — every year, hiring a professional tax lawyer or accountant can really pay off, and it's deductible, too.

However, we understand if you'd prefer not to spend a lot of money paying for a tax lawyer or accountant just yet. If that is the case for you, you can still employ a variety of strategies to reduce your tax burden. Consider the following list of sometimes-overlooked ways to save on your taxes:

✔ **Maximize your vehicle deduction.** You can choose between the standard mileage deduction (40.5 cents per mile in 2005) or the actual costs of operating your vehicle, which includes fuel, maintenance, taxes, and license fees. Runzheimer International (www.runzheimer.com), which analyzes the cost of owning and operating a vehicle in cities across the United States, found it costs over $11,000 to operate a mid-size vehicle in Detroit in 2004 but only $7,485 in Portland, Oregon. So taking the standard deduction may make more sense in Detroit, Los Angeles, and other higher-cost places than in does in Portland and other lower-cost places. Note, however, that if you use the actual cost method in the first year you use a vehicle, you must stick with this method ever after. Where you live can determine whether choosing to use the standard deduction will save you more money than reporting actual costs. Unless you use a vehicle 100 percent for business, you will need to keep a log of your business use, including dates, mileage and the purpose of your business travel.

✔ **Make the most of hiring employees.** If you need an employee, consider hiring a family member. Your spouse or child in a lower tax bracket enables you to keep income in the family. Depending on how much the family member earns, no tax at all may be owed on his or her earnings. Sometimes tax credits are available for hiring designated workers, such as Native Americans, or if you live in an economic empowerment zone.

✔ **Reduce your taxes with a retirement plan.** Putting money into a retirement fund reduces your Adjusted Gross Income, which is what you use to calculate your self-employment tax and make calculations for other deductions, such as a casualty loss. The self-employed are able to invest more money using a Keogh, SEP, or SIMPLE plan than with an IRA. To learn more about retirement plans for the self-employed, obtain IRS Publication 560 (www.irs.gov/pub/irs-pdf/p560.pdf).

✔ **Make the most of a bad year.** Because it's possible to carry business losses both back as well as forward, consult a tax professional to determine if you can get an immediate tax refund or would be better off carrying your loss into your next business year. Keep in mind that the tax law on handling losses changes frequently.

Of course, it's against the law to evade paying your taxes, but it's your duty to avoid paying more taxes than you're legally obligated to. The IRS is not going to give you any gold stars or special privileges for paying more taxes than you have to — you're throwing away your money if you do. And that's the last thing any home-based businessperson should ever do.

Tax software to the rescue

When home-based businesspeople prepare their taxes, they have two key options: pay someone to do them or do the taxes themselves. If you decide to do your own taxes, you may find that tax software makes the process much easier and far more accurate than filling out forms the old-fashioned way. Here are a couple of reliable tax software packages to consider:

✔ **TaxCut:** www.taxcut.com

✔ **TurboTax:** www.turbotax.com

Uncovering the Ins and Outs of Sales Tax

According to the people who keep track of these things, there are more than 10,000 different sales tax rates nationwide, and these rates are in a constant state of change as voters approve rate changes to fund needed local improvements or vote to scale down their sales tax bite. But although sales taxes are in a constant state of change, one thing is sure: If you sell products or provide certain kinds of services to people within your state (the exact services taxed differ from state to state — check with your local tax authorities to find out whether or not the services you offer are subject to sales tax), you had better be sure to collect sales tax while you're at it.

As of this writing, only five states — Alaska, Delaware, Montana, New Hampshire, and Oregon — don't have sales tax. All other states do have sales tax, and they do expect you to collect each and every dollar and cent owed and then submit them to the appropriate tax authorities regularly.

Here's how the sales tax setup and collection process generally works:

1. **File an application with your state sales tax authority to obtain a** *reseller's permit,* **also known as a** *certificate of authority, sales tax permit, resale permit, or sales tax number,* **depending on the state in which you reside.**

2. **File appropriate sales tax forms with your state or local tax authorities, with estimated collections for quarter or year (or whatever period of time requested).**

3. **Receive instructions from state or local tax authorities with information on how often to submit tax collections and where to send them.**

4. **Submit taxes at the time and place directed by the state or local tax authorities.**

Although the collection of sales taxes is a fairly routine and straightforward process (perhaps even boring), one thing that has brought a lot of excitement to the topic is the ongoing debate over collecting sales taxes for products sold over the Internet. Congress has temporarily exempted Internet sales from the payment of sales taxes, much to the delight of e-commerce firms such as Amazon.com and others, but much to the consternation of the states that cannot collect the sales tax revenue that is increasingly being lost to online sales. Although online companies still have to collect sales taxes for sales made within their home states, just as mail-order companies do, they don't have to collect sales taxes for sales made to people or companies outside their states.

Stay tuned to the debate in Congress over sales taxes for sales through the Internet — it promises to be a long (and loud!) one.

Part III
Avoiding Problems

The 5th Wave   By Rich Tennant

Paul's Petsitting

"I have read your resume, Ms. Cothman. Now please, come... sit... speak..."

In this part . . .

There is far more to starting a business than just hang-ing an *Open* sign on your door. You've got to create a foundation that will last for years. In this part, we review the most common legal do's and don'ts and explore how to leverage outside resources to your advantage. Finally, we take an in-depth look at home-based business ripoffs and scams.

Chapter 11

Legal Do's and Don'ts

· ·

In This Chapter

▶ Choosing a form (legal structure) for your business

▶ Selecting and registering your business's name

▶ Dealing with trademarks, copyrights, and patents

▶ Complying with zoning requirements, licensing, and permits

▶ Considering your tax situation

· ·

*I*f you think you have enough laws, statutes, and regulations to worry about now, just wait until you start your own business — you haven't seen anything yet! Actually, it's not quite that bad, but depending on what kind of home-based business you plan to start, you may be surprised at just how many city and local agencies and departments will play some role in your life, and how many rules and regulations you'll need to comply with. And it's not only the government you've got to take into account. Your own neighborhood or development may have restrictive covenants (that you agreed to honor when you bought your house, whether or not you noticed them in the fine print of your purchase agreement) that determine whether you can run a business out of your home. And you're wise to pay attention: The consequences of not doing the right things include fines, penalties, and even closure.

Laws and regulations determine where you can locate your home-based business and during what hours it can operate. Laws and regulations require you to get permits if your business prepares and sells food or if you have an alarm to protect your premises. And if you're a private investigator, hairdresser, masseuse, building contractor, plumber, or any of hundreds more occupations, you need a license (and you need to pay a licensing fee) before you can operate your business. The government, to some degree, determines which kind of business form (*sole proprietorship*, *partnership*, *limited liability company*, or *corporation*) that you're eligible to use and also decides the financial and tax implications on your business as a result of your decision.

In this chapter, we discuss a wide variety of legal issues that every home-based business owner faces, including the various forms of business available for you to choose among. We also tell you how to select and register a company name and consider the potential impact of zoning, licensing, and permits on your business. We take a look at trademarks, copyrights, and patents. Finally, we briefly visit the potential impact of tax considerations on your home-based business (see Chapter 10 for the lowdown on taxes).

Our aim isn't to turn you into a lawyer or an accountant (not that we've got anything against lawyers or accountants) but to arm you with enough knowledge to take care of the basics and to know where to turn when you need more information.

Understanding the Forms (Legal Structures) of Businesses

One of the first decisions you make after you decide to start your own home-based business is what *form* — that is, what *legal structure* — of business it will take.

You may have noticed a few interesting words or initials after the names of some of your favorite companies. Global fast-food giant McDonald's, for example, isn't simply named *McDonald's* — it's *McDonald's Corporation* — which means that McDonald's has decided to organize as a *corporation form* of business. LucasArts Entertainment Company LLC — producer of, among other things, the popular *Star Wars* and *Indiana Jones* computer games — is organized as a *limited liability company*.

Each of the different forms of business (and their accompanying alphabet soup of letters) comes with a wide variety of legal implications for many facets of your business, including legal liability in case of lawsuit, taxes, and more. It is important, therefore, that you take time to understand all of these implications up front — as you make and implement your business plans.

Which form of business is right for you? This section gives you some basic guidelines to consider as you weigh the options available to you; they are certainly sufficient to help you get your business off the ground and help you become an informed home-business owner. Our advice, however, is to contact an attorney or accountant to discern the specific advantages and legal requirements of each form of business and to decide which is best for you. The money you save over the years will probably pay for this advice many times over.

Some things to consider when you decide what form of business to use include the following:

- The impact on your business's image
- The impact of planned business growth
- The cost to start up your business
- The cost to maintain your business
- Your tax goals
- The impact of government regulation
- Your financing needs
- The amount of personal risk you're willing to take for your business

In each of the sections that follow, we consider the four major forms of business listed in the introduction to this chapter, discussing the pros and the cons for home-based businesses. As you review each, think about the kind of business you want to run — not just today, but also years into the future. We know it may be difficult to picture what your business will be like a couple weeks into the future, much less a couple of months or a couple of years. The good news is that you can change the form of your business most any time you like with a minimum of muss or fuss (corporations are the exception here, because they require the filing of special forms with your state government). But give it a try anyway; settling now on a form that will carry your business for many years into the future may be easier in the long run.

Sole proprietorship

By far the vast majority of home-based businesses are *sole proprietorships,* which means that you are the one and only owner of the business. You are the boss, the leader, the one to congratulate when the business does well and the one to blame when the business goes bad. In a sole proprietorship, the income you derive from your business is reported on your Form 1040 along with any other personal income that you make during the course of the year — you don't need to file a separate tax return for your business. Similarly, any debts you incur as a sole proprietor are the same as your personal debts.

Why are so many home-based businesses sole proprietorships? Perhaps one reason is that if you do nothing at all to formally organize your business, it will by default be considered a sole proprietorship. In other words, by doing nothing, you're automatically making a decision to become a sole proprietorship. Another reason may be because it's more difficult to create a partner-ship or corporation, which require creating partnership agreements or filing incorporation forms with the government.

Fortunately, this isn't a bad form for many home-based businesses to take. A sole proprietorship is the simplest and least regulated form of organization. Startup costs are minimal or nil, and one person owns the business and wields full control over it. He or she is also responsible for securing financing, and he or she receives all company profits. Business income under the sole-proprietorship form of business is taxed as personal income, which works out just fine for most home-business owners. On the minus side of the column, a sole proprietorship offers major disadvantages in the areas of legal liability for the owner (who can be personally sued for business-related issues) and potential dissolution of the business upon the owner's death. Table 11-1 summarizes the good and bad news of a sole proprietorship.

Table 11-1	Sole Proprietorship
The Good News	*The Bad News*
Owner has complete control over all aspects.	Sole proprietorships are considered less prestigious than some other forms of business.
Inexpensive.	It can be particularly difficult to create and maintain secure outside financing.
Easy to start and to close.	The business dies when the owner does.
Owner gets to keep all profits.	Owner is personally liable in the event of a lawsuit (as a result of malpractice, product failure, and so on).

Partnership

If you have two or more owners of your home-based business — perhaps you and a close friend or relative — consider choosing the partnership form of business. In a *partnership,* each partner commits to providing specific skills, expertise, and effort — and to share the partnership's expenses — in return for an agreed-upon portion of the company's profits. The agreement spelling out these terms is called (not surprisingly) a *partnership agreement.*

Partnerships take advantage of the different skills, expertise, and resources — including cash — that the different partners bring to an organization. On the plus side, partnerships are fairly easy to put together and administer; all you really need is a simple agreement (a verbal agreement works, although written partnership agreements are much, much better), which you can make more complicated if the stakes are high. Be sure, however, to have a lawyer take a look at your partnership agreement before you sign it. Because partners have a legally recognized ownership stake in the business, each is an agent for the partnership and can hire employees, borrow money, and operate the business.

Profits are taxed as personal income, but on the minus side of the ledger, partners are personally liable for debts and taxes. Not only that, but also, personal assets can be confiscated if the partnership can't satisfy creditors' claims. If you've got a nice home or a car or two, keep that in mind before you enter into a partnership. Table 11-2 shows the advantages and disadvantages in detail.

In the event that partners want to avoid personal liability, they can form a special legal arrangement available called a *limited partnership*. Limited partnerships must be registered and must also pay a *franchise fee* charged by the state to file a certificate of limited partnership. Don't forget: While it's legally possible to create a partnership with only a handshake and sometimes less, in the event of disagreement or when it comes time to dissolve the partnership, you will wish you had a written agreement. Consider having a lawyer either draft or review your partnership agreement. Remember: The money you pay now for a lawyer's help will save you many headaches and, potentially, big stacks of cash down the road.

Table 11-2	Partnership
The Good News	*The Bad News*
Get the skills, expertise, and efforts of two or more people.	Partners don't always agree on every course of action, a situation that may eventually become acrimonious and could harm the business.
Business risks are diffused across one or more partners.	Each partner is legally liable for actions of the other partners, including hiring employees, borrowing money, operating the business, and more.
Partners support one another and provide stimulating social environment.	Just as in marriage, partners almost always have disagreements and quarrels.
Government exerts little direct control over partnerships.	Like divorces, when partnerships break up, things can quickly get messy.
Expenses are shared by all partners.	Profits are distributed to all partners.

Limited liability company

The *limited liability company* (LLC) is a fairly recent innovation, providing flexibility in management the way a general partnership does while offering the limited liability of a corporation. On one hand, LLCs are treated as partnerships for U.S. income tax purposes, but they are also granted the protection from personal liability that corporations enjoy. Limited liability companies are now legally recognized in all 50 states, in the District of Columbia, and in many foreign countries.

For many, the LLC form of business may be the preferred choice for certain new operations and joint ventures. Owners of LLCs are known as *members* — comparable to stockholders in a corporation or limited partners in a limited partnership. If you decide to create an LLC, you need to file articles of organization with your secretary of state. Each LLC member must also execute an operating agreement that defines the relationship between the company and its members. Check your state's procedures to find out the requirements that apply to you.

The pluses and minuses of LLCs are similar to those of partnerships, with the exception of the limitation of liability that corporations enjoy. Table 11-3 gives you some other pluses and minuses.

Table 11-3	Limited Liability Company
The Good News	**The Bad News**
Limited liability for company's principals (owners).	Many states require that the business include more than one person.
Treated as partnerships for federal taxes, though some states, including California, treat them as corporations.	Dissolve on the death of an owner.
Cost less to form and maintain than do corporations and require less paperwork.	Cost more to set up and maintain than do sole proprietorships.

Corporation

Without a doubt, *corporations* are the most complex form of business. Corporations are unique because they are legal entities that exist separately from their owners. This is exactly why corporations limit the personal liability of their owners. While limiting the owners from personal liability, however, a *double taxation on earnings* (corporate tax and personal tax) may result, putting corporations at a tax disadvantage in certain circumstances. Corporations are identified by having the words *Incorporated (Inc.)* or *Corporation (Corp.)* in or after their names.

On the positive side, the corporation form may be advantageous for financing your company, because it allows capital to be raised easily through the sale of corporate stocks or bonds. And because a corporation exists apart from its owners, it can function even without key individuals. The corporation form of business also enables employees to participate in various types of insurance and profit-sharing plans that may not be available to sole proprietorships, partnerships, or LLCs. On the minus side, corporations can be expensive to start and maintain, and the requisite paperwork may be a nightmare for people who dislike red tape. Costs and procedures for incorporating vary from state to state. Contact your secretary of state for more information (you may find this on your state's Web site). Table 11-4 shares more of the ups and downs of corporations.

A special type of corporation — an *S corporation* — allows owners to overcome the double tax problem of regular corporations (called *C corporations*) by allowing shareholders to offset business losses with personal income. And as if the government (in this case, state government) didn't already charge enough to incorporate, S corporations are subject to an additional annual surcharge from the federal government. Everyone, it seems, wants a piece of the action.

Table 11-4	Corporation
The Good News	***The Bad News***
Best overall business image.	Expensive to start and operate.
Personal liability of owners and stockholders is limited.	Mountains of paperwork.
Can (and generally do) survive their owners.	Tax benefits may be little or nil compared with the other forms of business.
Easier to sell, though majority of voting stockholders required to do so.	All those mountains of paperwork required to form a corporation require quite a bit of effort to make changes to.
Can sell stock and bonds, making raising capital easier than with other forms of business.	Corporations are double taxed in some states, and insurance may be more expensive than for other forms of business.

Despite all the options available to home-based businesses, most start out as either a sole proprietorship or a partnership. This is the simplest thing to do, and forming a sole proprietorship or partnership costs little or no money. Eventually, though, many home-based businesses consider the other available forms of business, because each offers unique advantages and disadvantages to home-based businesses — especially when it comes to liability and taxes (and because it's actually kind of cool to have some of those extra letters trailing after your business name).

Name Registration

Choosing the name of your company is one of the most critical decisions you make as you set up your business. We're not exaggerating when we say that the right name can help pave the way to sales and success, and the wrong name can lead to all kinds of problems for you and your business — success not being one of them. According to business naming consultant Naseem Javed, quoted in a recent article in the *San Diego Union Tribune,* "If you don't have a good name, you'll be throwing away advertising money and profit potential."

Here's an interesting bit of information: An average of 4,000 to 5,000 commercial messages are aimed at each person each and every day. Think about it for a minute: television and radio ads, newspapers, magazines, ads on the sides of buses, company names on sports stadiums, junk mail, junk faxes, junk email . . . the list goes on and on. How will your home-based business cut through all that noise and capture the interest and attention of your prospective customers? A good name can make all the difference.

The best business names

- ✔ Describe the service or product that the business offers
- ✔ Are protectable by trademark or service mark
- ✔ Are novel

Naming your business is not something to do with friends over a few beers while you're grilling burgers in the backyard — it requires careful thought and planning. Your business name should give people some idea of the exact nature of your business (*The Pink Poodle* would be much better for a pet grooming business than for a tree-trimming business), and it should also project the image you want your business to have. Names can be simple, sophisticated, or even silly (not too silly, though).

Think several years out into the future; try to pick a name that will grow with your business over time instead of limiting it. The Pleasant Hawaiian Holidays travel agency, for example, had to change its name to Pleasant Holidays when its trip offerings expanded beyond the Hawaiian Islands.

Here are some tips on selecting a name:

- ✔ Your own name — if you have a reputation or plan to grow one. Peter's home-based business, for example, is titled Peter Economy Incorporated.

- ✔ Your name with a tag line or motto (for example, Sara's Place: Where Cookies Are Number 1).

- ✔ A super-catchy Web site name (freecash4u.com, no-homework.com).

- ✔ A name that communicates a primary benefit (No Mess Chimney Sweep).

- ✔ A name that describes your specialty (Fantastic Fabric Creations).

- ✔ A made-up name that suggests what you do or how you do it (Springfield Hand-Built Log Homes).

Of course, just as you can find general guidelines about what kinds of names you should go with, think about the kinds of names you should avoid. Here, according to naming consultant Naseem Javed, are some to avoid:

- ✔ Overused (says Javed, "There are 53,573 U.S. businesses or products with the name *King* in them and 5,730 with *Mr.*")

- ✔ Politically incorrect (Aunt Jemima)

- ✔ Sound-alike (General, International, Dynamic, U.S.)

- ✔ Neutral (Gold Seal, Lucky, Micro, Data)

- ✔ Confusing (Ben Gay)

Along with a name, many businesses develop a logo — the graphic symbol of the business. As they say, a picture is worth a thousand words. As with your name, your logo should be carefully designed to project the exact image you want for your business. See Chapter 14 for more on creating a logo.

After you have decided on a name, the next step is to make sure it is not already in use by another company. If the name you use is trademarked or otherwise legally protected by another business, not only can you be sued to stop using the name, but also, thousands of dollars of advertising and promotion may go right down the drain along with your name.

You can look up business names in a variety of different places. For starters, try your local telephone book (understand, however, that many home-based businesses don't list business phone numbers) and government offices, or do a search on Google. After you go through those sources, try trade directories, the Federal Trademark Register, and listings of corporate business names from your secretary of state. If that all sounds kind of like a pain in the neck (and it does to us), hire someone to do a search for you. When you have finally settled on a name, it may be worth your time and money to obtain a trademark from the U.S. Patent and Trademark Office to protect your business name and logo. If you don't, someone else may well take them away from you — along with all the customer goodwill that took you years to build.

Here are a few places to check whether your proposed business name is already in use:

- ✔ Local phone books (call information for the most recent listings)
- ✔ Local courthouse, county recorder, and the office in your state responsible for registering business names
- ✔ Internet Yellow Pages such as `www.switchboard.com` and `www.info space.com`, and search engines such as `www.google.com`, `alltheweb.com`, `msn.com`, and `yahoo.com`
- ✔ Trademark search using a database, such as the U.S. Patent and Trademark Office (`www.uspto.gov`) or NameProtect (`www.name protect.com`), o, better yet, an attorney specializing in trademarks and patents

If the name you have chosen is not your name, you will be required to file a fictitious-business-name statement (also called a *doing business as . . ., DBA,* or *d/b/a*). This is also necessary if the business name implies greater ownership with such words as *And Company*, or *Associates*, or *& Son/Daughter*.

The actual registration process is pretty much the same throughout the United States. Although regulations vary from state to state (check with your local authorities to be sure to get the exact information for where you plan to do business), fictitious-business-name statements are generally filed with the county clerk and may also have to be published in a newspaper of general circulation once a week for four successive weeks in the county where the principal place of business is located. Because the cost of publishing legal notices, such as fictitious-business-name statements, varies widely from newspaper to newspaper, it pays to shop around.

After your legal notice has been published for the required period of time, an affidavit of publication must be filed with the county clerk or requisite local or state agency within 30 days after publication. Again, check the requirements in your locale to be sure that you have a complete understanding of the filing requirements and that you dot all the *i*'s and cross all the *t*'s.

Trademarks, Copyrights, and Patents

When you think of the word *asset,* the first thing that comes to your mind may be cash, a computer, a company car, or perhaps the equipment you use to make the items you sell to customers. However, one of the most important assets for many businesses today is not any of those things — it's a company's *intellectual property,* the unique ideas and knowledge that give it a competitive advantage in the marketplace.

Intellectual property can range from a unique product design or the ingredients in your award-winning chili recipe to your company's name, a song or photograph, or the exact words that you wrote in a newspaper or magazine article. The value of your intellectual property depends on the nature of the ideas and their demand in the marketplace. But one thing is for sure: The value of your intellectual property is in jeopardy if you don't take steps to protect it from theft. That's where trademarks, copyrights, and patents come in.

Trademarks

A *trademark* (™) is a distinctive word, name, symbol, or device — or combination of any of these — used to distinguish a product or service from those of competitors. A *service mark* (℠) is simply a trademark for services. The word, name, symbol, or device you select to trademark must be sufficiently unique to separate your products from their generic source. You can't, for example, trademark the generic word *cola,* but you can trademark a trade name for your unique brand of cola known as *Coca-Cola* (or, that is, you could have if someone hadn't beaten you to it 100 years or so ago).

Anyone can apply the trademark or service-mark symbols to their distinctive word, name, or symbol at any time; you don't have to get anyone's permission to do so. If, however, you want to legally protect the trademark to ensure that someone else doesn't steal it away from you (not a bad idea, in our humble opinions), you should consider registering it. Trademarks and service marks can be registered through some state governments, for protection only within the state in which your business is located, or through the U.S. Patent and Trademark Office (USPTO) if you would like nationwide protection. When your trademark is registered on a nationwide basis, you're able to use the familiar ® symbol on your products and product information.

If you're wondering whether someone has already registered a trademark or service mark, you can look it up on the USPTO trademark database online at www.uspto.gov.

A trademark may not prevent someone from stealing (or mistakenly using) your unique word, name, or symbol, but it will provide you with legal recourse in court in case someone does. And in the long run, that may be worth its weight in gold to you and to your business.

Copyrights

Copyright is a form of protection provided to the authors of "original works of authorship," including literary, dramatic, musical, artistic, and certain other intellectual works, both published and unpublished. This book is copyrighted. The script for the latest *Harry Potter* movie is copyrighted. That song you were humming in the shower this morning is probably copyrighted. The 1976 Copyright Act generally gives the owner of copyright the exclusive right to reproduce the copyrighted work, prepare derivative works (a *derivative* work is one taken from something that preceded it and owes its existence to the original work), distribute copies or phonograph records (those big, round, black things that people used to buy before the invention of compact discs) of the copyrighted work, perform the copyrighted work publicly, or display the copyrighted work publicly.

A copyright is automatically created when the work itself is created — no need to file any forms or pay someone a bunch of money to copyright your work for you. As is the case with trademarks and service marks, you can apply a copyright symbol (©) to your work at any time without getting anyone's approval to do so. If, however, you want to be able to legally protect your work (again, a smart move, in our humble opinions), you should register your copyright and apply the © to it. You'll discover plenty of advantages to registering your copyright:

- ✔ Registration establishes a public record of the copyright claim — extremely valuable evidence that you have a right to it.

- ✔ Before an infringement suit may be filed in court, registration is necessary for works of U.S. origin.

- ✔ If made before or within five years of publication, registration will establish that the facts stated in the certificate of copyright are presumed to be true unless proven otherwise.

- ✔ If registration is made within three months after publication of the work or prior to an infringement of the work, damages specified by statute (or law) and attorney's fees will be available to the copyright owner in court actions. Otherwise, only an award of actual damages and profits is available to the copyright owner.

- ✔ Registration allows the owner of the copyright to record the registration with the U.S. Customs Service for protection against copies being imported that infringe on your copyright.

Getting information about trademarks, copyrights, and patents

If you need more specific information about trademarks, copyrights, and patents, help is on the way. Simply surf your way over to any of the following Web sites for lots more information:

✔ **Trademarks and patents:** U.S. Patent and Trademark Office, www.uspto.gov, (800) 786-9199 or (703) 308-4357

✔ **Copyrights:** Copyright Office, Library of Congress, www.copyright.gov, (202) 707-3000

Registering your copyright gives you, as the creator of the work, protection for your entire lifetime plus 70 years (ideally, that should be long enough to cover you). Registering your copyright is simple: Fill out a brief form, and submit it with a check for $30 and a copy of your work to the Copyright Office at the Library of Congress. For complete details, visit the Web site for the Copyright Office at www.copyright.gov.

Patents

A *patent* for an invention is the grant of a property right to the inventor, issued by the USPTO. The term of a new patent is 20 years from the date on which the application for the patent was filed in the United States and, in special circumstances, from a filing outside the United States at an earlier date. U.S. patent grants are effective only within the United States and its territories and possessions.

The idea of patents is to allow the inventor or patent holder an exclusive right to obtain the full financial benefits of his or her invention — allowing his or her investment of time and money to be recovered — before others are allowed to help themselves to a piece of the financial pie. You can appreciate the value of such protection if you spent ten years of your life designing a new kind of mousetrap — far superior and more cost-effective than any currently on the market — and began selling it, only to have someone immediately copy it and undercut your price, putting you out of business in the process. In such a case, a patent is essential.

What can and can't be patented has been subject to much debate over the years — witness the current furor over the patenting of genetically modified seeds for corn and other crops, and unique software programs such as

Amazon.com's 1-Click ordering process. But the law says that any person who *invents or discovers any new and useful process, machine, manufacture, or composition of matter, or any new and useful improvement thereof, may obtain a patent,* subject to the conditions and requirements of the law.

If you think you have an item that can and should be patented, our advice is to run — don't walk — to a competent patent attorney. The patent application process requires considerable research, and the appropriate forms have to be filed the right way and at the right time and place. When we're talking about something that may turn out to be your source of income for many years into the future — and could very well make you rich — this is not the time or place to try doing it yourself. Although filing a patent isn't inexpensive, a competent patent attorney can save you lots of time, money, and heartache.

Zoning, Licensing, and Permits

Uh-oh — this is where the red tape really gets sticky . . . and thick. No matter which governments — federal, state, or local — have jurisdiction in your particular place of business, you can bet they all have something to say about how, when, and where you can and can't run your business. Although you may have an easier time sticking your head in the sand and ignoring all the rules and regulations that these different government organizations want you to follow, you do so at your risk. When sufficiently motivated (as they will be if your neighbors complain to elected officials about cars that suddenly start parking in front of your house), most government agencies and departments aren't the slightest bit shy about issuing fines, imposing penalties, and — if compliance is not forthcoming in a reasonable amount of time — closing down offending businesses.

Working your way through the maze of government regulations can certainly be one of the most confusing aspects of doing business, but it is critical for your success in the long run. Yes, the process can be intimidating, and yes, you'd probably much rather be selling your products and services than messing with all this red tape and paperwork, but it will definitely be worth your while to dig in.

Instead of ignoring government regulations and requirements, consider this step as one that will enhance the professionalism of your business. In order for people to take you and your business seriously, you need to establish your business in a professional way. And for many home-based businesses, being taken seriously is one of the key steps to finding long-term success.

Zoning

For some reason, many homeowners — particularly ones who live in quiet residential areas — don't much like the idea of having a busy (or loud, or spotlit, or junky, or otherwise obnoxious) business move in next door. Just the thought of a constant parade of customer cars coming and going at all hours of the day or night, the clatter and noise coming from a makeshift appliance-repair shop out in your garage, or the vision of partly assembled cars littering the driveway is enough to send many homeowners into a fit of concern or even anger. And indeed, when people buy their homes, they (surprise!) generally expect to get some measure of peace and quiet along with them. Few homeowners awakened to the sound of grinding metal at 7 a.m. are happy homeowners.

Peter remembers the time a few years ago when one of his next-door neighbors decided to open an automobile-restoration business in his backyard. That wouldn't have been so bad in itself except for the loud air compressor that the neighbor found necessary to run 12 hours a day to drive his sandblasting equipment — waking Peter's year-old daughter and making writing his books and articles a difficult proposition during daylight hours. It took Peter six months — from the day he first complained to his neighbor about the noise (and being told to jump in a lake) to the day that the city zoning department finally shut down the operation — to get relief. But he did eventually get relief.

Zoning laws are, among other things, the government's favorite way of trying to keep residential areas residential and business areas business — making everyone (well, almost everyone) happy in the process. And in general, zoning laws do work. After a citizen makes a complaint, most jurisdictions follow an established procedure to determine whether a business owner is breaking the rules or not — and take action only when necessary. Unfortunately, the very zoning laws that attempt to ensure that someone doesn't decide to build a coal-fired power generation plant across the street from your house are also the same laws that may restrict (and in some cases prevent) you from starting a business in your own home.

Here are some of the categories of rules that zoning laws may impose in your particular city or county:

- ✔ Advertising signage
- ✔ Parking and vehicle traffic
- ✔ The percentage of your home devoted to business

> ✔ The number of people you employ and the jobs you employ them to perform
>
> ✔ The use of hazardous materials and chemicals
>
> ✔ Noise, smoke, and odor

One more thing: While your local zoning laws may permit you to run your home-based business as you intend, your particular neighborhood may have covenants or other deeded restrictions on those very same activities. Check your real estate purchase documents to see if such covenants or restrictions may apply to you.

So what can you do if zoning regulations make your home-based business illegal or are so restrictive that you can't operate your business effectively? You can certainly ignore the regulations and hope you don't get caught, but that's not really the best long-term solution. You are apt to discover that at least one of your neighbors is not going to be happy about some aspect of your business and will file a complaint. Not only that, but also, if you operate an illegal business, you're breaking the law. And if you break the law, you had better be ready to pay the consequences (we'll keep an eye on the Court TV listings just in case you make an appearance).

A better idea is to try one of the following approaches:

> ✔ **Request a variance.** Government agencies and departments routinely grant variances to rules and regulations. Often, you only have to fill out a short form. In other cases, your request may have to be publicly heard before your city council, zoning board, or other body (in the case of conflicts with neighborhood covenants, you may need to appeal to your neighborhood association). Check with your zoning or planning department to find out what options are available for you.
>
> ✔ **Fight city hall.** In some cases, you may have no other choice but to take action to change the rules or regulations that restrict your ability to start and operate a home-based business. A variety of approaches are available to you, from buttonholing your district's council member, to circulating a petition, to lobbying for legislative change, to filing a lawsuit. The exact action you take depends on your community's political environment. If you have any friends, relatives, or business acquaintances who have had to take on city hall, ask what worked for them.

Although zoning regulations can get in the way of your home-business plans, they don't have to be the end of your dream. If the rules aren't in your favor, you have legally viable options for either bending them or changing them.

Licensing and permits

There really is a business license or permit for most any occasion. Which ones does your home-based business need? It really depends in which city, county, and state your business is located.

Ask questions, starting with your city and/or county government. Describe the kind of business you have in mind, and a friendly worker will likely direct you to the appropriate forms and requirements. They may even have a special booklet or package of forms specifically for new or home-based businesses. After you check with your local government, contact the state and federal agencies that apply to your business.

Some of the most common licenses and permits include the following:

- **Business license:** This is the standard permit to operate a business locally, and it is required of most every business, no matter how large or small. Check with your local business agency for details.

- **Home occupation permit:** If your community restricts home-based businesses, you need one of these.

- **Miscellaneous local permits:** Contact your local business agency to see if any other business permits are required.

- **Police permit:** Some businesses require police clearance or permit. You may also need a police permit if your business has an alarm that generates a police response when it goes off.

- **Food permit:** For businesses that make or sell food.

- **Seller's permit:** Required for businesses that sell taxable products in states with sales tax (there are just a few that don't have sales tax).

  The definition of taxable products varies from state to state. Graphic design services, for example, may be considered a nontaxable service in one state but taxable in another.

- **Building permits, fire certificates, and zoning permits:** Check with your local planning department for restrictions on the kinds of business activities that can be conducted in your home. Some localities, for example, restrict home-based businesses that operate in residentially zoned communities from having customers come to the place of business.

- **State occupational licenses:** Certain occupations (for example, doctors, lawyers, general contractors, day-care providers, and so on) require a special license. Check with the state agency regulating consumer affairs.

✔ **Federal export licenses:** If you want to export goods to another country, your business will be subject to all kinds of federal regulation. Get more information on this from the U.S. Department of Commerce at www.doc.gov. A number of optional certifications can help in some situations: You may want to look into being certified as a small business, minority-owned, woman-owned, or disabled-veteran-owned enterprise.

Don't get discouraged by all this paperwork and red tape. Your own business is the light at the end tunnel created by all of these blasted forms. Remember that people are ready, willing, and able to help if you feel overwhelmed. Contact your local Small Business Development Center, chamber of commerce, or other local economic development organization for guidance on these local and state and federal issues; you'll be glad you did.

Tax Requirements

You can be sure that your business is going to owe taxes to somebody, somewhere, particularly if your business is making a profit. Depending on the state where you're located, the kind of business you conduct, and the form of business you select, you may owe taxes to many different people in many different places.

Take a look at the following list for a hint of the kinds of taxes you can look forward to paying when you own your own home-based business. Now you know why good accountants and tax advisors are so popular with all kinds of businesspeople, including owners of home-based businesses.

✔ Income tax

✔ Self-employment tax

✔ Estimated tax

✔ Social Security tax

✔ Unemployment tax

✔ Sales tax

✔ Excise tax

✔ Use tax

✔ Business tax

For much more information about taxes — including what taxes you need to pay and ten key ways to reduce your income tax burden — take a look at Chapter 10.

Starting a collections agency

Q: I am interested in starting my own collections agency, but I'm unclear about the rules and regulations I will have to follow in doing this business, as well as the types of software and other materials I will need.

A: We dropped starting a collections agency as a home-based business from the new edition of our book *Best Home Businesses of the 21st Century* for two reasons. The first reason is because of the hostility we experienced toward home-based collection agencies when we listed the industry trade association as a resource in the first edition of the book. The second is that when we called the home-based collections agencies we'd previously interviewed, none was still in business.

Furthermore, one of the previously most successful specialties, collecting court-ordered child support, has been pre-empted by state governments, which can now, as a result of federal legislation, garnish the bank accounts of delinquent parents.

However, if you can find a viable niche such as collecting on day-care accounts, heating-oil accounts, veterinary bills, or some other types of collection, this business may work for you. An example of a home-based agency that is doing well can be found at www.madagency.com.

The major piece of legislation you need to become familiar with is The Fair Debt Collection Practices Act. That, a telephone, a computer, and some clients are all you need to get started. Collections software programs include Debtmaster from Comtronic Systems, (509) 674-7000, www.comtronic.com; Collect!, (250) 391-0466, www.collect.org; and Collection Resource System, (703) 934-9060, www.crsoftwareinc.com.

Chapter 12

Using Outside Resources and Experts

· ·

In This Chapter

▶ Creating trade accounts

▶ Taking advantage of support services

▶ Using professionals in your business

· ·

*O*kay. So you're the boss, owner, and chief bottle-washer of your very own home-based business. Now what? In theory, you could probably do each and every thing on your own — from reviewing contracts to picking the best insurance coverage to representing your business in court to designing and printing your own letterhead stationery — but you really should think twice before doing so. Specialists — lawyers, certified public accountants, insurance brokers, and others — are much more knowledgeable and up-to-date about certain topics than you can ever be, and using their services frees you to focus on doing the things that you do best.

Beyond these outside professionals, there are a variety of outside resources that you should (and likely will have to) consider using when the opportunities present themselves. Establishing trade accounts with the outside vendors you'll rely on to sell you the products and services you need to do business is just one example.

In this chapter, we look at why, when, and how to take advantage of outside resources. Doing so can give you a real edge against your competition and help you provide your customers with the best products and services possible.

Establishing Trade Accounts

A *trade account* is an informal agreement between you and a supplier or vendor — such as an office supply store, printing company, or warehouse superstore — that allows you to purchase goods or services on credit and be billed by the supplier on a regular, usually monthly, basis. Trade accounts are a win–win situation for both parties — you can purchase whatever you like whenever you want, and your supplier gains a steady customer.

The care and maintenance of trade accounts is essential for almost any business, because they speed the purchasing process and remove much of the red tape that can slow vital business transactions. Not only that, but also, when a company agrees to establish a trade account with you, its management is essentially agreeing to extend a short-term, interest-free loan to your company — allowing you to pay your bill anywhere from a few days to a month or more after you complete your purchase and receive your goods or services. That is a good deal for your company, and one worth actively pursuing and maintaining.

You may find that some of the following trade accounts will be beneficial for you to establish in your business:

- ✔ **Product vendors:** If you sell products on a retail basis, you have to buy them from vendors or purchase the raw materials from suppliers. Establishing trade accounts will make your life much easier; you'll be able to place orders now and be invoiced for your purchases later.

- ✔ **Office supplies:** If you regularly purchase large quantities of office supplies, consider building a relationship with one office supply vendor that can meet your needs quickly and accurately. The big office supply chains Staples and Office Depot offer *frequent buyer* programs that provide customers with a variety of financial rewards in return for their loyalty.

- ✔ **Warehouse superstore:** Warehouse superstores, such as Costco and Sam's Club, offer everything most home offices ever need — from appliances to office supplies to groceries and baked goods — at great prices.

- ✔ **Copying/reproduction:** If you constantly find yourself sending jobs out for printing or copying, you may want to establish a trade account with your printer so that you're billed monthly instead of having to pay every time you run a job. Copy centers such as Kinko's offer their own charge cards to business customers, which are billed out on a monthly basis. The monthly invoices, which present detailed information about each order, are also a great way to keep track of your copying and reproduction jobs.

- ✔ **Office equipment repair:** Has your computer's hard drive ever crashed? If so, you know just how scary life can be — and how dependent you are on office machines and equipment. It can really pay off to have an established relationship with a good computer/office equipment repair person *before* — not after — your equipment goes down. The question isn't whether your office equipment will break, but when. Even if you don't go through the trouble of establishing a relationship with an office equipment repair company before you need it, do take some time to become familiar with who's good and who's not so good. That way, when the inevitable emergency does occur, you'll know right where to take your sick machine.

✔ **Support services:** Numerous support services are available to you, depending on the nature of your business. From typists and architects to paralegals and consulting engineers — you can establish relationships and trade accounts with most anyone you like. (In the next section, we address how to decide which support services you need and then how to identify and hire them.)

✔ **Courier/messenger services:** Although more and more transactions are being handled over the Internet, some items, such as products and signed documents, must be physically received. When you establish an account with an overnight courier service such as FedEx, UPS, or DHL, or with a local messenger service, you'll receive preprinted, multipart shipping documents or air bills. Even better, most of these companies now allow you to set up your shipments online, printing out shipping documents on your own computer and making it easy to track your package's progress — from your home office to your customer's front door.

Trade accounts are a good thing, and you should try to establish them with all your regular vendors, suppliers, and service providers. Not only will they streamline your business dealings, but because you hold onto your money for a longer period of time, your cash flow will be improved as well.

 It also works the other way — other businesses may want to establish trade accounts with you. Allowing them to do so may make a lot of sense, because it can encourage repeat business and the development of long-term business relationships. You must, however, protect yourself from customers who don't pay their bills. Check credit references scrupulously. Don't just take their word for it — especially if you've got a lot of money on the line. Do a Google search for *credit application form,* and you'll find plenty of sample forms that you can easily adapt for your own purposes.

Using Support Services

With just 24 hours in a day, if you're the sole proprietor and only employee of your home-based business, you may find that you have difficulty doing day-to-day support and administrative tasks while still doing the work that your customers pay you to do. This is where using support services comes in.

Using a service to take orders

Q: I sell several different mail-order products, and things have gotten too busy for me to take all the orders. Can a service take orders for me?

A: Absolutely. They'll also print address labels for you and provide your customers with personalized service. Look in the Yellow Pages under *Telemarketing* or *Answering Services,* or use these same key words to search Internet Yellow Page services such as

✔ www.switchboard.com

✔ www.anywho.com

✔ www.superpages.com

✔ www.canada411.ca

The costs for such a service — according to Howard Goodman, president of the telemarketing company Goodman Communications West and author of *Seven Steps to Successful 800, Radio and TV Direct Response Campaigns* — begins at around $500 a month after an initial setup fee of $1,500. Setup fees include the first month's service and 500 minutes of phone time. Goodman's booklet is available free by calling (800) 466-8595.

Support services include everything from short-term employees to temporary employment firms to hiring professionals such as lawyers, accountants, and consultants — in fact, they potentially include just about any business service you can imagine.

Consider using support services for the three following reasons:

✔ **People out there have more experience than you.** Do you know how to file a patent application? Or the best way to set up a computerized accounting system? Or which health care plans are the best deal for home-based businesses in your state? If not, support services providers — many of whom are owners of home-based businesses themselves — do. People who provide support services are specialists at what they do, just as you're a specialist at what you do. One of the great things about using support services is that you can take advantage of as much or as little of their experience as you like — usually for a reasonable hourly fee.

✔ **You can leverage your experience.** Certain support-services use, such as hiring a temporary employee as an assistant, can allow you to leverage your own experience — greatly increasing your effectiveness in the process. By teaching another person to perform a high-dollar-return task that you're expert in, that person can then do the same thing you're doing, instantly multiplying the effort spent on that task while substantially increasing the financial return. For example, why not consider hiring someone to make cold calls to prospective customers or create and distribute flyers advertising your business? While you're busy working, she can be drumming up new customers.

✔ **You can focus your efforts.** Instead of getting caught up in all the details of running a 500-copy brochure (finding the right kind of paper, using the right machine, dealing with jams and equipment breakdowns, collating, and folding), why not just drop it off at Kinko's or another copy center, and let them worry about it? That way, you can focus your efforts on the things that bring money into your firm — such as selling products and writing proposals.

ASK PAUL & SARAH

Leasing employees

Q: I have a home-based medical-billing business, and I am ready to hire employees. Because I didn't want to hassle with payroll, workman's comp, and so on, I called several employee- leasing companies. To my surprise, none would provide me with employees, because I'm home based. What should I do?

A: We're surprised and appalled to discover that some employee leasing companies are discriminating against home-based businesses! Like many home-based companies, we use employee leasing ourselves. We've worked with two different companies for over five years, and the results have been more than satisfactory. So we recommend that you keep looking to find more-enlightened companies.

Be sure that you're actually contacting employee-leasing companies — not temp agencies. *Professional employee organizations,* as they are called, carry out the administrative functions of having employees. You recruit the personnel, interview them, and select them. When you're ready to put them to work, you contact the leasing company, which puts them on the payroll and handles all aspects of their employment for you. Temporary-help agencies,

on the other hand, recruit, interview, and train employees whom they send out to work with companies on a short- or long-term basis.

For many years, we've been aware that some temporary agencies will not place their temps in home offices. But according to Bruce Steinberg, director of Research and Public Relations for the National Association of Temporary and Staffing Services, some temp agencies do. He recommends that if you have an employee in mind or want to find someone yourself, you should work with an employee-leasing company. If you want an agency to find and place someone to work in your business, you should contact a temporary-help agency.

To locate such companies, you can contact the following:

✔ The National Association of Professional Employer Organizations, 901 N. Pitt St., Suite 350, Alexandria, VA 22314, (703) 836-0466, www.napeo.org

✔ American Staffing Association, Suite 200, 277 S. Washington St., Alexandria, VA 22314, (703) 253-2020, www.natss.org

So what kinds of support services should you consider using for your home-based business? Here's a partial list (many more are available to home-business owners):

- ✔ Copying, printing, and graphics design
- ✔ Public relations
- ✔ Packaging and shipping
- ✔ Professional services such as accounting, legal, banking, and so on
- ✔ Temporary help
- ✔ Advertising
- ✔ Cleaning

Although you may have plenty of time to do these tasks when your company is new and has little business, after it starts to grow, you'll want to devote more time to the selling and customer-fulfillment processes and less to the kinds of tasks that don't directly generate cash for the business.

Finding Good Lawyers, Accountants, and Other Professionals

When you own your own home-based business, you're responsible for just about everything. Whether you're selling your products, paying the bills, or taking out the trash, the business begins and ends with you — without you, you have no business.

This doesn't mean, however, that you have to go it alone. Any number of outside professionals are ready, willing, and able to help you build and expand your business while ensuring that you're on a firm footing — legally and financially. By leveraging the services of key professionals such as lawyers, accountants, bankers, insurance agents, and others, a small business can be just as effective as a much larger organization — perhaps even more so.

No matter what kinds of professionals you decide to affiliate with, check them out thoroughly before you commit to doing business with them. Don't forget: Your goal is to find someone who is not only talented and affordable, but who also can grow with you and your company, and become a long-term partner and trusted associate. Take your time in the selection process; believe us, the time you invest in the process now will pay off many times over in the years to come. Consider the following when selecting:

- ✔ **Qualifications:** Hire professionals who are as qualified and experienced as possible; your business is not the place where you want them to learn the ropes. Do not hire someone who merely dabbles in an area of professional expertise or who does it as a hobby. You need someone who is a pro and is fully committed to your success.

- ✔ **Accessibility:** You may have a difficult time getting their attention when you really need them. Make sure that the professionals you hire aren't already so overcommitted with other clients that they can't meet your needs quickly, when you need them the most.

- ✔ **Price:** Although you should never select a professional on price alone, price certainly does enter into the equation. With some lawyers charging well over $300 an hour, every dollar really does count. Don't be afraid to shop around for the best combination of skill, experience, and price.

- ✔ **Ethics:** Your professionals should have ethical standards that are just as high as the standards you uphold. Choosing someone with flexible ethics is asking for trouble.

- ✔ **Compatibility:** None of the preceding means much if you aren't compatible with your chosen professional. Conversely, you may be willing to give up some experience or price in exchange for someone you really get along with. The ideal situation is to find someone who meets all your criteria and is also compatible with you and any business partners and associates you may have.

In the sections that follow, we take a close look at some of the kinds of professionals that home-based business owners most often turn to for help and support.

Lawyers

Question: How many lawyers does it take to change a light bulb? Answer: How many can you afford? Actually, most lawyers really are nice people to work with, and they do have other things on their mind besides emptying your bank accounts. In fact, an attorney's services are an important part of any business's — including any home-based business's — support team.

What can attorneys do for your business? Here are some of the most common tasks attorneys take on for their small business clients:

- ✔ Choosing a form (legal structure) for your business

- ✔ Writing, reviewing, and negotiating business contracts

- ✔ Dealing with employee issues

- ✔ Helping with credit problems and bankruptcy

- ✔ Addressing consumer issues and complaints

- ✔ Working with rental or leasing agreements

- ✔ Outlining workers' compensation and Social Security benefits

- ✔ Advising you on your legal rights and obligations

- ✔ Representing you in court

Be sure to seek out an attorney who specializes in working with small businesses and startups. Any other attorney may not have the exact skill set that you need. If you have a family attorney, start there. If he or she isn't the best person for the job, chances are you'll get a good referral to someone who is. One more thing: Make a point of asking your attorney how much a particular task is going to cost — *before* you engage his services. There's nothing worse than getting a bill that's in the thousands of dollars when you expected to pay far less.

Accountants

If you're not an expert in accounting — and even if you *are* but would rather devote your precious time to taking care of your customers' needs — getting a good accountant is a definite must. Why? Because as the owner of your own business, you need to know exactly how much money is going in and out of your business and for what purposes it is being used. This knowledge will allow you to assess the financial health of your company while assisting you in making plans for the future. Not only that, but also, the information contained in your accounting system provides the basis for determining how much you'll owe the government in taxes and other fees.

Inadequate recordkeeping is a principal contributor to the failure of small businesses. A good accountant can be a tremendous help in setting up a useful financial recordkeeping system, as well as providing ongoing financial advice.

Here are some of the most common tasks that accountants perform for their small business customers:

- ✔ Small business startup, business sale, or business purchase

- ✔ Accounting system design and implementation

- ✔ Preparation, review, and audit of financial statements

- ✔ Tax planning

✔ Preparation of income tax returns

✔ Tax appeals

Handle finding and choosing an accountant in much the same way that you select any other professional adviser. Check with friends and business associates for recommendations. Interview at least three candidates to be sure that your personalities are compatible.

You want to interview your prospective candidates (either in person or over the phone), asking and watching for the following:

✔ Does your candidate have specific experience working with home-based businesses?

✔ Does your candidate show an active interest in the financial aspects of your business operations (cash flow, inventory, and so on)?

✔ Does your candidate have specific experience with income tax, and does he or she keep abreast of the latest changes in the tax law as it pertains to your industry?

✔ What do the candidate's references say about his or her performance and reliability?

✔ What is the candidate's fee structure?

✔ Does your candidate have a network of other potentially beneficial financial contacts within your community (for example, loan officers at local banks)?

✔ Are you comfortable with the candidate, and are your financial philosophies compatible?

One thing you'll notice as you search for the right accountant for your business is that some have the initials *CPA* following their names. A *certified public accountant* (CPA) is an accountant who has met his or her state's minimum educational requirements and passed a rigorous examination covering accounting, business law, auditing, and taxes. CPAs are required to have a college degree (this can be offset by extensive work experience, in some cases) and must meet an annual continuing-education requirement. This all means that when you choose to affiliate with a CPA, you're getting someone who is at the top of his or her profession. A CPA may be more expensive than a regular accountant, but depending on your specific needs, the extra cost may be well worth your money.

Any skilled accountant — whether or not she has *CPA* after her name — may be just right for you and your business. It all depends on the experience and expertise that she brings to the table, as well as her willingness to be available to help you when you really need it. Don't exclude good candidates merely because they lack the letters *CPA*.

Be sure that you have at least a basic understanding of accounting and the particular bookkeeping system you're using. Even if you decide to hire an accountant to take care of the details, as owner of your own business you should and must understand how the financial side of your business works. Take advantage of the financial reporting functions of your system, and know how to read and interpret your company's financial reports. For more information on doing just that, be sure to check out Chapter 7.

Bankers

You want to have a relationship with your bank already in place when you need it. You never know when you may need financing. It may be when you're in the startup phase of your business or when you get a huge order from a customer and need to pay your suppliers before you receive payment. Or it could be when your business starts to grow, and you need to finance your expansion. And — even if you don't plan to expand any time soon and have no need for a loan or financing — depending on the size of the checks you deposit, you may not have immediate access to your funds. That often depends on your banking relationship, how long your account has been open, and your average balance. These ongoing financial needs make finding and establishing a relationship with a good local banker a must.

Peter was shocked to learn, soon after he established a business account for his new corporation at a large local bank, that any checks over $500 would be put on hold for a week or more while the bank waited for them to clear. Such an unexpected outcome can really put the hurt on your fledgling business if you're not ready to deal with it. In Peter's case, a combination of lots of begging, sweet-talking, and threats to move his account to another bank helped keep his cash flowing.

Establish a relationship with your banker (which most often means the branch manager) *prior* to applying for a loan and *before* depositing a $10,000 check that would normally take 10 days to clear. The relationship that you have with a banker at the time you apply for a loan can make the difference between getting approved and getting turned down.

The big question is: What kind of financial institution is right for your kind of home-based business? Several different kinds of financial institutions are available to you, and each has its unique spin on the world of money and banking.

 ✔ **Banks** are the first choice of many home-based businesses, and they include savings banks, savings and loans, and commercial banks. Banks traditionally make a wide variety of loans, both commercial and consumer, and they are the place to go for special small business loans offered in conjunction with the Small Business Administration (SBA). Most also offer special accounts designed specifically for businesses, along with a wide array of business-oriented products and services, all of which makes them the logical first choice for most businesses.

- ✔ **Credit unions** are similar to banks but differ in that they are owned by their members. This results in lower costs of operation, which are passed on to members in the form of interest rates on loans and higher savings interest rates. Most credit unions specialize in consumer loans rather than commercial loans, although many offer special loans to buy home computers. Credit unions are less likely than regular banks to offer special accounts and products and services for businesses, and in some cases (for example, if your home-based business is a corporation that issues stock), they may not even be able to accept your business as a customer.

- ✔ **Credit card companies** offer interest rates that are often significantly higher than the rates you would get on the same amount of money from a bank or credit union, yet thousands of companies regularly use credit cards to finance purchases. Why? Because using credit cards is usually far more convenient that applying for a loan every time you want to make a major purchase or make some other financial move. Keep in mind that even if the credit card has your company name on it, it's likely that you are personally responsible for the charges, and even if your business fails, the credit card company will be looking for you when the monthly payment is due.

- ✔ **Commercial finance companies** specialize in working with businesses, usually in financing equipment leasing or purchases or the acquisition of inventory. The deals that commercial finance companies offer — particularly leasing — may offer attractive tax advantages and are worth checking out.

- ✔ **Consumer finance companies** are businesses that specialize in making loans to borrowers who have a hard time obtaining loans from their banks or credit unions, perhaps because they have defaulted on loans in the past or because their credit is already overextended. Because those borrowers are considered to be a higher risk for defaulting on loans, consumer finance companies generally charge significantly higher interest rates than do banks and credit unions. Consumer finance companies should, therefore, be considered a funding source of last resort for most businesses.

Be sure that you anticipate your needs well in advance. Waiting until the last minute to develop a relationship with your banker or to apply for a critically needed loan is a recipe for financial disaster.

Business consultants

Everyone has talents in many areas, but even you can't be the master of everything. Help is on the way, however: *Consultants* are available to assist in those areas in which you need expert help. You can hire business, manage- ment, and marketing consultants; promotion experts; financial planners; and a host of other specialists who can help make your business more successful.

Regardless of exactly which kind of consultant you decide to hire, we give you nine steps for selecting the right one, adapted from the Institute for Management Consultancy Web site at www.imc.co.uk:

- ✔ **Clearly define the objectives you hope to achieve.** Describe the job you want done, and specify the things you expect from the assignment. Understand precisely how you expect your business will benefit from the work. Decide on the time frame, scope, and any constraints on the assignment. Clarify your own role and how the consultant's time will be made available.

- ✔ **Short-list no more than three consultants, and ask them to provide written proposals.** Make sure you ask for quotes only from consultants qualified to carry it out. Good consultants will be more than happy to send you basic information about them and talk with you about your needs, without charge. Invite your best prospects to submit written pro- posals, which should include the following:

  - Their understanding of the problem

  - Their approach to solving the problem

  - Names and resumes of the consultant(s) who will do the work

  - Experience of the firm

  - References

  - Other support provided by the firm

  - Work plan

  - Reports and/or systems that will be supplied to you

  - Fees, expenses and schedules of payment

  - Any inputs required from you

- ✔ **Brief the consultant properly.** Prepare a concise brief that clearly defines the objectives, scope, time frame, reporting procedure, and constraints of the project. Remember that the cheapest quote will not necessarily give the best value for your money and that consultant fees may be negotiable.

✔ **See the individual consultant who will do the job, and make sure that the chemistry is right.** Successful consulting requires goodwill in human communications. Meet the consultant who will be doing the job, and brief him or her well, using a written brief and any background information that you think necessary. Talk through your chosen proposal with the consultant before making a final decision to ensure that you have any concerns answered. If you're not happy with any aspects of the proposal, don't feel pressured to accept them. Continue discussions with the consultant until you reach a full agreement on the proposal. Select the firm or individual that you feel has the best qualifications and experience and that you feel you can work with comfortably.

✔ **Ask for references from the chosen consultant, and follow them up.** Ask the firm or individual for names or written references from former clients in order to verify the consultant's suitability for the assignment.

✔ **Review and agree to a written contract before the assignment starts.** This almost goes without saying, but we're going to say it anyway. And while you're at it, have your lawyer take a look at the contract before you sign on the dotted line.

✔ **Be involved and in touch during the assignment.** Using consultants effectively demands a commitment of time as well as money by clients. Remember that you must keep in touch with the progress of the assignment if you're to get the most from it. Consultants are likely to be most cost-effective when working on an agreed program and time frame. Make sure that you hold regular progress meetings and that the consultant keeps you fully briefed on progress against the program.

✔ **Ensure that the consultant doesn't save surprises for the final report.** The consultant's report is often his or her most tangible *deliverable* (what you provide in fulfillment of a contract), but it must be in a format that's beneficial to you. If necessary, ask the consultant to produce a draft report so that you can review the findings and recommendations before the final report is produced. The final report should contain no surprises.

✔ **Implement the recommendations, and involve yourself as well as the consultant.** You may need to make arrangements for the consultant to help with the implementation. This can be done cost-effectively by involving the consultant in regular progress meetings. Get a written fee quotation and proposal for any implementation work, even if it follows directly from an assignment.

Hiring the right consultant for your business at the right time can mean the difference between just getting by and achieving tremendous success.

Insurance agents and brokers

Not only are there a dizzying array of different insurance policies and programs available to businesses, but there also are hundreds of insurance companies to choose among. Which offers the best coverage for you? To get an inkling of the answer, you have to extensively research insurance policies and companies — definitely not the best use of your time.

A better way to find out what insurance is available (and necessary) for your business, and which deals are the best for you, is to use insurance agents and brokers. Insurance professionals can save you precious time and money — sometimes thousands of dollars — while providing you with the peace of mind that comes from knowing your insurance needs are being met.

Not only can a good insurance agent or broker advise you about the type and amount of coverage that is best for your business, but he or she can probably also tailor a package that meets your specific needs at reasonable rates. All of these services are worth their weight in gold to busy home-based business owners who have neither an extensive knowledge of insurance and risk management nor the time to mess with it.

What's the best way to choose an insurance agent for your business? Here are our suggestions:

- ✔ Solicit bids from two or three established agents to see who can deliver the lowest price for a specified level of coverage.

- ✔ Evaluate the professional experience and qualifications of prospective agents as though you were choosing a new attorney or accountant.

- ✔ Interview prospective agents with an eye toward the same qualities you seek in a key employee.

The following steps can help you find the agent or broker who will be the best person for your business:

- ✔ Look for an agent who is knowledgeable about your industry and who regularly works with home-based businesses; different companies have different needs. A wildlife photographer, for example, has much different insurance needs than does a home inspector. And what's good for a high-tech company may not necessarily be right for an e-commerce operation or retail outlet. One thing is for sure: No one agent can effectively keep up with every different kind of insurance for every different type of business.

- ✔ Ask your friends and business associates for referrals to good agents or brokers, or check with professional and trade associations. Be sure to look for someone who regularly handles accounts of your size (many agents and brokers consider one-person businesses too small to be worth the "trouble" to service). Expect your agent to add value to your enterprise, just as an attorney or accountant does.

✔ Choose an agent who is knowledgeable, dependable, loyal, and a good communicator. You want the agent to work well for you and know how to expedite claims when necessary. Check out the agent's support structure to make sure it is adequate to handle your account. Visit the agent's office, and meet the people who handle day-to-day operations. Confidence in them will increase your confidence in the agent or broker.

Insurance is an important part of every business, and it will pay off for you to get the best advice possible. Although most home-based businesses never have to use their insurance, if you need it — because of an auto accident, fire, product-liability lawsuit, or other covered risk — you'll be glad you have it.

Cashing In on Barter

Bartering means trading goods or services without exchanging money. Even so, bartering does have implications for your cash flow. Can home-based businesses benefit from bartering? The following story can illustrate.

"Barely surviving" is how Gilles Tessier of Moncton, Nova Scotia, described himself when in 1998 he needed to come up with $400 to print flyers for his lawn care and landscaping business. He was beginning the spring with only 14 customers and a broken-down truck, and he needed more to make a living. It was during this low point that he saw a television news story about a man who had put his son through flight school through bartering. Gilles, who has a college degree in small business management, immediately contacted Maritime Barter Associates, a local barter exchange, which had grown out of the reorganization of a franchised barter operation.

After paying a membership fee of $375, he immediately bartered his lawn-care services in exchange for printing and a van to replace his truck. Tessier, whose work at North of Eden Landscaping is seasonal, now hires up to four employees to help him. During the long Canadian winter, he uses his van to pick up and deliver goods for business customers in Canada and down the eastern seaboard of the United States. Barter plays a role in this, too: He has gotten his van repaired on the road and hasn't paid for a hotel room in five years.

His barter exchange works as many do. In addition to joining and annual membership fees, he pays the exchange 10 percent of the value of what he receives in barter — in cash. When his services are used, he provides the equivalent of 3 percent of his services to the barter exchange. So when Gilles receives barter goods or services worth $10,000, he pays the exchange $1000. If he provides $1,000 worth of services to an exchange member, the exchange credits itself with an additional $30 worth of his lawn care.

Tessier observes, "When you first start a business, you have little cash flow. You must depend on your customers to pay you on time, and if someone doesn't, you have to phone to ask for payment. By bartering, I can in effect keep cash in my business by in effect borrowing from other businesses."

Here are six tips for taking advantage of bartering in your business:

- A *bartering exchange or club* is a company that serves as a clearinghouse for getting barterers together. Another way to think of a bartering exchange is as a bank for keeping track of barters in terms of barter points, credits, or "dollars," rather than direct barter, in which you swap your service or product for the service or product of someone else.

- Membership in a bartering exchange costs money. Besides the initial registration fee, exchanges charge a 12 to 15 percent fee per transaction, due in cash. Some exchanges also charge monthly fees. You can find local bartering exchanges through one of two bartering organizations: the International Reciprocal Trade Association (IRTA) and the National Association of Trade Exchanges. Both have online directories listing their member exchanges on their Web sites (www.irta.net and www.nate.org). IRTA has a checklist of things to consider before joining a bartering exchange. Another way to learn about local bartering clubs is through *BarterNews* magazine (www.barternews.com).

- If you don't want to join a bartering exchange, you may be able to find barter partners on www.craiglist.org, for which there is no charge. Some Web sites also post a notice that they will barter.

- Take into account that *barter is considered a form of income and has tax consequences.* Whether or not you join a bartering exchange, the fair market value of goods and services exchanged must be reported as income in the year you receive them, but you may deduct costs incurred to perform the bartered work. Barter exchanges must comply with their own reporting requirements on Form 1099-B for all transactions.

- Beware of scams on the Web, and check out local exchanges as you would any other business, using perhaps the Better Business Bureau (www.bbs.org). And be sure your barter exchange is filing the proper tax reports. Existing members can tell you if they've been getting 1099s.

- Be selective about what and how much you barter. Read barter contracts in detail to be sure you have legal recourse if something goes amiss.

Chapter 13

Eluding Scams, Rip-Offs, and Other Headaches

. . . .

. . . .

*I*f you compare statistics from the Federal Trade Commission and the Small Business Administration, you'll find that just about as many people are victims of business-opportunity scams as actually start new businesses each year. Why do more than half a million people a year fall victim to fraudulent business opportunities year after year?

✔ Although the business world has long been fertile ground for scams, cons, and outright fraud, the Internet has made it easier and cheaper for scamsters to reach more victims. Also, seeing how other scammers work, they each become better at pushing the buttons of the desperation and desire so many people have.

✔ Most people do not complain about being victimized. Some are embarrassed; others regard collecting "business opportunities" like a crapshoot ("Maybe this one will work"). And a few, despite experience and the warnings they read and hear, including what they'll read on these pages, believe that if something were really bad, the government would have closed it down.

✔ Despite hotlines and Web sites where potential victims can check out business-opportunity vendors, many, if not most, scams never get listed — and often when they do, the scam's perpetrator has changed its name or moved onto a new scam.

As a result, many people find it hard to tell whether a promising opportunity is real or a scam.

Sniffing Out the Scams

Can you tell a scam from legitimate business opportunity? Are you certain? Here's a sample. Is it a scam, or is it real?

It's So Simple To Earn $2,000 - $5,000 Per Week Nowadays . . .

We're searching for only ten elite individuals with the work ethic necessary to generate a cash-flow for themselves of $2,000 to $5,000 per week, and to increase that to over $20,000 per month in as little as four to six months. And you know what? If you really have a burning desire and commitment, we guarantee that you'll reach this explosive income!

Can you read a short script to our qualified leads, and then turn the interested prospects over to our electronic sales medium? (You will not be required to do any selling.)

Do you have the self-discipline to ignore the TV for a couple of hours per day?

Are you looking for a legitimate home-based business opportunity that is not multi-level marketing or a chain-letter scheme?

If you would like to build an amazing income that will grow lightning-fast and have you profit $1,000.00 every time only one prospect makes a purchase, this is for you!

You can build the business under our guidance and support without having to attend meetings or sell people things they don't need.

Call NOW our TOLL FREE, PRE-RECORDED Message: 1-888-555-5555 [note: number changed to protect the guilty!]

We market a real product that pays real commissions to you, $1,000.00 per sale, just for making the initial contacts. With our turnkey lead generation systems, you always talk to people who actually WANT to talk to you.

You have nothing to lose and there's no risk involved, nor is there any obligation whatsoever, and you may be qualified to earn thousands of extra dollars per month!

So call now! The call is FREE, and there is absolutely no obligation, so what have you got to lose? Call toll free 1-888-555-5555.

So what do you think — scam or real? Not sure? Tempted?

Well, it's a scam, and we believe that if you do two things when reading an ad like this, you won't become another unhappy statistic. These are:

1. **Temper the enthusiasm** with a large helping of restraint in the face of a business opportunity that sounds "too good to be true" — it is. As Professor Barry Commoner observed, "There are no free lunches." Of course, the meals served by scamsters aren't free; they're out to take your money. But consider this in the context of being skeptical of — no, allergic to — promises of hundred- or thousandfold returns.

   When someone makes the kind of return promised by some scams, it makes the news. Consider that when Char Crawford, the "Toaster Lady," whom Paul and Sarah interviewed on their radio show (www.wsradio. com/entrepreneur_homebasedbiz), bought a 1939 toaster for $20 and sold it for $5200 on eBay, she got on CNN. How often does this happen?

2. **Be alert to red flags.** This ad had plenty of them. In the sections that follow, you find out how to identify *red flags* — the warning signs that something isn't quite right — that should cause you to pay extra-special attention to a seemingly reputable opportunity. Then you must take the time to thoroughly check out the red flags before you shell out your hard-earned money.

Let's consider the red flags you want to look for. This section highlights some of the most common ways people lose their money to false opportunities and often outright scams.

Job-at-home

Yes, this book is about self-employment, but it's important to erect some warning signs if you're tempted to seek hourly or salaried work at home based on an ad.

Red flags

- ✔ Charging a fee for job listings or a job directory even when there's no refund promised if you do not find work.

- ✔ *Previously undisclosed* government jobs. All federal jobs must be advertised, and state and local governments typically have a similar requirement.

- ✔ Anything involving envelope stuffing or coupon clipping. For examples of other scams, go to the Federal Trade Commission's Web site (www.ftc. gov), and search *job at home*.

If you are seeking fill-in work while you are developing your business or during a slack time, consider bidding for project work on such sites as www.elance.com and www.guru.com instead of falling prey to job-at-home come-ons.

Business opportunities

Any "formula" business you buy is a business opportunity, but certain types — multi-level marketing and franchises — have special characteristics. Although many, if not, most business opportunities are indeed legitimate, as often as not, *the ones that solicit you* are suspect. But if a business opportunity interests you, research it thoroughly to determine whether it's a legitimate opportunity — and whether it's a fit for you — before you invest your hard-earned time and money in it.

Red flags

✔ You're told that you won't have to sell, that the product sells itself, or that it's *easy work*.

✔ You're pressured to make an immediate decision to buy into the business opportunity.

✔ Earnings claims sound too good to be true.

✔ You're discouraged from letting an attorney review contracts or other materials.

✔ For whatever reason, you cannot talk to prior investors in the business opportunity.

✔ When you call the company's phone number, you never get a live person, only an answering machine, and the company's address is a post-office box.

✔ The Web site or seller sells many different kinds of "biz ops" and is not someone who actually does or has done this business him/herself.

✔ You live in one of the 23 states that require registration of business opportunities (California, Connecticut, Florida, Georgia, Illinois, Indiana, Iowa, Kentucky, Louisiana, Maine, Maryland, Michigan, Minnesota, Nebraska, New Hampshire, North Carolina, Ohio, Oklahoma, South Carolina, South Dakota, Texas, Utah, Virginia, Washington), and the business opportunity is not registered. However, many states have thresholds, like $500, before a business opportunity must be registered. Some scam operators take advantage of this — and you guessed it — price the business op at $495 or some number that will enable them to avoid registration.

✔ Testimonials use only people's initials or names that when you try to locate the people using directories like switchboard.com and anywho.com there's no listing. Legitimate businesses want to be listed; they aren't hiding.

✔ Your gut tells you something is wrong.

Franchises

Most franchises are legitimate, because the amount of money and legal compliance involved in offering a franchise is substantial, but this does not necessarily make them good investments.

Even with "good" franchises, serious disputes sometimes arise between the franchisees and franchisors. As discussed in Chapter 2, the law requires that they give you a detailed disclosure statement, called the Uniform Franchise Offering Circular (UFOC). However, this documentation does you no good unless you verify everything asserted and have the contract reviewed by an attorney who is qualified to do franchise work.

Red flags

✔ The franchise has been around for less than five years. You're most apt to be successful with a franchise that was in business for five years before it was franchised — and then has been franchised for five years.

✔ You don't receive a copy of the disclosure documents required by law _the first time you meet,_ or you are told you don't need to read them.

✔ A list of current franchisees doesn't exist or is curiously short.

✔ You're pressured into signing a franchise agreement without having it thoroughly vetted by your attorney.

✔ You feel that the focus of the franchisor is on selling you a franchise. A good franchisor does not necessarily assure that you're qualified. They are searching for the right person to add to their organization.

✔ The franchisor is new to the business but not new to franchising — or the franchisor is new to the business _and_ new to franchising.

✔ Your gut tells you that something is wrong or any of the red flags for business opportunities are present, such as claims of making big profits from a small amount of work.

Direct-selling, network marketing, multi-level marketing

More than 90 percent of the individuals who work in direct-selling programs do so part time. A major reason for this is because less than 2 percent in most organizations do well enough to produce a full-time income. Regardless, the promise of fast (and big!) riches draws a constant stream of people to direct selling.

The reality of the situation, however, is that few people make much money. As these disenchanted individuals drop out of the system, established distributors feel intense pressure to find and sign up new recruits — recruits just like you!

But there are stellar performers — people like Bea Sherzer in Fern Park, Florida, who extols the benefits of the health products she sells. "They improved my health so much that everyone began asking me about them." Bea told us. "This was the best thing that ever happened to me."

Unless you're as thoroughly sold on the products you'll be selling — as Bea is — and are good at recruiting and selling, which most people are not, do not expect significant earnings. Quixtar, the Internet marketing arm of Amway's parent company, Alticor, is one of the few companies that reports distributor earnings. It does so because of a court settlement many years ago. The company reported in its October 2003 SA4400 that the typical distributor earned $115 month, the same as for the previous three years. From this amount, distributors must pay their own overhead costs, including training, samples, and selling materials. As you can see, even for a big player in the direct-selling market such as Quixtar, the vast majority of distributors aren't exactly getting rich quick.

Sometimes, we meet home-business owners who, trying to supplement their income from a principal business that is not producing the earnings they want, take on a direct-selling company "on the side." Rarely does this work unless it's a natural fit, such as a chiropractor selling supplements to his or her patients.

If you think you're being hustled or pressured to sign up for a program before you have a chance to thoroughly check it out, including time to use the products or services, take a step back. The opportunity will be there — if the company is still around (direct-selling companies have a high mortality rate) and if you come to feel enthusiastic about what you'll be selling.

Red flags

The following should get your attention and make you think twice before you commit to a particular direct-selling opportunity.

- ✔ You're told that you can achieve great success without having to actually sell anything.

- ✔ You aren't provided with the name of the company until after you listen to a canned sales pitch.

- ✔ You are required or pressured to buy inventory. You should be able to get started with a kit costing less than $100 and never more than $500.

- ✔ The company does not specifically agree to buy back any of your unsold inventory.

- ✔ The direct-selling company is not a member of the Direct Selling Association (www.dsa.org/directory). In order to belong, companies agree to a code of ethics and have been in business for at least two years.

- ✔ Your gut tells you that something is wrong.

Keep in mind, if a direct-selling opportunity is a *legitimate* one, it's not going away overnight. (It's estimated that almost nine out of ten direct-selling companies do not last five years.) And if one does, you're better off without having invested your time or credibility with the people you contact, so take the time to thoroughly check out any company you're considering. The time you spend now is an investment in your future that will pay for itself many times down the road.

Places to Check

Unfortunately, most people do not lodge complaints about being victimized by scams and rip-offs with official agencies, but here are some ways that you can sometimes flush out a company you will not be happy with:

- ✔ Better Business Bureau (www.bbb.org), as well as contacting the BBB office in the community where the seller is located

- ✔ Federal Trade Commission (www.ftc.gov/ftc/complaint.htm)

- ✔ The National Consumer League's National Internet Fraud Watch Information Center (www.fraud.org)

- ✔ State consumer protection agencies, sometimes in attorney-general offices; sometimes called Bureaus of Consumer Protection when located in a state agency other than the attorney general's office

✔ US Postal Service warnings about phony job opportunities and work-at home schemes (www.usps.gov/websites/depart/inspect/work home.htm)

✔ A Web search using the company or product name and words like *scam* and *fraud*

Finally, Be Wary of . . .

Aside from the above tried-and-true scams, there are plenty of new and innovative ones out there — with more popping up every day of the week. Be very careful about these new approaches to separating you from your hard-earned cash!

✔ Online "shills" who post messages in Internet forums and discussion groups. They are apt to describe others as frauds while extolling their own company, making false claims about their earnings.

✔ *Due diligence* sites, which either for free or a fee promise to purport to differentiate honest business opportunities from frauds.

✔ If you're purchasing something, you can only use a foreign payment service — not a recognized service like PayPal — or you're asked to pay in advance or by way of a bogus escrow site. Bogus sites are not always easy to identify, because they may use fake logos and graphics from verification services like "VeriSign" and confusingly similar names. Using the list of places to check in the previous section of this chapter — as well as search engines, using phrases like the escrow service's name plus *fraud* and *complaint* — gives you a fighting chance to spot the frauds.

A Final Word

Despite the scamsters and the clever ways in which they snare the unsuspecting *as well as* people with experience, thousands of people find their way to self-employment through formula businesses: franchises, business opportunities, and direct sales. If you find the right match, you can save yourself weeks and months of time by putting someone else's business model to work for you.

Network marketing over the Internet

Q: What do you think of direct-selling or network marketing, especially over the Internet?

A: Network marketing is part of the direct-selling industry, and the Internet does play a role in network marketing, though small in proportion to face-to-face sales, which account for three out of four sales. The most recent statistics from the Direct Selling Association indicate that almost 11 percent of direct sales are made over the Internet, up from 8 percent two years earlier. So most sales are made the customary way of making direct sales and recruiting people into a downline.

Beyond using e-mail, the Internet can be useful by having a Web site where you support your downline and attract buyers looking for your products and others looking for a business opportunity. You will need to use a domain name that does not duplicate or infringe upon the name of the network-marketing company.

The Internet is used successfully by some people to attract a downline in still another way. Although junk e-mail may the way you think of first, it's not used by those who are most successful. Instead, they actively participate in online forums or discussion groups, usually related to the product they are selling, where they are helpful to others by answering questions and offering advice that earns people's trust and interest.

One less obvious benefit of network marketing is that you can learn about the skills needed to operate a business, such as selling, managing time, and keeping yourself motivated in the face of rejection. In this sense, network marketing can be a good training experience based on the help and strength of your upline. While such skills are primarily "offline" ones, with every passing year more and more of what we do involves connectivity to the web.

You can find the current research on direct-selling and network marketing at www.dsa.org. Network marketing has its share of critics. A comprehensive site is www.mlmsurvivor.com.

Part IV
Making It Work: Moving Ahead

The 5th Wave   By Rich Tennant

"It's your wife Mr. Dinker. Shall I have her
take a seat in the closet, or do you want to
schedule a meeting in the kitchen for later
this afternoon?"

In this part . . .

Having an office in your home creates both opportunities and problems. While you may long to have an office in your home, your loved ones may not share your enthusiasm. In this part, we discuss the importance of having the right attitude in your business and coexisting peacefully with those who share your home with you. We wrap up this Part with a look at how to grow your business.

Chapter 14

Staying on Track with a Serious Business Attitude

In This Chapter

▶ Having a serious business attitude

▶ Keeping your work life and personal life separate

▶ Avoiding interruptions and distractions

▶ Creating positive work routines

▶ Getting organized

Many people talk about their dreams of starting and running their own businesses, but relatively few actually do it — and even fewer start businesses that turn out to be successful for the long haul. What makes the difference between those who succeed and those who don't? In many cases, it's all about attitude.

How important is it to be serious about your business? Incredibly important. Why? There are two main reasons, both of which involve perception, and they both have a way of becoming self-fulfilling prophecies:

- ✔ **If you're not serious about your business, you probably won't put your all into making it a success.** You won't be able to imagine that your modest little enterprise will ever have the potential to provide you and your family with a livable wage or that it can provide you with an alternative to the regular 9-to-5 job you may have faced your entire working life.

- ✔ **If you're not serious about your business, no one else will be either.** Why should your potential clients and customers take your business seriously if you don't? The answer to that question is easy: They shouldn't. And if your potential clients and customers don't take your business seriously, you have no business at all.

In this chapter, we examine exactly what having a serious business attitude is all about — and why it's so important. We also discuss how to keep your work life and personal life separate, at least enough to get some work done!

We assess two of the most common problems facing home-based business-people — interruptions and distractions — and provide you with a variety of tips to help you beat them. Finally, we consider the importance of developing regular work routines, as well as the whys and hows of getting organized.

It All Begins with a Serious Business Attitude

Most successful businesses are successful in part because the people who own and run them are serious about doing business. Employees and customers may have fun, but make no mistake about it: Businesses have products and services to sell and money to make. If you don't sell your products and services, and you don't make money, you don't have a business — it's just that simple.

Your home-based business is no different from any other business. Most likely, you originally chose to start it because you were looking for something that working for someone else couldn't provide. Maybe it was freedom, autonomy, control, flexibility, money, or any number of other reasons. A home-based business, though, is a business first and foremost, and if you hope to be successful (and we're sure you do), you have to treat it like a serious business.

This means your business is not:

- A hobby
- Something you do just every once in a while
- Merely a tax shelter
- A get-rich-quick scheme
- A lark

It's fine to have fun in your business — in fact, you should — but don't forget that your home-based business can be your ticket for leaving the rat race behind once and for all. Many successful home-based business owners have done just that. You can, too.

It's what's inside that counts

Starting your own business can cause nervousness and trepidation. If you've always worked for someone else, the thought of working for yourself can truly feel like a step into the great unknown. And in many ways, you are braving an unknown world: Will customers buy your products? Will you be able to make enough money to support your family? Will you be able to get health insurance? What happens if a competitor tries to steal away all your business?

Having a serious business attitude starts on the inside. It starts with being knowledgeable about your services and products, and having the confidence that comes with that knowledge. Above all, it starts with a decision: that your dream of starting your own home-based business is no longer going to be just a dream, but a reality. Here are some of the things that come from inside you that can make building a home-based business a successful proposition:

- ✔ **Have confidence.** Confidence — or the lack thereof — can make all the difference in the world when starting and growing your own business. When you're confident, you feel as if you can overcome any hurdle that's put in your way. And you know what? You probably can!

- ✔ **Keep a positive attitude.** Most successful entrepreneurs tend to be optimistic about themselves, their businesses, and the future. They see the glass as half full rather than half empty. A positive attitude can take you far in this world, both in business and in your personal life.

- ✔ **Expect the best from yourself and others.** Set your standards high, and refuse to settle for less. The quality of your products and services begins — and ends — with you.

- ✔ **Care about your customers.** Whom would you rather do business with: someone who really cares about you and who takes the time to show it or someone who doesn't? If you take care of your customers and clients, they'll take care of you.

- ✔ **Make the decision.** Plant your foot firmly on the other side of the fence, and make the decision once and for all to turn your home-based business dream into reality. Quit talking about it; just do it!

Take the time to build your serious business attitude from the inside out. If you already have all the self-confidence and positive attitude in the world, that's great — you've got a big head start toward business success!

If, however, you still have some way to go, don't be afraid to work into your business slowly, one step at a time. Instead of leaving your regular job to start your own business, consider starting your home-based business while still working your regular job. Not only will this take much of the pressure off you to create an immediately successful enterprise — boosting your self-confidence in the process — but it will also give you the time you need to really get to know your products and services and to network with potential customers and clients.

Creating an identity

One of the first things most home-based businesspeople do is to order business cards and stationery for their new home-based businesses. That raises a question: Should you develop a logo design to represent your business while you're at it?

If you're serious about building your business and committing to it for the long haul (and we're sure you are), you need to create an identity that will help your business stand out in the crowded marketplace. And although you may be able to create a logo yourself, it's probably a better idea to hire a professional graphic artist to develop a logo for your business. Your logo will be used for a variety of purposes, including business cards, stationery, your Web site, advertising and promotional materials, brochures, reports, and more.

Your graphic artist may present you with a wide variety of options and alternatives. Remember that the logo design you select for your home-based business should be:

✔ **Simple.** A logo design should never be so complex that it becomes confusing. In the case of logos, simpler usually means better. Think McDonald's golden arches, AT&T's globe, or Nike's swoosh.

✔ **Unique and recognizable.** Take a look at the cover of this book. What do you see? The Dummies Man — the mascot in the Dummies Press logo — is at once unique and recognizable. After you've seen him on a ...*For Dummies* book, you'll always associate his face with this brand, no matter which book it is.

✔ **Compatible with your business's image.** Is your business conservative, such as a management consulting or investment firm? Then you want to have a conservative logo that reflects the rock-solid image you want your firm to project. But if your firm is dynamic, exciting, and takes chances, your logo should, too!

Keep in mind that other things help create an identity for your business besides a logo: the way you answer your phone, the color and type of paper that you use in customer correspondence, the design of your Web site, the friendliness with which you handle customer problems, even the message you leave on your answering machine or voice mail . . . all build the image that people have of your business and, therefore, its identity in the marketplace.

Take the time to step outside your business from time to time to experience what your customers and clients experience. Are you happy with what you see? If not, what can you do to improve your business's identity and image?

What's outside counts, too

Of course, though we all know you can't tell a book by its cover, that doesn't stop people from making judgments about you and your business based on what they see on the outside. People make superficial assessments all the time. Whether their ultimate judgments are right or wrong, these judgments can mean the difference between getting new customers or clients and losing them.

So what's outside really does count. Here are some ways to make sure that what's outside (and easily seen) reflects what's inside (and not so easily seen):

- ✔ **Create a top-notch Web presence.** The days of being able to get away with an amateurish-looking, clunky site are gone. Invest some money in building a top-notch Web site that absolutely exudes quality and experience. The good news is that many Web hosting services now offer inexpensive and easy-to-use templates that instantly give your business a professional look.

- ✔ **Create a custom logo, stationery, business cards, and promotional materials.** If it's good enough for a multibillion-dollar corporation, it's good enough for you. The money you invest in making your business look more professional will pay off many times over in the number and quality of clients that you attract.

  The quality of the paper and other materials you deliver to your client says a lot about the quality of your work and the importance you place on delivering a quality product. What does the paper you use say about you and your business?

- ✔ **Incorporate.** Those three little letters — *Inc.* — say something about your business. They say that you're established, that you're serious, and that you're in it for the long haul. Not a bad impression to leave with your potential customers. (See Chapter 10 for more information on incorporating your business.)

- ✔ **Dress for success.** As a general rule, you should always dress one level higher than the client you're meeting with. If your client is dressed casually, you should have a jacket and tie (for men) or a dress (for women). If your client goes for jacket and tie, wear a suit. Of course, if you're at home — and there's no chance a client will be popping by unannounced — you can wear whatever makes you comfortable.

- ✔ **Get a dedicated phone line.** There's nothing that screams "unprofessional!" louder than a five-year-old answering a client's call. You'll make a much better impression by having a dedicated phone line for your business, hooked up to a dedicated answering machine or voice-mail system.

Make sure that the message you project on the outside reflects the high level of quality and commitment to your customers that you hold so dear inside.

Serious doesn't mean you can't do it your way

Some of the most liberating things about having your own business are that you get to decide when and where you're going to work, what work you're going to do, and whom you're going to do it for. Here are some statistics on the different approaches people working at home are taking to doing things their way:

✔ Fewer than 10 percent work a traditional, 9-to-5 schedule.

✔ Eighty-one percent dress casually (6.5 percent don't wear anything at all!).

✔ Half don't wear shoes while they work.

✔ Eleven percent wear formal business attire.

✔ Sixty percent play music while working.

Separating Your Work from Your Personal Life

Although being closer to those you love (even if it's just your goldfish) is one of the big attractions to working at home, you will clearly have times when you have to draw a line between your home life and your work life. By taking the time to anticipate this requirement up front, you can make the transition to your own home-based business smoother — not just for you, but for your clients, customers, family, and friends as well.

You can use a number of barriers to separate the business and personal sides of your life. Here are some of the most important ones for you to consider:

✔ **Use a separate room.** Having a room apart from the hustle and bustle of your regular home life — one that is dedicated *exclusively* to your business — is the first step in making your home office into a real office.

✔ **Set a work schedule.** When you own your own business, you can work whenever you like. You may find it easier (and more productive), however, to establish a regular work schedule. That way, those around you know when it's okay to interrupt you and when it's clearly not okay.

✔ **Have a separate entrance.** Should your clients really have to pass through a gauntlet of toys, cereal bowls, and cranky children (or spouses!) to get to your office? A separate entrance helps keep your work life separate from your home life. Many home-based business-people may not currently have this luxury, but it's something to think about if you have the opportunity to build, buy, or rent a new house in the future. If not, you always have the option of meeting your clients at a convenient off-site location such as your local Starbucks or favorite lunch spot.

✔ **Get help!** Instead of trying to juggle your obligations at home while trying to keep up with your work obligations, consider getting the help you need to allow you to focus exclusively on your work when you need to do just that. You could, for example, hire a housekeeper to clean your home and relieve you of that burden. Or you could hire a babysitter to come into your home to watch your young children. Or you may be able to get your spouse or a relative or friend to help cover for you. The main thing to keep in mind is that you do have alternatives available to you if you feel overwhelmed.

Keep in mind that the degree to which you separate your work and personal lives is totally up to you. The good news is that you can be far more flexible than you ever could be working for someone else. You can strengthen the separation when you're under the gun at work and loosen up when things are a bit more relaxed. In this way, you really can enjoy the best of both worlds, where you're able to do the work you love in the place you most want to be — your own home.

Getting off the preschool bus route

Q: Once when my neighbor was in a jam, I offered to pick up her son from preschool. She has since asked me to repeat this favor several times. How can I explain to her, without damaging our friendly relationship, that just because I'm working at home doesn't mean I'm not working as hard as her corporate acquaintances?

A: You don't need to explain. The way to let her know that you're working as hard as corporate acquaintances is to tell her that even though you'd like to help, you can't pick up her son because you're working. Be warm. Be sincere.

But be clear and definite that your business is such now that you can no longer take time off during working hours. She will probably be disappointed, as she has come to rely on you. But if you want her to take you off her emergency help list, you may need to reinforce your message several times, repeating that you're sorry and wish you could help, but because of your work, you simply can't. She may call you several more times, just to be sure. But if you continue to be clear that you'd like to help but can't, she'll eventually get the idea and find new resources.

Avoiding Interruptions and Distractions

Every job has its interruptions and distractions. When you're in a regular office, you may have a coworker who drops in on you regularly to unload his or her latest thoughts about your company's management team. Or you may have a boss who is so busy assigning you new tasks that you never seem to be able to get around to the old ones.

Without a doubt, however, working at home offers its own unique set of interruptions and distractions. From television soap operas to rambunctious kids to your neighbor's ear-splitting leaf blower — almost an unlimited number of interruptions and distractions are waiting to take you away from your work. Your job is to find ways to ignore them or to avoid them altogether.

Dealing with interruptions

You can't always prevent interruptions, but you can do things to remove them after they occur and then get back on track and back to work. Here are some ways to deal with interruptions:

 ✔ **Focus on your goals and priorities.** Although you may not be able to keep from being thrown off track when an interruption occurs, you should be able to quickly return your focus to the goals and priorities at hand. How? By resolving the interruption as quickly as possible and then refocusing your full attention on your work.

 ✔ **Be kind, but firm.** The wrong way to deal with interruptions is to get mad at the person who is interrupting you. The right way is to firmly explain, in a loving and supportive way, that the interruptions will have to stop while you're working. Kids especially need this kind of caring treatment. They probably aren't aware that they're interrupting your work; they simply want a chance to spend some time with you.

 ✔ **Take action.** Don't try to simply ignore interruptions — chances are they won't go away, no matter how little attention you pay them. In fact, by not taking action, you're sending the person doing the interrupting the message that it's okay to interrupt you — or even that you actually welcome it — all the while building resentment within yourself.

 ✔ **Stay loose.** No matter what you do, someone, somewhere, will interrupt you. The key is to stay loose and not let the interruption totally destroy your ability to jump right back onto task. Learn to be flexible, and find ways to get back on task quickly.

With a bit of practice, you'll soon be able to deal with your interruptions like a pro, and you'll find that you can take charge of them instead of letting them take charge of you.

Is TV the problem or the symptom?

Q: I am often tempted to watch TV during work hours. At first, I set a rule that I would watch for only one hour during my lunch break; however, I sometimes have gotten sucked into a show and watched longer than I should have. Then I rationalize by saying I'll work longer hours. Sometimes I'll have the TV on in the background and then press the mute button when I get an outside call. Do you have any suggestions on how I can break this bad habit?

A: Take the television out of your office. Watching TV is one of the top five home-office bad habits. Get a VCR (or, even better, a digital video recorder such as Tivo) if you don't have one, and tape your favorite daytime shows. If you don't like a show well enough to watch it after work hours, something must be missing from your workday. Find out what it is, and replace your bad habit with new, more appealing habits that serve you better. For example:

✔ **Are you bored with your work?** What has happened that watching daytime TV is more interesting to you than the work you do? There will always be a few tasks in any business that are so mindless, you may as well be watching TV while you're doing them, but you're in the wrong business if that's how

you feel about most of your workday. Has your business lost its magic — or never had it? How could you make what you do more exciting and challenging? What attracted you to go out on your own in the first place? What do you like best about your work? What could you do more of in your work that would make you forget all about watching TV?

✔ **Do you miss the social interaction of an office setting?** Arrange to have more contact with people you enjoy. Call up a colleague. Get active in a local business or professional organization. Join an Internet newsgroup. Sign up for a class or ongoing social activity you enjoy.

✔ **Are you stressed out and working too hard?** Give yourself something else to look forward to, such as planning an exciting evening for when you've finished working. Or replace your bad habit with a better one. Many home-business owners, for example, enjoy listening to talk radio or music while they work. Others walk in nature over the lunch hour or take an exercise break like running, biking, or taking an aerobics class. What would you enjoy most?

Dealing with distractions

Interruptions generally occur when people take you away from your work — by walking into your office and demanding your immediate attention or calling you on the phone and talking your ear off for half an hour. Distractions are often more subtle. For home-based businesspeople, common distractions include the Internet, a favorite soap opera broadcast for an hour every day, or a refrigerator down the hall that's full of goodies.

Here are some ways for dealing with distractions:

- ✔ **Remove the sources of distraction.** Is that television on your file cabinet begging you to turn it on? Does that America Online chat room have your name on it? Are you spending more time looking through your magazines than producing billable work? One of the best ways to avoid distractions is to remove their source. Turn them off, throw them out, or move them to another room. If the Internet or e-mail is a problem, set definite times — perhaps during lunch or maybe no more than five minutes every hour — during which you allow yourself to spend time on those activities.

- ✔ **Avoid procrastination.** Putting work off until later, sometimes much later, is a powerful enemy of the home-based businessperson. And it's an enemy that you must defeat in the short run if you hope to be successful in the long run.

- ✔ **Reward yourself for achieving your goals.** Don't forget to give yourself some sort of reward for accomplishing a significant task or achieving an important milestone. Take a day off. Meet your significant other for a long lunch. Go shopping. Go for a bike ride with your kids. Whatever makes you feel good. Not only will these rewards make you feel better, but they'll also motivate you to stay focused on your work while tuning out distractions.

- ✔ **Schedule (and take!) regular breaks.** Do you find yourself fidgeting or unable to stay focused on your work? Take a short break from your work. Forward your calls to voice mail, and get out of your office. You can relax and take your mind on a brief vacation by going for a brisk walk outside or enjoying a cup of coffee or tea on your back porch. And don't leave taking breaks to chance; schedule regular breaks into your daily work plan.

You can control the effect of distractions on you and your business by taking action to remove their source and by providing sufficient structure and motivation in your work. Don't let distractions get in the way of your doing the best job you can — and building the best business you can.

The last resort

Sometimes, despite all your efforts to deal with interruptions and distractions, they may get the best of you. Peter, for example, is usually able to keep his work separate from his very active kids, but occasionally, the thin line that divides them is broken. And more than once, Peter has thought about how nice it would be to rent an office in a small building down in the village — a place that would be a guaranteed refuge from the demands of three busy kids.

Resisting the call of the fridge

Q: I'm embarrassed to say that I've gained some weight since I began working at home. I think part of the problem is that I eat out of stress, and of course, the refrigerator is now just a few steps away from my desk. Do you have any suggestions for how I can moderate my eating habits?

A: You're not the only one to gain weight in the comforts of working from home. But although you have more access to excess at home, you also have more control over what you do and how you do it.

The best way to beat this problem is to find new ways to de-stress: Take a walk, call a friend, or lean back and listen quietly to some of your favorite music. Thinking of something, anything other than food will help you relax. It may take a while to find what will satisfy you more than food, but on the way to the kitchen, take a deep breath, and think of what else you may enjoy at that particular moment.

Also, stock your refrigerator and kitchen cabinets with lots of low-calorie, low-fat, healthy-but-filling foods that don't make you want to eat until the bag is empty, the way that chips and cookies do. Apples or rice cakes are good examples. We find that eating small, balanced snacks can also help keep snacking within bounds. For example, you might have half an apple with an ounce of cheese and a couple of almonds or a teaspoon of almond butter. Alternatively, you can remove the incentive to visit the kitchen between meals by keeping the beverages of your choice in your office. Consider picking up one of those mini shelf-top refrigerators if you like cold drinks.

Be aware, too, that evidence is beginning to show that one's blood type makes some foods fattening for one person that are not fattening for someone else. If you'd like to check this out, see the book *Eat Right for Your Type,* by Dr. Peter J. D'Adamo, or check out his Web site at www.dadamo.com. Following his guidelines, if you do snack, you shouldn't put on pounds.

But that thought passes quickly (when he remembers just how much he would have to pay each month in rent), and Peter again remembers all the advantages of having an office in his home. When interruptions and distractions get the best of you, you'll certainly do whatever you can to resolve them. But what happens when you can't resolve your interruptions and distractions and they actually begin to threaten your ability to get any work done at all?

It may be time to take drastic action. Here are a number of different ways that you can really shake things up and get back on track:

> ✔ **Change your schedule.** Work when your chances of being interrupted or distracted are minimized. If you can't seem to avoid being distracted by your noisy roommates who party late into the night, do your work in the morning and afternoon — well before the partying is set to begin.

✔ **Learn to live with it.** Of course, this is easier said than done, but perhaps you can learn to live with the distractions — accepting them, but tuning them out and ultimately ignoring them.

✔ **Move your work.** Sometimes a temporary change of scenery can do wonders for your concentration, especially when the source of distraction or interruption is a short-term one. Try out an outside deck or even a local café, library, or park. With a cell phone and a laptop computer, you can take your work wherever you want, most any time you want.

✔ **Move your office.** If you have a long-term, ongoing problem with distractions and interruptions, and it doesn't appear that you can solve the problem with a temporary change of scenery, consider moving your office altogether. At a minimum, choose a different room or other location within your home. In a worst-case scenario, you may need to move your office out of your home and into a regular, leased office space.

Don't let interruptions and distractions get in the way of your success. If you're serious about your home-based business and about the potential for succeeding at it (and we're sure you are!), take action before things get so bad that your business suffers irreparable harm.

Routines Rule

Routines are a part of life. They help you stay focused on the things that are most important. They provide the structure and continuity that you — and your clients and customers — rely on to do business efficiently and effectively. Routines are a good thing.

Of course, some routines are better than others. Here are some tips for establishing the right kinds of routines — the kinds that can bring you success rather than failure:

✔ **Establish a regular work schedule.** Maintain regular business hours just as you would working for a regular business. It doesn't matter if you decide to work from 9 to 5 or from 5 to 9, so long as your schedule meets your needs and the needs of your clients and customers. As the owner of your own business, you get to decide!

✔ **Take plenty of short breaks.** When you work in a regular business, you have lots of opportunities to take breaks from your routine. A phone call from a friend, a visit from a vendor, a lunch break with your associates, or a quick walk to a nearby deli — all offer a break from the routine. When you work at home, such breaks are much fewer and farther between, and you have to make a point of taking them.

ASK PAUL & SARAH

Missing the hustle and bustle

Q: I know home-based business owners often complain about noise distracting them, but my problem is the opposite: Sometimes it gets so quiet in my home office that it unsettles me. Do you have any suggestions for creating a little bit of good old-fashioned "office noise"?

A: You're not the only one who doesn't work well in silence. This is undoubtedly why home-based business owners avidly listen to talk radio. Of course, background music helps many people stay productive, and rather than being a distraction, it can energize your brain and your work. We sometimes like to have Steven Halpern's album *Productivity* playing in the background while we work. It's available on both tape and CD (call 800-909-0707 or visit his Web site at www.innerpeacemusic.com). We set our stereo tape system on continuous play and get to work. Alternatively, you can listen to radio stations, music or talk, over the Internet. Check out the amazing array of listening options available to you at Launch (launch.yahoo.com).

We've also met people who spend part of their day working over lunch at a restaurant or coffeehouse. Others prefer to work on their corporate client's premises several days a week. When graphic designer Nancy Rabbit couldn't stand the sound of silence, she decided to expand her business by bringing several coworkers into her home.

We like the sound of water, so we keep a small fountain gurgling. While once fairly expensive, these are now quite reasonably priced.

As for "office noise," if that's what you miss, you can most likely find a client or colleague who will let you tape 10 or 15 minutes of office sounds on an endless-loop tape that you can then play in the background while your work. Or if you like the idea of creating your own soundtrack, you can find collections of sound clips on software. Try ClickArt by Broderbund (call 800-395-0277 or visit the Web site at www.broderbund.com), or have someone create one for you.

✔ **Schedule appointments for yourself, friends, and family.** The everyday events that take place in a typical business — home-based or not — can quickly fill up your schedule. While you may have planned to get out for a relaxing lunch with friends, go to the gym to work out, or attend your daughter's awards ceremony, you may find yourself glued to the phone or computer instead. Instead of "trying" to do the things you want to do, schedule firm appointments to do these things instead. Just as you would schedule an appointment to meet with a client, schedule an appointment to meet with your spouse over lunch or go for a walk.

✔ **Start your workday the same way every day.** Create a routine around starting your workday. For example, you may make a pot of coffee, check your e-mail and voice-mail messages, read *The Wall Street Journal,* and then begin making sales calls. You decide what to do in your routine; the point is to have a routine and to follow it.

> ✔ **End your workday the same way every day.** So many businesspeople complain about not having enough time to sit down and really think ahead and to plan, but few do anything about it. Here's your chance to do just that. At the end of your workday, take 15 minutes to go over what happened that day and then review your priorities and schedules for the next day. File away any papers that need filing, and straighten up your desk so that you come back to an organized workspace on your next day of work.

If you feel that your work life — and maybe even your personal life — is chaotic and out of control, perhaps you should step back for a moment and take a close look at how you run your life. Using the preceding list, create routines in your life that you can rely on day after day, week after week.

An Organized Home Office Is a Happy Home Office

Some people can have stacks and stacks of seemingly random pieces of paper all over their desks and around their offices and still be right on top of things. For many people, however, this would be a recipe for disaster. People are organizational creatures who are much more effective when work and tools are organized and easy to access.

Don't underestimate the power of organization. Being organized, efficient, and effective can mean the difference between being successful in your home-based business and being less than successful — perhaps far less. The following sections show you how.

Managing your office

So where should you start in your efforts to get your work life organized? We start with the one place where you probably spend more time while you're working than any other place: your home office!

> ✔ **Clean up your desk.** Yikes! What's that mess on your desk? The busier you get, the less time you have to clean up the paper, the old coffee cups, the pencils and pens, the Post-its, the cell phone, the sunglasses, and all the other things that accumulate on your desk. The trouble with that is that the more stuff that accumulates, the harder it is for you to do

your job. Not only do you have less space in which to work, but things also mysteriously begin to disappear. That phone number for a prospective client whom you need to call in a few minutes — gone. That report you just saw a few minutes ago — where did it go? Begin your office organizing efforts with the place that you spend most of your working hours: your desk. After you have your desk under control, you can move on to other areas.

✔ **Clean up your office.** After your desk is a model of organization, turn your attention to the rest of your office. What's that pile of paper in the corner? File it or pitch it! And those boxes stacked over in the other corner? How about moving them into your basement or garage? Or straight into the recycling bin? An organized office is so much easier to get around in, and you have far less chance of losing something important in your daily shuffle.

✔ **Revisit your office layout.** After you've had a chance to get settled into your newly cleaned-up office, take some time to assess whether it's really set up as effectively as it could be. Is the file cabinet in a convenient place? How about your fax machine or your paper supply? Periodically revisit your office layout to make sure it's working for you, and don't be afraid to make adjustments as you need to.

✔ **Buy an appointment calendar, daily planner, or electronic organizer, and use it.** Organizers and planners — whether electronic or paper based — can be effective tools for keeping your life organized. It's not important what kind of organizer you use; the best organizer is the one that you use.

✔ **Schedule regular office-organizing sessions.** Avoid the temptation to organize your office once and then forget about it. If you do that, you'll soon find yourself up to your ears in paperwork, products, faxes, and whatever else wanders through your door. Make a regular habit of keeping your office organized and clean.

✔ **Work as paperlessly as possible.** Do you really need to print out a copy of every single document that you create on your computer or every Web page that you visit? Probably not. If you're like us, you've grown up with lots of paper in your life, and you may be comforted by having lots of paper all around you. We believe that most of the documents you create can be stored more efficiently on your computer. And if you use your computer as a fax machine, you can store all your incoming faxes on your computer, too.

✔ **Do it now!** You've read about what to do to organize and manage your office. You know what you need to do. Now you just have to do it!

Managing your time

You still only get 24 hours in a day; no one has yet been able to figure out how to make any more than that (if they do, we'll be first in line for our share). Given that you have a finite number of hours in which to get your work done, the secret to getting the most out of each and every workday is to manage your time.

Time management is a topic familiar to most in business. Done right, time management can indeed be an effective technique for focusing on what really needs to be done while removing the clutter and distractions that may get in the way of achieving your goals.

Here are some tips for managing your time:

✔ **Get organized!** There's nothing that slows you down faster than having to wade through a messy desk or office searching for a missing address, phone number, or report. Take time to get and stay organized. After you do, the amount of time you set aside to perform ongoing maintenance will be substantially reduced. (See the "Managing your office" section, earlier in this chapter.)

✔ **Review your priorities at the beginning of the day.** Each workday, before you do anything else (okay, go ahead and grab a cup of coffee first, if you like), review your priorities for the day to see what you need to work on right away.

✔ **Do your first priority first, and drop your last priority.** Instead of jumping to an easy, low-priority item on your list, always take on your first priority first. And instead of letting your lowest-priority items languish at the very bottom of your list — never to be acted on — drop the lowest one from your list. Chances are you'll never miss it. (See the "What's a priority and what's not?" section, later in this chapter, for more tips on establishing priorities.)

✔ **Lose your junk mail (and junk e-mail).** Junk mail (and junk e-mail, also known as *spam*) is an incredible time-waster. Whenever you find it in your mailbox, don't pass Go, don't collect $200 — simply pitch it into the trash can or recycling bin. And as for junk e-mail, use your e-mail program to filter out messages from junk senders before you even see them. Out of sight, out of mind. One more thing: Be careful about giving your e-mail address to people and Web-site operators who may just turn around and sell it to the highest bidder. You may want to create a free Web-based e-mail address for just such use while keeping your real address more private.

✔ **Get a faster computer.** How much time have you spent watching that little hourglass mouse pointer while the machine crunches a big chunk of information or waiting for your ancient modem to download a Web page from the Internet? If you still have a slow computer and modem, all the time you spend waiting could easily add up to several hours every month. This is time down the drain. Do yourself (and your customers and clients) a favor, and get a faster computer and modem. Buy the fastest computer you can afford, and be sure to get plenty of RAM while you're at it — this will ensure that your computer can work at its fastest. And if DSL or cable modems are available in your location, spend the extra money to sign up. You'll more than make up the extra cost in greatly improved productivity and effectiveness.

For more detailed information on time management and ways to take advantage of every minute of every day, check out *Time Management For Dummies,* by Jeffrey Mayer (Wiley).

What's a priority and what's not?

Priorities can — and should — have a significant impact on what work you decide to do and when you decide to do it. Most people think they know what's most important in their businesses, but many don't follow through on this knowledge and instead let trivial events and distractions rule their schedules.

Here are two ways to separate your real priorities from the wannabes. Ask yourself:

✔ **What's the impact to your firm's bottom line?** Everyone has reasons for being in business for themselves, but one of the main reasons for creating a business is to make money, pure and simple. Sure, you want to do fulfilling work that taps your creativity, but if it doesn't pay the bills, you won't be doing it for long. What kind of impact will the action have on your bottom line — will it reduce your expenses or increase your revenues? The greater the impact on improving your bottom line — your profitability — the higher it should rate on your list of priorities. If an action has little or no impact on your bottom line, give higher priority to other actions that do have such an impact.

✔ **Is the action in response to a client emergency?** Another reason that many people start their own businesses is to solve their client's problems and to provide them with solutions. Because clients in many ways are the heart and soul of any business, solving their problems is clearly a priority. And when your clients have an emergency, the actions you need to take to solve them should be top priorities for you.

It all comes down to doing first things first: consciously identifying a business's highest priority actions and then taking a single-minded approach to tackling them. This may mean ignoring the calls of a salesperson, forwarding your phone to voice mail for a day, or even throwing your priority list into a drawer and working only on your number-one priority until it's done. The good news is that prioritizing gets easier with experience.

Don't forget, you hold the key. It's up to *you* to decide what's most important to your business and then to act on it. You're the boss now; no one else is going to decide for you.

Chapter 15

Coexisting with Kids, Relatives, Neighbors, and Pets

*W*ould it surprise you to learn that many of today's most successful companies started out as home-based businesses? It's true. Global computer and electronics powerhouse Hewlett-Packard was started by cofounders Bill Hewlett and Dave Packard in a garage behind Dave's house in Palo Alto, California. Apple Computer — which today pulls down annual revenues in excess of $6 billion — was cofounded by Steve Jobs and Steven Wozniak in Jobs's parents' garage.

The number of home-based businesses is growing. In 1997, Dunn and Bradstreet found that 38 percent of all businesses were based at home. By 2002, the percentage grew to 53 percent, the same percentage given out by the Small Business Administration. The Gallup Organization has found that 7 of every 10 (71 percent) businesses started from scratch were based in the home. Who knows — maybe your home-based business will be the next big business success story.

Of course, nobody said having your own business at home was easy. Indeed, when you run a business at home, you face a variety of challenges rarely encountered by people who work in a regular office.

When you're at home, you're accessible. The boundaries that would typically separate your work life from your personal life in a regular job don't exist. Although one of the greatest rewards that home-based business owners get from working at home is being closer to family and friends, this closeness can also be a huge liability if it isn't controlled. It can be a big enough challenge keeping your focus on your work instead of on the many distractions all around your home office. Add to that the stress of juggling a house full of active kids and visiting friends, neighbors, and relatives. Believe us — it can be a real challenge.

In this chapter, we take a look at the issue of coexisting peacefully with those likely to be in or around your home-based business. We give you some idea of what to expect and suggest solutions to common dilemmas. We discuss the importance of setting aside time for yourself. Finally, we take a close look at one of the most fulfilling ways to work at home: working with a spouse or significant other.

Some home-based business owners find that they miss not having an office full of coworkers swirling around them every minute of the workday. Others find that it's not easy keeping their personal lives, kids, and significant others separate from their business lives when they need to. (What do you do when you're with an important client on the phone, and you hear a loud knock on your front door — or your 4-year-old screaming in the backyard?) And some have no difficulty at all making the transition to a home-based business; in fact, they soon realize that their newfound freedom and the control they now wield over their work and personal lives are things that they should have made happen sooner.

If there's anything we have learned as home-based business owners ourselves, and from the hundreds of home-based business owners we've met and interviewed over the years, it's this: You can expect the unexpected!

What to Expect from Your Kids

If you have kids, you know there's nothing they like more than attention, and the less they get, the more they want. And you know what? They really deserve the attention they seek. It's natural that they want to spend time with you, to play and experience the reassuring security of knowing that you're there. The problem is that kids never really seem to get *enough* attention, and you *do* have to work every once in a while if you hope to make a go of your new enterprise.

If you have kids and decide to start a home-based business, inevitably you'll have competition between the time that you need to devote to your business to make it a success and the demands of your children. The decisions you make early on in dealing with this natural conflict can have a dramatic impact both on the ultimate success of your business and on your relationship with your children.

Finding good child care

Many owners of home-based businesses find that the best way to get quality work done while ensuring their children are well cared for is the same way many regular workers and employees already use: child care outside the home. You won't find a shortage of child-care providers, but you may find a shortage of good ones. So how do you know if the child-care provider you've found is good or not? Here are five steps for choosing a good child-care provider, adapted from the National Association of Child Care Resource and Referral Agencies (NACCRRA) Web site at www.naccrra.net:

✔ **Look.** Begin by visiting several child-care homes or centers. On each visit, think about your first impression, but don't stop there. Does it look safe for your child? Do the caregivers enjoy talking and playing with children? Do they talk with each child at the child's eye level? Are plenty of toys and learning materials within a child's reach? Always visit a home or center more than once, and continue to come back and check it out. Unannounced visits may give you a more candid view of what's really going on at the home or center than if you call ahead or announce your visit ahead of time.

✔ **Listen.** What does the child-care setting sound like? Do the children sound happy and involved? What about the teachers' voices? Do they seem cheerful and patient? A place that's too quiet may mean not enough activity; too noisy may mean a lack of control. If you have the opportunity to meet other parents during your visit, ask about their own experiences, and listen closely to what they have to say.

✔ **Count.** Count the number of children in the group and then count the number of staff members caring for them. The fewer children per adult, the more attention your child will get (and, therefore, the greater the opportunity for meaningful play and learning). A small number of children per adult is particularly important for babies and younger children. Older children are naturally more independent and self-directed but still benefit from interaction with care providers.

✔ **Ask.** It's important that the adults who care for your children have the knowledge and experience to give them the attention they need. Ask about the backgrounds and experience of all staff: the program director, caregivers, teachers, and any other adults who will have contact with your child in the home or center. Find out about the special training that each one has and whether the program is accredited by the National Association for the Education of Young Children (NAEYC) or the National Association for Family Child Care (NAFCC). Quality care providers and teachers will be happy to have you ask these questions. At a minimum, your care providers should have Red Cross training in first aid and CPR in the event of an accident or medical emergency.

✔ **Be informed.** Find out more about efforts in your community to improve the quality of child care. Is your caregiver involved in these activities? How can you get involved? Does your community require child-care providers to be licensed, and are certain minimum standards required to be maintained? If so, is your provider licensed, and are the standards adhered to? Be knowledgeable about legal requirements for caregivers in your community, and ensure that the people to whom you entrust your children are following the rules.

Kids do eventually grow up, and as you may be surprised to find out, you will someday be working away for hours at a time without interruption (an event that Peter can only dream about right now). Until that day arrives, however, try these suggestions:

- ✔ **Keep them busy.** If you're going to let your kids hang out with you in the office, set them up with things to do: an easel for painting, lots of crayons, paper, glue, scissors, or whatever else keeps them busy and creative. Here's a tip, though: Make sure that whatever you give them to keep them busy does not require your constant intervention or attention. Avoid anything that may result in a big, sloppy mess.

- ✔ **Involve them in simple work tasks.** Nothing is more boring for most adults than folding letters or brochures and stuffing and stamping envelopes. Guess what? Your kids probably won't find those things boring at all. Not only will they enjoy helping you, but they will also feel that they are doing something important and worthwhile. And, of course, they are.

- ✔ **Hire a nanny or sitter.** If you can't (or don't want to) juggle your kids and work simultaneously, by all means hire a nanny or a sitter to come keep your children occupied and out of your hair. You can have the best of both worlds: working at home while still having your kids nearby and accessible.

- ✔ **Work around their schedule.** Because you're the boss, you get to decide when you'll report to work (that alone is why many people long to start their own business). Why not set aside a certain time each day to take your kids to play in a park, go to a library, ride bikes, or simply go for a walk? If you want to stay accessible to your clients, just bring your mobile phone along.

- ✔ **Keep your office your office.** Although many people integrate their offices throughout their home, we believe your office should be your office. It should be the one place that, when you close the door, you're removed from the day-to-day distractions of friends and family. A closed door means others, including children, need to respect your privacy, peace, and quiet. You can decide to make your office off limits to your kids — and you may need to, depending on your particular situation. Just be sure your kids know that you're available in case of emergency, which includes emotional traumas when they're in dire need of a shoulder to cry on and a big hug!

Kids and home-based businesses aren't necessarily mutually exclusive. Coauthor Peter has proved this with three young, busy kids of his own. Involving your kids takes a bit of extra work and a lot of flexibility, but if you're really motivated, you really can have the best of both worlds.

What to Expect from Relatives, Friends, and Neighbors

As much as you think they should understand your new work status, chances are many of your relatives, friends, and neighbors *will never really get it.* Because you're at home all day — and how can you be at work if you're at home? — they may decide you're able to talk on the phone for hours on end, run errands, pick up their kids at school, or even babysit. Not only that, they may start bugging you about getting a "real" job — meaning one in an office building with a receptionist.

You can head off a lot of these misconceptions and problems by taking the following steps, and the sooner, the better:

- ✓ **Send out an announcement.** Create a postcard or e-mail message announcing your new business, and send it out to all your relatives, friends, neighbors, and business contacts. Include your business address, phone and fax numbers, Web-site URL, and e-mail address. This will go a long way in making your business seem more real — both for you and for your friends, relatives, neighbors, and clients.

- ✓ **Establish regular hours of business.** By establishing regular hours of business, you draw a line that tells others when you're available for socializing and when you aren't — just as the line is automatically drawn for those who work a regular job in a regular office. Not only does this help reinforce your own self-discipline, but it also sends a clear message spelling out exactly when you are available and when you're not.

- ✓ **Be firm, but polite.** Sure, your relatives, friends, and neighbors may want to pop in any time they like or to ask you to do favors while they are at work. Tell them firmly, but politely, that you won't be available while you're at work; you have to take care of your customers and clients first.

- ✓ **Hire them!** What's the old saying? If you can't beat them, join them! In this case, however, they can join you. You may find that hiring relatives, friends, and neighbors to help you in your business is a good way to make the time you spend with them more productive while enabling your business to grow and building stronger and deeper relationships — all at the same time.

Just as it will take some time for you to transition into the new culture and work habits that go along with owning a home-based business, so, too, will it take time for your relatives, friends, and neighbors to adjust to the change. It may take them longer, in fact, than it takes you. Throughout this transition, be firm, but be considerate of their feelings. Give them time; they'll come around.

What to Expect When Working with Pets

Pets can be great company for the home-based businessperson. Whether you have a dog or a cat — or some other fuzzy, furry, or slinky little creature (Peter's pet ball python, Poki, has been his constant companion in his home office for the past ten years) — you never have to worry about your pet gossiping behind your back, and you can be sure that his or her loyalty will be absolute and unquestioning. Pets can, however, be a problem for your home-based business. If your dog likes to bark at the most inopportune times, or if your cat enjoys nothing better than to jump onto your head while you're making phone calls to clients, you have to take action.

Here are a few tips for ensuring that your pets and your business can coexist peacefully:

✔ **Get a mellow pet to begin with.** Although you can never be sure what kind of pet you'll end up with when you get one that's young, you can be pretty sure what kind of pet you'll end up with if you get one that's already fully grown. Visit your local animal shelter, pound, or rescue center to find a pet that meets your needs. Low-maintenance pets such as fish, birds, reptiles, and large spiders and insects make perfect office companions.

✔ **Get an outside versus an inside pet.** If the idea of a dog or cat hanging out with you all day doesn't appeal to you, get a pet that likes to spend most of its days outside your home, rather than inside. Just be sure your outside pet doesn't spend all day barking or scratching your door to be let back in the house.

✔ **Have your pet properly trained.** If you do decide to get a puppy, train it properly early in its life. Although it's really not impossible to teach old dogs new tricks, it's certainly easier when they are young. A well-trained pet will make your life at home — and in your home-based business — much more enjoyable.

✔ **Give lots of praise.** Most pets want nothing more in the world than to please you, and they respond eagerly to positive reinforcement. Whenever your pets do what you want them to do, give them lots of praise and affection.

✔ **Be patient.** If things aren't going the way you hoped as quickly as you like, be patient, and don't give up. If you keep at it, chances are that your pet will come around to doing things the way you want.

Problems with pets

Q: My dog occasionally barks when I'm on important phone calls. What can I do to control this problem?

A: Boy, do we know this problem! We have a little barker lying at our feet right now. Here's what to do:

✔ Make sure the phone in your office has a mute button so that you can discipline your dog without interrupting your phone conversations.

✔ Train your dog not to bark, but keep in mind that this takes time and energy. If you're willing to make this investment, we suggest professional trainer Matthew Margolis's *The Ultimate Guide to Dog Training: How to Bring Out the Best in Your Pet,* coauthored with Mordecai Siegal. For more information about "Uncle Matty's" other books, videos, products, and services, call (800) 334-3647 or visit www.unclematty.com.

Alternatively, you can use a phone headset, such as the Jabra, produced by GN Netcom (www.gnnetcom.com, widely available at office supply retailers), which has a special microphone that filters out room noise.

✔ Ignore the barking. You say that your dog only barks occasionally. Unless it really drives you crazy, just relax on those occasions. And if the barking is quite audible, jokingly apologize to your caller for the enthusiasm of your home-office mascot.

Paul and Sarah are big believers in the sock method of training; it has worked wonders with their dog and has made sharing their workplace not only tolerable, but also enjoyable. Simply toss a pair of socks near the dog — you don't need to hit it — so that you startle it, interrupting the barking or other behavior you want to stop. Paul and Sarah have graduated from socks and use a small dog toy, which Billy picks up and plays with for a few minutes. They've stopped the annoying behavior, and Billy's happy, too.

Workaholics, Unite! (It's Time to Get a Life!)

Although work is fun, pays the bills, and can be one of the most fulfilling aspects of our lives, there can be too much of a good thing. Just as alcoholics are consumed by liquor, workaholics are consumed by their work — always focusing on getting more work done and meeting a never-ending succession of deadlines.

Sound familiar? In an article for an online magazine, here's how Peter described his own brush with workaholism during the time that he was transitioning from a regular career to having his own home-based business:

> *I became a workaholic, slogging through the standard eight hours a day plus an hour for lunch at my regular job and squeezing in my writing projects whenever and wherever I could. This meant stealing away with my laptop to a local coffeehouse for the previously mentioned lunch hour and firing up my home-office computer at about 9 p.m. — routinely hitting the keyboard until 2 or 3 in the morning. Day in and day out, week after week, month after month. Whenever a friend or coworker complained about working late the night before — until 9 or 9:30 — I'd wince, because that was when my second shift had only just begun.*

The trouble is, no matter how hard they work, workaholics never catch up with their work and never have a chance to take time off or to relax. In fact, just the thought of taking a day or two away from work is enough to make many workaholics break out in a cold sweat and start shaking.

"So what?", you may ask yourself. "Why is this a problem?" Workaholics jeopardize their physical and mental health by not taking time to relax fully from their work or to get the rest and sleep they need to recharge their batteries. They often fail to get the exercise they need to build a strong body and mind. Workaholics jeopardize their personal relationships with family and friends by putting their work before those they love. Finally, they also jeopardize their work relationships when they become unstable and unreliable because of overwork, delivering poor-quality or late products or services to their customers or clients. And guess what? That is a sure going-out-of-business plan.

Are you a workaholic? Are you sure? Here are some warning signs:

- ✔ Are you always working, even when you're not "at work"?
- ✔ Do you feel uncomfortable about the idea of taking time off or a vacation?
- ✔ When you do take a vacation, do you bring your cell phone, laptop computer, organizer, and other equipment with you to conduct business?
- ✔ Are the majority of your friends also your business associates?
- ✔ Do your friends and family complain that you never spend enough time with them?

Recognizing workaholic tendencies is the first step, but breaking the cycle of overwork can be difficult. If you are a workaholic, though, the state of your health and your relationships — both personal and business — may depend on it.

Here are a variety of tips for breaking the cycle of overwork and workaholism:

✔ **Schedule breaks, time off, and vacations.** Just as you schedule business appointments in your calendar, schedule vacations and regular breaks (15 minutes here and there throughout your workday) in your calendar as well. Making plans for taking time off of work will increase the probability that you'll actually follow through with them.

✔ **Get voice mail — and use it.** Don't leave your business phone on all the time. Set regular business hours and then forward your calls to voice mail outside those hours. When work is over for the day, *it's over.* Here's a tip: When you want to take a mini-vacation in the middle of your workday, set your phone so that it rings directly to voice mail. You can pick up the messages later, after you return from your "vacation."

✔ **Maintain an active social life.** There is life outside of work! Stay active socially, and build and maintain relationships with friends who have nothing to do with your work. Invite your neighbors over for impromptu parties; join a rock-and-roll band; become active in your community.

✔ **Engage in hobbies and other interests.** Many workaholics allow their personal interests and hobbies to go by the wayside as work overwhelms their every waking moment. This is a huge mistake but one that can be easily rectified. Revisit your hobbies and other interests, and take time to pursue them.

✔ **Hire an assistant or farm out tasks.** Sure, you can work every waking hour of every day, if that's what you want to do. But that's definitely *not* an effective approach to doing business. If you're so busy that you really don't have time to do anything else, hire someone to help you out. Try to find a stay-at-home mom or dad, or another home-based worker who is looking for some extra, part-time work. Get the word out through friends and family or through your children's school.

Teaming Up with a Spouse or Other Loved One

You can find countless examples of husbands, wives, siblings, and kids who have pulled together to build successful enterprises: the Wright Brothers of Dayton, Ohio (later of flying fame), and their bicycle shop; brothers Walt and Roy Disney, who founded the Walt Disney Company and built it into a global entertainment powerhouse; and International Fieldworks, Inc., a multimillion-dollar company that Barry Allen and Pauline Field created from their home that provides work for hundreds of others through project-management contracts. The list goes on and on.

For many home-based businesspeople, teaming up with a spouse, boyfriend, girlfriend, sibling, parent, son, or daughter may seem like the ultimate dream. And for many home-based businesspeople, this dream is a reality. After all, if working at home is the right answer for you, why not for those you really care about as well? But unfortunately, for others, teaming up can also turn into the very worst kind of nightmare — scary beyond all belief. The secret is knowing when to team up and when not to — and what to do when a good team goes bad.

In the sections that follow, we take a look at when to team up with people you care about; how to team up; and how to build a successful, long-term relationship — at work and away from the job.

Knowing when to team up

As in the rest of life, some times are better than others to team up with a significant other. You definitely do want to team up when doing so will create a positive experience for you, your partner, and your customers. You definitely don't want to team up when doing so will create a negative experience for any of you.

Here are some good times to team up:

- ✔ **When a significant other has common skills and interests.** If you decide to start a plumbing business in your home, and your spouse has solid bookkeeping skills that will help you better keep track of the financial end of your business, teaming up makes perfect sense.

- ✔ **When a significant other purchases a business opportunity or franchise.** What better time to team up than when a close friend or relative buys into a business opportunity or franchise? This assumes, of course, that the business opportunity or franchise is something that you want to do, too.

- ✔ **When a significant other can make a positive contribution to your business.** There will be times when a significant other is at the exact right time and place in his or her life to make a positive and substantial contribution to your business and to your customers and clients. This is definitely the time to team up, and it's a time when 1+1 can truly add up to more than 2.

- ✔ **When a significant other has a resource that you need.** What if you need a large amount of cash to get your business off the ground, and your significant other would like to help by providing you with a loan? Or what if he or she has a network of contacts that would be very beneficial for you to approach? Such resource synergies can make teaming up a very smart move.

✓ **When a significant other has more work than he or she can handle.** Nothing succeeds like success, as they say, and there may be times when a significant other is so successful that he or she needs help, and needs it fast. Teaming up can be a win–win in this kind of situation.

Not every business team or partnership is going to work. Working closely together — day after day — may bring out the worst in your partner, and you should always be ready to break up your team if necessary. *Do not* — we repeat, *do not* — allow a bad situation to become worse just because you are afraid to tell a friend or relative that your partnership is not working out. Always be honest — with yourself and with your partner. And never team up out of weakness or pity for a significant other who just can't seem to get his or her act together. Finding the right time to team up is a must if you want your business relationship to be successful over the long run.

Figuring out how to team up

How you team up with a significant other is just as important as — if not more important than — *when* you team up with them. Doing it the right way can help reinforce your relationships and increase the likelihood of your success. Doing it the wrong way can be a recipe for disaster — not only for your business, but for your relationships, too.

When teaming up with significant others, be sure to consider taking the following actions:

✓ **Define clear goals, and assign clear responsibilities.** Although you may have different approaches to getting there, you and your partner should agree on definite and clear goals and on who will be responsible for different jobs and tasks within the business. Confusion is not a good thing in business or in relationships; clarity is.

✓ **Get important agreements in writing.** Of course, you should be able to trust your significant others without question, but it is always better to get your important agreements in writing. Sometimes these agreements are incorporated into legally binding contracts. People forget; misunderstandings arise; relationships are broken. Why rely on your memory when a piece of paper will perform the same function without fail?

✓ **Encourage each other to communicate openly.** Communication is incredibly important to the success of a business, and it's equally important that you and your partner communicate openly and honestly with each other about all aspects of your relationship and your business. Always be up front and open with your business partners, no matter who they are or how closely you are related.

✔ **Treat each other with respect.** You treat your clients and customers with respect, and you should treat your partner with respect, too. If you don't respect partners enough to treat them like you do, don't team up with them in the first place — and you may want to reconsider your entire relationship.

✔ **Take a break from each other whenever necessary.** People get on each other's nerves from time to time, no matter how good the relationship is. Rather than getting mad or stewing on it, take a break from each other for a while. This gives you both time to get over whatever issue is bugging you and to remember what it is that drew you together in the first place.

If you do it right, teaming up with a significant other can strengthen and deepen your personal relationship. Work hard on bringing out the best in both of you instead of the worst. For more information on collaborating with others, see Paul and Sarah's book *Teaming Up: The Small Business Guide to Collaborating with Others* (co-authored by Rick Benzel).

Working at home with a baby

Q: Though I've just had a baby, I obviously can't take maternity leave from my home-based business. How do I balance the needs of my business and my clients with a demanding newborn, each of which take an incredible amount of time?

A: Get help. Most women home-business owners take some type of maternity leave. They stagger contracts or clients so they have a one- or two-month break, hire temporary or part-time personnel, or subcontract work to colleagues for a period of time. Get help caring for your baby, get help running the business, or arrange for some combination of the two. Begin by deciding what kind of assistance will be most helpful. Ask yourself the following:

✔ How much time during each day do you want to devote entirely to your baby?

✔ What aspects of your baby's care could you use help with? What do you want to do yourself?

✔ Which business tasks are the most burdensome right now? Which demand your full attention without interruption?

✔ Which tasks must you do? Which can others do?

By working from home, you have many more options for tailoring child-care arrangements to your particular needs. For help with your newborn, for example, you can hire a nanny to come to your home for a few hours each day while you work. We hired an elderly woman to help us when our son was an infant. Alternatively, you may be able to line up help from family or friends, or exchange babysitting hours with other new mothers. When you feel comfortable taking the baby out, you can place him or her in a nearby family day-care home for several hours a day.

Sometimes new fathers can take paternity leave. Having Dad at home, even part-time, can be a big help. Mom and Dad can care for the baby in shifts, and Dad can help answer the business phone and do other business-related tasks. Taking simple steps, such as getting a voice-mail service or hiring an answering service to take your calls, can free you to better concentrate on both family and business matters. Hooking up a baby monitor between your baby's room and your office may also help.

Set up a schedule that suits both your needs as a new mother and your work habits. For some people, this means working only mornings, afternoons, or evenings. For others, it involves fitting work around the baby's sleep times. To keep your sanity, remember that this is a special time. It can be exhausting, but it will pass all too soon, so do arrange your schedule to enjoy it while you can.

Building a healthy, long-term relationship

If all goes well, working with a significant other in your home-based business can go a long way in helping you build a deeper and even more profound personal relationship. And if you decide to team up with someone you love, nurturing your personal relationship should be just as important as developing a healthy business relationship. If one suffers, the other is sure to suffer as well.

The following are some tips for building healthy, long-term relationships — both personal and business — with your significant others:

✔ **Be clear about who's in charge.** In most businesses, one person is ultimately in charge and has the right to veto the suggestions or actions of others, including partners. Make this clear at the outset, but be sure to ask for the input of your partner and to give that input serious consideration. If your business is a true, legal partnership — with ownership shared in equal amounts — be sure that you establish a system for making decisions when you are in disagreement with your partner. If making decisions becomes problematic for you and your partner, you probably should not be in a business partnership in the first place.

✔ **Don't interfere with how your partner achieves his or her goals.** Focus on agreeing on what your goals are and on letting your partner decide how he or she will reach them. Avoid the temptation to micromanage your partner's efforts or to interfere with or second-guess them. You'll only build resentment and erode your long-term relationships.

✔ **Don't forget to nurture your private lives.** Every couple working together needs to take time away from the demands of their business to focus on themselves and on their relationship. You can find a number of ways to be fun and spontaneous in your relationship. Close the office for a day, and enjoy a long weekend at a resort or on a trip to the beach or mountains. Take a long lunch together, or treat yourselves to an afternoon of pampering at a spa or health club. Or simply turn off the phone and sleep in late one morning.

✔ **Seek the help of a professional counselor if needed.** Sometimes relationships can be broken, and the help of a professional is needed to put them back together. Don't hesitate to seek counseling if your relationship is broken — the sooner you do, the easier it will be to get things back on track.

Long-term relationships can be the most meaningful relationships in your life, and there's no reason why you can't share a meaningful and productive business relationship with someone with whom you share a close personal relationship. It has worked for Paul and Sarah, and it has worked for Peter and his wife, Jan. Explore the possibilities!

Chapter 16

Don't Just Stand There, Grow

In This Chapter

▶ Understanding success

▶ Deciding whether or not to grow

▶ Partnering with others

▶ Expanding operations

▶ Moving on

A time comes in the life of every business owner when he or she has to make a decision: whether or not to grow the business. If you're good at what you do, and your customers love the products and services that you sell them, don't be surprised if after you start your business, you're soon faced with more customers and clients than you can handle.

When your business increases to a point where you can't accommodate it in the normal course of your day, you have to make a conscious choice: Reject this extra work and maintain the status quo (or perhaps even cut back the time and effort you devote to your business to allow yourself to spend more time with loved ones, volunteer in your community, or just relax), or take on the extra work and grow. For many home-based business owners, this isn't even a question. For them, being in business means growing the business, pure and simple. For many others, however, the prospect of growth is something they prefer not to embrace. They're comfortable with things the way they are, have made a decision to spend less time working and more time with family and friends, or have any of a thousand different reasons why growth is not something that holds an attraction for them.

 In the case of growth, the right answer is the one that's best for you. And what's best for you may or may not be what's best for your clients and customers, your family and friends, and any employees or contractors that you may have.

In this chapter, we consider what makes a business a success and examine the good and the bad news about owning a growing company. We take a close look at bringing partners into your business and expanding your operations. Finally, we explore strategies for selling your business and moving on to other opportunities.

Becoming a Success

Success is a relative thing. While one home-based business owner may be pulling down a $25,000-a-year, part-time salary — considering himself a smashing success while enjoying lots of time with family and friends and making a nice contribution to the family finances — another may consider that minimal level of income to indicate failure. As the owner of your home-based business, *you* get to decide how to define what success means *to you;* no one else can or should define it for you. You may decide to measure your own success in terms of money or in terms of how many clients you can help. You may also measure success in terms of your ability to achieve an equal balance in your work and personal lives. When you're the one who decides what success means to you, there is no wrong answer.

After defining what success means to you, though, like anything else that you want to achieve in your life, you have to have a strategy for achieving the goals you've set for yourself. Although anyone who puts his or her mind to it will find some measure of success, starting up a successful enterprise involves more than just working hard. William Bygrave, former director of the Center for Entrepreneurial Studies at Babson College and one of the nation's top experts on entrepreneurship, describes nine keys to success for an entrepreneurial business in his book *The Portable MBA in Entrepreneurship.* Bygrave calls these keys the *Nine Fs:*

- ✔ **Founders:** Every startup must have a first-class entrepreneur. (That means you.)

- ✔ **Focused:** Entrepreneurial companies focus on niche markets. They specialize. (Fuzzy companies lead to fuzzy customers; people are willing to pay top dollar for products and services that clearly appeal to their wants and needs.)

- ✔ **Fast:** They make decisions quickly and implement them swiftly (but never so quickly that they don't take time to understand and consider the alternatives before they implement their decisions).

- ✔ **Flexible:** Entrepreneurial companies keep an open mind. They respond to change. (Small, home-based businesses can often respond much more quickly to change than larger businesses — a key advantage in today's fast-changing, information-driven marketplace.)

- ✔ **Forever innovating:** They are tireless innovators (at least until 2 or 3 in the morning, when most of them make sure they go to bed and get some sleep).

- ✔ **Flat:** Entrepreneurial organizations have as few layers of management as possible. (This is quite easy when you're a sole proprietorship and have no employees.)

- ✔ **Frugal:** By keeping overhead low and productivity high, entrepreneurial organizations keep costs down (which means they are more profitable).

- ✔ **Friendly:** Entrepreneurial companies are friendly to their customers, suppliers, and workers. (And because of that, their customers, suppliers, and workers are friendly right back, demonstrating their friendliness with orders for products and services.)

- ✔ **Fun:** It's fun to be associated with an entrepreneurial company. (Owning your own home-based business doesn't mean you can't have fun — indeed, if you're not having fun, why bother?)

Compare the way you do business with Bygrave's Nine Fs. Do the two have any similarities, or are they miles apart? The more Fs you find in your own home-based business, the greater your chances of finding success at the end of your rainbow.

Identifying the Upside and Downside of Growth

Business growth has ramifications that extend far beyond the simple day-to-day running of an organization:

- ✔ Growth means new work, new clients, and new opportunities.

- ✔ Growth means more money coming into your business, but it also means more money going out.

- ✔ Running a growing business can make your life incredibly busy and hectic, but it can also be incredibly rewarding — financially and personally.

What are your long-term goals for yourself and for your business? Do you want to make a certain amount of revenue every year — enough to allow you to support yourself and your family? Do you want to make a certain level of profit or service a certain number of customers or clients? Do you want to work for a certain number of years or save up enough money to travel the world — or retire early? Whatever your long-term goals, if you decide that growth is indeed in the cards for your business, you can't leave it to chance — you have to have a plan to get there. And don't forget: Your business will change, as will your feelings about it. Be flexible and prepared to change your plans as your goals change.

Growth has both good and bad aspects. In the following sections, we explore growth in detail so that you can decide what growth means to you, helping you decide whether you'd rather grow, maintain the status quo, or perhaps even shrink your business operations.

Understanding why you may want to grow

Although the pressure to grow seems inevitable for many businesses — especially ones that do a good job for their customers and clients — growth is something that is within your power to control. Too many clients? Trim back your client list. Too much work? Turn down new work until you catch up. Not enough time for yourself? Do less work. You're in charge; you're the boss. The decision is yours.

So given the possible attraction of maintaining the status quo, why grow? Here are a number of good reasons:

- ✔ **Increased revenue and profits:** The immediate impact of growing your business is an increase in revenues and — as long as your costs of doing business don't grow out of proportion — an increase in profit. And if we're not mistaken, that's probably one of the reasons you're in business for yourself in the first place.

- ✔ **Building equity:** *Equity* is the amount of money left over after you subtract all of your company's liabilities from its assets (see Chapter 7). If your business is profitable over a long period of time, this number can be quite large. Growing your business is likely to grow your equity as well.

- ✔ **Take advantage of economies of scale:** The larger your business, the more you can take advantage of *economies of scale* — that is, paying lower prices for items you buy in larger quantities. You can, for example, purchase a case of laser printer paper at your local Costco warehouse store and pay far less per ream than you would if you bought each ream individually at Kinko's.

- ✔ **Why not?** In the absence of any compelling reasons not to grow, why not grow? Growth can be exciting and fun, and who knows — it may lead you to new and more exciting adventures down the road.

Of course, it's okay not to grow, if that's the way you decide to run your business and your life. Many people have become home-based business owners for just that reason — to leave the rat race and to get off of the never-ending treadmill of business that devours their personal lives. *Propreneurs* — business owners who make a conscious choice not to grow — are active and vital players in the marketplace, and they tend to be just as happy as their entrepreneurial (and more growth-oriented) counterparts.

Recognizing the many different ways to grow

If you've made the decision to grow your business, you have a number of ways to do it. The exact approach depends on your growth goals and plans and on the nature of your business. The following are some of the most common approaches for growing a home-based business:

✔ **Expand beyond your locale.** Do you do work only for people who live within a few miles of your home or only for close personal acquaintances? If that's the case, one of the quickest ways to grow your business is to expand the area in which you do business. What if you decided to do business citywide or countywide? Or perhaps even beyond the boundaries of your state? Expanding beyond your locale dramatically increases the number of potential clients and customers available to you — potentially increasing sales and profits.

✔ **Get on the Web.** With the right Internet presence (be sure to check out Chapter 5 to find out exactly how to establish the right Internet presence), the number of people who view your product catalog or see your work can mushroom. Many home-based businesses have seen tremendous growth after capturing the imagination of their customers on the Internet.

✔ **Go international.** It's a great big world out there, and depending on the products and services you sell, a huge, underserved international market may be waiting for you to tap it. For many growing businesses, a plan for expanding into international markets is a key success strategy.

✔ **Expand your product line.** If you currently carry ten different products, and you want to double your business, what's the quickest way to achieve your goal? Carry 20 different products. Although the exact impact that decision ultimately will have on sales depends on the products, their pricing, and the extent to which you promote them, expanding your product line is a quick and easy way to grow your business.

> ✔ **Add employees.** Adding employees to your business by definition means that you're growing it. Just be sure that you never hire new employees until you have sufficient business to support them. If your revenues are flat or decreasing as you add employees, you have what's commonly known as a *going-out-of-business plan,* and that is not a plan for home-based business success. For lots of information on the right way to interview and hire employees, check out *Managing For Dummies 2nd Edition,* by Peter Economy and Bob Nelson (Wiley Publishing).

You know your business better than anyone else, so think about what you can do to grow your business. One of the benefits of being your own boss is that you can do whatever you like with your business, whenever you want. Think you have a good idea? Give it a try. The more things you try, the higher the probability you'll find something that works.

To grow or not to grow

If you've anguished over the decision of whether or not to grow your business, you know that the decision isn't just a business decision — it's a personal one as well. Because you're the one who has to live with the consequences of the decision to grow or not, it's in your interest to thoroughly examine yourself, your business, and the marketplace to make sure that whatever decision you make, it's the best one for you and for your business.

Here are four key places to look as you consider whether or not to grow your business:

> ✔ **Check your heart.** The first place to look when you're thinking about growing your business is deep inside your heart. Take some time to get away from the hustle and bustle of your business ,and really listen to what your heart tells you. Are you looking forward to the excitement that business growth with bring with it, or are you secretly dreading the possible consequences of such a choice? What does your heart say?

> ✔ **Check your lifestyle.** Will your preferred lifestyle support or be in conflict with the growth of your business? If, for example, the growth of your business will take you away from your family — and spending more time with your family is one of the key reasons why you started your home-based business in the first place — you'll likely resent the extra time you have to devote to your business, as will your family, who will have less of your time.

> ✔ **Check the numbers.** Of course, your heart and lifestyle may say "go," while your business (more specifically, your business's financials) says

"no." If your company's sales are too low or costs too high, growing your business probably isn't the best thing to do. Can you somehow increase sales or decrease costs enough for growth to make sense? If not, either figure out some way to put your financials on the right track or put your growth plans on the back burner until the numbers do make sense.

🗸 **Check the market.** You may think it's time to grow, but the market in which your business operates may not be ready for you. Before you invest lots of time, money, and effort in growing your business, be sure that enough potential customers and clients are interested in buying your products and services. If they aren't, you're just wasting your time and your hard-earned money — two things that are especially precious for every home-based business owner.

Diversifying your client list

Q: I've been in business for three years, and about 80 percent of my work comes from one client. How could I possibly find the time to diversify while still keeping my client satisfied?

A: As great as the steady cash flow is, getting the bulk of your income from just one client puts you at great risk should that client suddenly decide to work with someone else. You sound as though you not only get 80 percent of your income from this one client, but also spend most of your time serving him or her. To free your time to market and serve new clients, you need to get some additional help. Evaluate what portions of your work can be done by an assistant, associate, or outside contractor. Arrange to free up at least two hours a week for marketing, and begin breaking in someone to work with you so that when you generate new business, you have dependable help to meet the demand.

Although you don't mention the nature of your business, in many fields, self-employed individuals can't or prefer not to market themselves, preferring instead to subcontract their services to someone else. Such individuals like to work with people like you. Be certain, however, that

all the billing and all funds come through you. Be sure you get clear, written agreements preventing associates or subcontractors from contracting directly with your clients. Also, you need to line up individuals you can depend on to do high-quality work within necessary deadlines.

To find associates you can count on, get referrals from sources you trust. Be sure to review their work, and talk with them about how they approach their work and what their priorities are. Ask for — and check — references. Most important, start with one small, low-risk assignment. Set a clear goal and a specific deadline. If the deadline is more than a week away, check progress intermittently and, if possible, ask that portions of the work be turned in as they are completed. This can help you identify possible problems before they develop.

Keep in mind that working with someone else will, in and of itself, take some additional time — especially at first. But by building a network of others you can rely on, you can expand without taking on debt or adding to your expenses until you have the business to cover them.

All of these factors play a role in the growth decision; the weight that you place on each depends on your own personal desires and goals. Many businesses have succeeded, for example, when the numbers didn't make sense or when there did not seem to be broad support in the market for a business's new initiatives. But behind businesses like these, there have been incredibly motivated and hard-working business owners.

Bringing In Partners

A partnership is when two or more people team up in the ownership and operation of a business. Many well-known businesses have started out as successful partnerships (and home-based businesses at that), including Microsoft's Bill Gates and Paul Allen; the Disney brothers, Walt and Roy; and Ben & Jerry's ice cream namesakes Ben Cohen and Jerry Greenfield. While these businesses quickly outgrew their original partnership structures — eventually becoming large, multinational (and publicly owned) corporations — the combination of the original partners provided the spark of creativity and energy that led to great success.

When a partnership works, the business will run like a well-played symphony. When it doesn't, it's more likely that things will be closer to a scene from the film *Titanic* (specifically, that part where the ship sinks). Unfortunately, you can't really know how things will turn out until a partnership is actually created and the partners begin to work together. It's sort of like a marriage; you really don't know how things are going to really work — or even if they will work — until the honeymoon is over.

More than a few friendships, families, and personal relationships have been destroyed by partnerships gone bad. Partners can clash in a variety of ways, and these clashes may only occur in a business environment under the pressures of a busy schedule. That's why you should always apply the same standards of care when you decide to partner with family or friends as you would when hiring a stranger.

The following are some tips for ensuring that your partnerships operate smoothly. (For more specific information on the partnership form of business — including advantages and disadvantages — take a look at Chapter 11.)

> ✔ **Date first.** Before you get married, it's a good idea to date your prospective mate for a while first — a few months or a even a few years would be good. Not only will this approach allow you to develop trust and find out how to communicate with each other, but it also allows you to see both the good and the bad sides of your partner. Business partnerships

work the same way: Get to know your prospective partner very well before you tie the knot. Consider doing shared marketing or a specific project together first.

✔ **Partner only with someone you trust.** Trust is the glue that holds a partnership together and allows you to achieve great things. Don't even consider — not for one second! — partnering with someone you don't trust or respect. The road to business success is littered with broken partnerships that fell apart as soon as the trust that kept them together vanished.

✔ **Don't partner until you can stand on your own.** You should partner from a position of strength, not weakness. Otherwise, your business will become a codependency and, thus, dysfunctional. And a dysfunctional company is a company that's going to have problems serving its customers well and making money.

✔ **Enlist partners who add to the business.** Ideally, your partner will complement you and bring positive personal value to the company. Short on cash? Then find a partner who will provide the cash you need. Need help marketing? Then find a partner who is a strong salesperson. Don't like managing the business? Then a partner who is a strong leader and administrator will be the right choice for you. Just as you should hire employees who shore up your weaknesses, choose partners to cover the skills or connections that you lack.

✔ **Share the equity (and the burden of risk).** Sharing equity means sharing ownership of the company with your partners. If you don't share ownership with your partners, they will not act as though they are owners — they won't value the business the same way you do, and they won't be willing to make the same sacrifices as you to keep the business alive and healthy. But if you agree to share ownership of your company, be sure to require partners to share equally in the risks associated with the business.

✔ **Create a written partnership agreement.** Formalize your partnership in a written agreement that spells out — clearly and unambiguously — the ownership stake of each partner, rights to business proceeds, and his or her responsibilities to the business. Our advice is to spend the relatively small amount of money necessary to have an attorney draw up a proper partnership agreement for you and your prospective partners to sign. Many business partnerships eventually fail; when they do, a well-written partnership agreement can help protect the huge investment of time and money that you have made in your business.

Follow these tips, and your partnerships should be happy ones. If not, you can always split up the partnership and try again, but you'll have a much easier (and more profitable) time by doing your homework and getting it right the first time. Keep in mind, too, that as Paul and Sarah and Rick Benzel describe in their book *Teaming Up,* partnership is only one of many ways of collaborating with others, many of which carry less risk.

Cashing Out and Other Exit Strategies

Although starting and growing a business is the common focus for most entrepreneurs whose businesses are young, eventually a business owner's thoughts turn to other goals — specifically, the goal of selling the business and retiring or moving on to a new business. For some people, this phenomenon occurs at an early age (coauthor Peter still dreams of retiring before he hits 50; however, the reality of his currently advanced years, along with three kids rapidly approaching college age, may have its own say in the matter). Others plan to work literally until they take their last breaths.

If and when you do decide to exit your business, you'll be faced with even more decisions — in particular, when and how to gracefully sever your ties to the business so that its value is not damaged in the process. You can find all kinds of strategies for exiting your business, from mild to extreme. Here are some of the most common:

- ✔ **Sell it.** Businesses are bought and sold all the time (take a look at sites like www.businessesforsale.com or your local newspaper classified advertisements). If you've built a strong customer base or have a valuable inventory, or if your operations are particularly profitable or otherwise attractive to a potential buyer, you may be able to make some significant money in the process. And that's not a bad thing!

- ✔ **Merge it.** Merging your operation with another business can create a new business that's more powerful and profitable than the two businesses were separately. In a merger, you have the option of stepping aside in favor of having the owner of the other company run and operate the combined companies while you maintain an ownership stake, or you can accept some form of one-time or ongoing payment or royalty while acting as a part-time consultant or adviser to the business. Either option can make a lot of sense, depending on your personal preferences.

- ✔ **Pass it to a family member, friend, or employee.** If you have a son, daughter, close friend, or employee who is particularly interested in keeping the business going, you always have the option of passing it on to the person or people of your choosing. You can choose to pass it on for free, sell it, or set up some sort of compensation arrangement such as an ongoing royalty or payment based on a percentage of sales.

> ✔ **Close it.** Of course, you can simply close the business, unplug your answering machine, and move on with your life. For many home-based business owners interested in exiting their businesses, this is the simplest option by far. If you decide on this option, it's good karma not to leave your customers hanging out to dry, wondering where their orders are. See the nearby "Shutting down your business" sidebar for ideas on how to make sure your loyal customers are taken care of.

Whatever decision you make, be sure to carefully match it with your long-term goals. If you merge the business with another or pass it to a family member, friend, or employee, you may have the opportunity to keep your finger in the business's operations if you desire. If you sell or close it, however, chances are slim (very, *very* slim, in the case of a closed business) that you'll be able to have anything further to do with it. Is that what you really want? Are you really ready to call it quits? Only you know the answer to that question, and only you can make the ultimate decision.

Shutting down your business

Unfortunately, not every home-based business is destined to last forever, which means that at some point, you may have to close it — whether by choice or due to circumstances out of your control. If this happens, here are a few tips to ensure that your customers aren't left out in the cold:

✔ Give your customers plenty of notice. A month is not too long.

✔ Refer your customers to companies like yours, including former competitors (you won't need to worry about them anymore, right?). The idea is to give your customers as many options and alternatives as possible.

✔ Offer to train your customers to do what you do. You might have a customer or two who

would like to start a business like yours or add your business to their own.

✔ Subcontract the work to another company or individual in your field.

✔ If you have a contract that is legally assignable, sell or transfer it to another company capable of satisfying your clients. It's always a good policy, whether required by your contract or not, to prepare the client for a change in who will be providing the goods or services.

✔ Sell your client list to another company or individual in your field, letting your customers know you're doing this and introducing them to the person or company who will be filling their needs.

Putting a value on your business

If you decide to sell your business, the first question your potential buyer is likely to ask is "How much do you want for it?" Do you have any idea how much it is worth? If you do, are you sure the price is right?

You can use a number of different ways to establish a price for a business. If you're thinking about selling your home-based business, consider the following methods:

- **The firm's earning capacity:** How much money does your business rake in every month or year? Are your sales high enough to offset expenses and leave a reasonable profit behind? The higher the earning capacity of a business, the more it will be worth to a potential buyer and the more he or she will be willing to pay you for it.

- **The value of its assets:** If you have a lot of money tied up in physical assets, such as inventory (the products you keep on the shelf to sell to customers) or machinery (say, medical transcription equipment or mechanic's tools), the worth of your business will surely be influenced — or perhaps even determined — by the value of your assets. The higher the value of your assets — and the ease with which they can be converted to immediate use by a buyer or into liquid assets such as cash — the more money you'll be able to demand for your business.

- **The market value of similar firms:** The value of firms similar to yours will inevitably have a significant influence on the value of your firm. You can get a rough idea of your firm's value by finding out what similar businesses are selling for. Try listings of businesses for sale in your local newspaper classified ads or check out the www.businessesforsale.com Web site.

- **The value of the company's stock:** If your business is organized as a corporation, and you have issued stock, that stock has value. Because buying stock in a company is the same as buying the company itself, the value of that stock can often determine the value of the business.

Now what?

You've sold your business or handed it over to your daughter, and you've done your best to keep your nose out of how she's running it. But for years, you've spent the better part of your waking hours working and, lately, running your own business. Now what?

Many people dream about retirement their whole working lives, but after they get there, they find that they miss the action and the demands and responsibilities of a busy business environment. Of course, others adjust to their retirement just fine and spend their days traveling the world, fishing, or enjoying a good book. If you're ready to take the next step, but you're not exactly sure what that step is, be sure to read Paul and Sarah's book *The Practical Dreamer's Handbook: Finding the Time, Money, & Energy to Live the Life You Want to Live* (Jeremy P. Tarcher).

Whatever you decide, don't forget that you always have one option open to you: starting another business. As this book describes, starting your own home-based business can be amazingly simple, and the rewards are many.

Part V
The Part of Tens

The 5th Wave   By Rich Tennant

@RICHTENNANT

"Oh, we're doing just great. Philip and I are selling decorative jelly jars on the Web. I run the Web site and Philip sort of controls the inventory."

In this part . . .

These short chapters are packed with lots of quick and powerful ideas to help make your home-based business the kind of success you've always dreamed of. Read them when you have an extra minute or two.

Chapter 17

Ten Tips to Succeed in Your Home-Based Business

In This Chapter

▶ Doing what you love — and becoming an expert

▶ Being businesslike in your dealings

▶ Selling yourself and charging what you're worth

▶ Avoiding unnecessary expenses and monitoring your cash flow

▶ Asking for referrals

Although no one can guarantee that your home-based business will bring you the fame and fortune you hope it will, if you work hard, price your products and services right, and keep your customers satisfied, you stand a good chance of doing just that. The results you get out of your business are a direct result of the work you put into it. That relationship between work and results is one of the real joys of having a home-based business. Plus you get to see the fruit of your labor every day, when satisfied clients and customers tell you how much they enjoy doing business with you — and buy more of your products and services.

The most successful home-based business owners — those who get the results they had hoped for — share a variety of traits. We discuss ten of them in this chapter.

Do What You Love

We all dream about the job that we would do if only we had the opportunity to do it. Unfortunately, for many of us, our current job is something we do because we have to pay the bills, not because we want to. What if you could do what you really loved to do? Wouldn't that be great? It is, and it's exactly the opportunity you get by starting your own business. But to do what you love, you first have to know what kind of work you really want to do. This requires intense introspection and an understanding of which kinds of work get your creative juices flowing and which kinds dry them up. Doing what you love also sometimes requires that you ignore what other people want you to do for a living. You may decide, for example, that you'd really like to start a recording studio in your home, but your spouse or best friend may think something more practical, such as buying into a fast-food franchise, makes more sense. Ultimately, you must decide what you're going to do for a living — even if it means you can't work at home.

It's *your* dream — you're the one who gets to choose it (and live it!). No one else has the right to tell you what kind of work you should love — and do.

Treat Your Business Like a Business

If you want your business to be a business — an organization that generates the kind of money you need to become financially independent — you have to treat it like one, not like a hobby or a momentary fling. Here are some ideas:

- ✔ Set aside a real home office — not just a closet or a shelf — exclusively for your business (see Chapter 14).

- ✔ Make an investment in business equipment and supplies: a decent computer, extra phone lines, a fax machine, and whatever else you decide you need to run your operation.

- ✔ Create a marketing plan and marketing materials (see Chapter 4).

- ✔ Publicize your company's products and services to a wide audience of potential customers and clients.

- ✔ Build a strong customer base and make plans for future growth (see Chapter 16).

Treating your business as such doesn't mean that you can't have fun, though, or that you can't make up your own rules along the way. Indeed, being your own boss means that you get to decide how you're going to run your business. If you want to work only on weekday afternoons, for example — setting aside mornings for exercise or spending time with your kids — you can do that and still have a serious business.

Become an Expert

People respect those who know more than they do. By specializing, you assume the role of a presumed expert, even if you've just started your business. It makes good business sense for your clients to hire an expert instead of someone less experienced. By avoiding the mistakes and dead ends that someone with less experience may make, your clients could end up spending less money by hiring you — even if your hourly rates are higher.

The interesting thing about becoming an expert is that the passage of time makes you increasingly more experienced in your field. As time goes on, potential clients and customers will seek you out just to get the benefit of the expertise you've developed through experience and education.

Don't Be Shy

There's a reason why companies spend millions of dollars advertising their products in the media: because it's a particularly effective way to get the attention (and, ideally, the business) of potential customers. Unfortunately, far too many people believe that a good idea is all a successful business needs. In the real world, it takes far more than that; the world is chock-full of good ideas that have gone nowhere fast. Even the best ideas have to be packaged, presented, and sold, and the key is to identify and use marketing methods suited to both your personality and your business.

While you may never have had to sell yourself or your products before, when you own your own business, this must change — and fast! After you generate momentum and build a strong customer base, you can rely more on referrals from your happy clients. But when you're getting your business off the ground, consider and attempt every possible method for selling your products and services.

For a complete discussion of the hows and whys of marketing your products and services, check out Chapter 4.

Charge What You're Worth

Here's an instant going-out-of-business plan, no matter how hard you work: Charge your customers less than you're worth. Why would you do that? Well, some people charge less than they're worth because they don't realize exactly how much they *are* worth. Others charge less than they're worth because they are embarrassed or afraid to ask for an amount that reflects their true worth. Whatever the reason, if you don't get paid what you're worth, you are putting your business at risk.

If you don't know what you're worth, find out what other companies charge for similar products or services by researching catalogs, price lists, stores, and e-commerce and auction Web sites. From there, develop a pricing or fee structure that will help you attain your personal goals.

After you figure out what you should charge, use the following tips to get the price you want:

✔ Become a master at selling the value that your products and services offer to your customers and clients. They won't know if you don't tell them, so tell them often and in a variety of ways.

✔ Get past any hang-ups you have about charging your customers and clients what you're worth. Practice, as you would a request for a raise or a speech, asking your price in front of a mirror or with someone you trust to give you constructive criticism.

Avoid Unnecessary Expenses

Shopping for the latest and greatest business gadgets and equipment is fun — a lot of fun. And it's a lot of fun to treat clients to expensive lunches and dinners, and to drive that snazzy new company car. The bad news about all this fun is that it can be expensive (and all of it may not be tax-deductible) and detrimental to your company's financial health and welfare.

Spend your company's hard-earned money only when you have to. A good example of this is your personal computer. Every other week, computer technology makes another great leap forward, which may constantly tempt you to upgrade to the latest and greatest and fastest computer with all of the latest bells and whistles. Unless your older, slower, and less flashy computer is actually getting in the way of your ability to do business efficently, stick with it for as long as you possibly can. Think about adding a bigger hard drive, more RAM, or other upgrades that cost far less than buying a new computer. Eventually, you'll need to replace that old slug of a computer, but the longer you can defer the expense, the better for your company's bottom line.

Do your best to hold the line on all the other expenses that simply drain your financial reserves while bringing in little or no additional revenue. If you're going to eat out, for example, go to less expensive places. Save the expensive meals for your highest-paying customers. Or consider inviting your best customers as dinner guests in your home.

Manage Your Cash Flow

Cash, or the lack of it, is one of the key indicators of a company's success over the long run. If you have cash, you can buy and stock new products for your customers, develop innovative new services for your clients, pay for your day-to-day operations, and expand your operations. If you don't have cash, your business will certainly suffer, and so will your customers and clients.

It's not enough to simply watch your cash flow — the money going in and out of your business — you've also got to *manage* it. This means looking to the future, planning and scheduling your projected cash inflows and outflows, billing quickly, staying on top of money owed you, and paying attention to the money that goes in and out of your business. See Chapter 7 for more ideas.

Keep Your Day Job

As we suggest in Chapter 6, the best way to work into your own successful home-based business is to try it out while retaining your full-time conventional job. This approach will not only keep your income safe and sound as your company revenues ramp up — a process that can take months or even years — but it also will allow you to keep your health care and other benefits in place, including allowing your employer to continue making contributions to the cost of these benefits, if applicable in your case. A rule of thumb for when to transition to your business full time is when your business income will sustain your minimal living expenses and you feel confident that by putting in more time, you will increase your business's earnings.

When Peter embarked on his new writing career a number of years ago, he did so within the safety of his full-time job. While he established his business on his own time — during lunch hours and after work — Peter drew a regular salary, health benefits, and a retirement plan. Finally, when the time was right, Peter left his day job and moved into his home-based writing career full time.

By approaching the transition to self-employment this way, you can discover whether you've picked the right business — and whether you're right for the business.

Build a Solid Customer Base

One of the most important ways to establish a successful business is to build a solid base of customers who stick with you through thick or thin. This solid customer base becomes the foundation on which you can grow your business.

Of course, building a solid customer base is much easier said than done. At the heart of the process is creating an organization that values its current customers and goes out of its way to ensure their satisfaction and happiness. Customers are smart — they can tell whether they are high or low on a company's list of priorities. If they sense that you don't care much about whether they do business with you, they'll likely jump ship as soon as another company that really does care about them comes along.

Always remember the feeling of getting your first customer and your first payment for your products and then treat every one of your customers as though they were your first. Value them every day, and they will in turn value you.

Ask for Referrals

The word-of-mouth referral is probably the least expensive and the most effective way of getting new business. This makes referrals the most important way for home-based businesses to market themselves. Here are several of the best ways of earning great referrals from customers:

✔ **Do great work:** When you do great work, your clients are happy to give you great referrals. Do less-than-great work, and you'll be lucky to get any referrals.

✔ **Do your work on time and within budget:** Do you want to know the quickest way to your customer's heart? Do your work on time and within budget. If you consistently deliver on your promises, you'll soon have more business than you could ever imagine possible. And you'll earn your clients' referrals.

✔ **Keep your clients well informed:** When clients spend their money on you, they want to be kept apprised of your progress, not only to stay in touch with the project, but also to keep a watchful eye out for problems before they get out of hand. Do your clients a favor, and keep them informed about your project's progress. Whether the news is good or bad, your clients and customers will appreciate your forthrightness and candor.

✔ **Be dependable:** If anything, you should always keep your word — even when it hurts. If you promise to do something, do everything in your power to keep your promise, no matter what it takes to follow through on it. Who would impress you more (and earn your referral) — a business owner who runs to you for schedule extensions every other week or an owner who delivers on time, every time?

✔ **Be flexible:** Customers and clients appreciate vendors who are flexible and willing to meet their needs, no matter what those needs are. Not only that, but also, they will pay more for that flexibility. Think what you can do in your business to better meet your customers' needs.

✔ **Thank your clients for their referrals:** Everyone likes to be appreciated for what they do. Your customers are no different. Be sure to thank them for their referrals with a hand-signed card or small gift.

Many small businesses get the vast majority of their new business through referrals. They really are worth their weight in gold!

Chapter 18

Ten Things to Avoid

. . . .

In This Chapter

▶ Letting your business take over your home

▶ Letting distractions get the best of you

▶ Eating junk food

▶ Expecting business to come to you

▶ Shutting out your personal life — or not letting it go as you work

. . . .

*E*very business is fraught with danger, and home-based businesses are no exception. In a perfect world, it would all go just the way you wanted — all the time. Unfortunately, you live in a less-than-perfect world where many things can go wrong with your business.

Stay alert to the potential problems outlined in this chapter, and take steps to avoid them before they have a chance to negatively impact your business. Your home-based business has a much better chance of surviving — and thriving — when you take steps to avoid the ten "don'ts" in this chapter.

Don't Turn Your Bedroom into Your Office

One of the first questions many new home-based business owners ask is this: "Where am I going to put my business?" For some people, the answer is easy: in an extra bedroom, an underused den, or in the basement. But for many, the answer is anything but easy, and finding the space necessary to run their business is a challenge.

One of the first thoughts for new home-based business owners short on space is to turn a bedroom into an office. If you're among that group of people, we have one word for you: Don't! The information revolution swirling all around you — pagers, cell phones, fax machines, voice mail, e-mail, and more — is conspiring to take the last vestiges of your privacy and nonwork time, and you need a safe place to get away from it all. Your bedroom is your inner sanctum, a refuge from the pressures of work and life where you relax and spend meaningful, intimate time with your spouse or significant other (or perhaps simply with your television set or a good book).

Don't Use Your Office as a Family Entertainment Center

Peter once put a television in a corner of his office. The reason? To keep up with breaking news reports or to relax for a moment in the middle of a project. He even went so far as to buy a videogame system as an occasional diversion during the workday.

Big mistake.

It didn't take long for his three kids to turn that corner into their new, favorite hangout. And although Peter loves to spend time with his kids, the sound of blaring alien attacks and grand-prix auto races made it more than a little difficult to focus on his work.

Your office is first and foremost for work. It's not for relaxing or socializing or hanging out with youngsters. Avoid installing anything that will attract leisure-seekers — especially distracting things that make a lot of noise!

Don't Work Morning, Noon, and Night

Most regular businesses have established starting and quitting times, holidays, and vacations. These boundaries not only help customers know when they can do business with the company, but they also give employees a chance to spend time with their families, get necessary errands done, or simply relax and recuperate from a hard day's work.

When your office is in your home, though, it's very easy to fall into the trap of not establishing a regular work schedule and then working 24/7/365. Not only is this a prescription for burnout, but it is also sure to put a strain on your family relationships. You don't want your child saying to you, as Paul and Sarah's did early in their home-based careers, "Is this a home or an office?"

Here are a few tips for avoiding the 24-hour-office situation:

✔ Establish regular work schedules — and stick to them!

✔ Build a couple of days off into your workweek.

✔ Avoid working holidays.

✔ Set aside sufficient time for yourself and your family.

✔ Take plenty of breaks during the course of the workday — and don't forget to take time for lunch!

Don't Allow Paperwork and Office Equipment to Take Over Your Home

Chances are you'll need more and more space as your business grows. Rather than allow your office stuff to take over your home, blurring the boundaries between your work life and your personal life, find other storage options.

If you have a garage, attic, or basement, consider boxing up infrequently used files and putting them in long-term storage. Go through them periodically, and throw out the paperwork and files you no longer need. There probably isn't too much that you've absolutely got to retain for more than four or five years; tax records and contracts are some things that you should hang onto for a while. Sell or donate obsolete or unused equipment. Use space-saving storage systems, and if you need help, consult a professional organizer. Check out Chapter 14 for more solutions you can put to use right away.

Don't Let Housework or Hobbies Distract You from Getting Your Work Done

Peter's cable modem is always hooked up to the Internet, and he finds himself constantly fighting the urge to jump online and check the latest news on CNN.com or see how his bids (for more guitars, of course) are faring on eBay. Sometimes he beats the urge, and sometimes it beats him.

Left unchecked, distractions can negatively impact your productivity and efficiency. Take regular breaks during the course of the workday — at least a few minutes off every hour — but don't let your breaks stretch into long periods of playtime that you had planned to use for work.

Don't Fill Your Cabinets and Refrigerator with Junk Food

When you work at home, you've got a virtual treasure trove of food just a few steps away in the kitchen. This constant temptation can distract you from your work and cause you to put on unwanted pounds. If you want to remain feeling and looking your best, avoid the temptation to fill your cabinets and refrigerator with unhealthy snacks. Instead, keep lots of healthy ones close at hand, such as:

- ✔ Fruit, including bananas, grapes, oranges, and apples
- ✔ Chopped vegetables, such as carrots, celery, and broccoli
- ✔ Salads
- ✔ Low-fat trail mixes or party mixes
- ✔ Smoothies and fruit shakes

Make your home office a junk-food-free zone. If you don't, you may soon find yourself shopping for a new wardrobe. And here's a little secret: Your new wardrobe is *not* going to be tax-deductible!

Don't Expect Business to Come to You

To be successful in your home-based business, you have to be proactive in developing a marketing mindset. Even the world's largest, most well-known companies have to spend millions of dollars each year to keep themselves in front of their potential customers and explain why people should buy their products or services. Companies like General Motors, Pfizer, and McDonald's have huge advertising budgets. You can bet they don't wait for business to come to them; they're out there every day of the week seeking it out.

Here are some tips for getting into a marketing mindset. Take a look at Chapter 4 for further details.

- ✔ Regularly think about how to get the word out about your business.
- ✔ Make a commitment to invest your time, energy, and money in marketing your business (and then do it!).
- ✔ Make personal contacts though direct solicitation, networking, speeches, and so on.

✔ Get others to talk about you through such avenues as referrals, publicity, radio, TV, and Internet forums.

✔ Show what you can do with business cards, audiotapes, photos, portfolios, and so forth.

Don't Expect to Be an Overnight Success

Some organizations recruit people to start home-based businesses using "proven" systems, especially multi-level marketing firms and companies that tell you that you'll get rich stuffing envelopes for them. They make it sound like you'll be rolling in cash within weeks or months. If this were really the case, every home-based business would be a certified cash machine.

In reality, building a business that will be profitable and survive over the long run takes a lot of hard work, and it takes a lot of time. Sure, there are occasional exceptions, but most every business that is a success today went through years and years of often grueling work to get there. If you work hard, you can turn your business into a success — but not overnight.

Don't Give In When Someone Tries to Occupy Your Precious Working Time

One of the hardest things that many new home-based business owners face is getting people to understand that just because they are working at home, this doesn't mean that they are available to pick up friends' kids at school, chat for hours on the phone, or join folks at the local bar for a drink. Some people seem to believe that anyone who is at home wants visitors to drop in and stay a while.

Wrong.

You can't get anything done if that's the way you do business. So what to do? Be assertive with your visitors and let them know that although you would love to sit around and talk all day, that's just not going to pay the bills. At the same time, tell them when you *will* be free to spend time with them. You don't want to hurt anyone's feelings, but your friends and relatives have to understand that when you're in your home office, you're working just as hard as if you worked in a big office tower downtown.

Don't Expect to Work Effectively with Children Underfoot

You can run a thriving home-based business with young kids around. What you can't have, though, are kids constantly underfoot and interrupting your ability to work and communicate clearly with your customers. Although being in closer proximity to your family is a real plus of having a home-based business, you must ensure that your business doesn't suffer unduly as a result.

Depending on the age of your children, you're likely to need some child-care help. In addition, don't let children play in your office if you don't want them to use your office as a playroom when you're not there. And for safety's sake, avoid keeping items that pose a danger when kids are reaching or running, including furniture with sharp edges that could cause running children to seriously injure themselves.

Chapter 19

Ten Myths about Working from Home

*T*here are many myths floating around about home-based businesses. No doubt you've heard some of them. You may even believe some of them. Regardless of what you may or may not have heard, the simple fact is that millions of people are making home-based businesses work for them, proving that the vast majority of home-based business myths are false. Perhaps you'll prove them wrong, too.

Here are some of our personal favorites.

You Have to Be a Salesperson to Be Successful

Home-based businesses come in all sizes, shapes, and flavors. While plenty of home-based sales opportunities exist — selling cosmetics and telemarketing, for example — that kind is just a small percentage of the entire universe of home-based businesses. Consider the following nonsales businesses and careers that can be done from home:

✔ Accountant

✔ Organic farmer

✔ Caterer

✔ Personal fitness trainer

✔ Income tax preparer

✔ Web-site designer

In each case, you could build a successful business with little or no sales experience. By doing great work or creating the best products, your first customers will tell their friends and associates, who will then tell their friends and associates. Of course, not everyone is a star. If you're not tops in your field, no matter your personality type, you can find ways other than directly selling to market yourself, as Paul and Sarah (and coauthor Laura Clampitt Douglas) describe in their book *Getting Business to Come to You* (Putnam Publishing Group).

Although being a good salesperson can be an asset to getting your business off the ground, it is by no means an indicator of your ultimate success.

You Can't Work with Kids at Home

Without a doubt, kids do put their own unique demands on a home-based business. But the belief that you can't work with kids at home simply isn't true. When everything works the way it should — and it can — nothing beats working from home, really being a part of your family, and getting to know your kids far better than most working parents can ever hope to. And for many individuals who start home-based businesses, being close to their families while making money is what it's all supposed to be about.

So how can you do it? Here are a few tips:

✔ Find a location for your office that's flexible — one where you can shut out all outside distractions when necessary or monitor your young children, if you desire.

✔ Set a regular business schedule — one that accommodates the needs of your children but that your customers and clients can rely on.

✔ Ask for extra help from your spouse or relatives, especially for those first few years before your children enroll in school.

✔ Bring a babysitter into your home during working hours. Four hours a day can keep the insanity away.

You *can* work with kids at home; thousands of home-based businesspeople (including Peter, with his three busy kids) prove that fact every day of the week!

You'll Get Rich Quick

This myth really brings smiles to our faces. Starting a home-based business is not the same as buying a lottery ticket and hoping your numbers come up. A home-based business is like most businesses — it takes a lot of hard work and no small amount of time to build sufficient income to make a full-time living.

Unfortunately, the world of home-based business is rife with all kinds of get-rich-quick come-ons, blue-sky promises, and overpromised-but-underperforming "opportunities." Our advice is to ignore the persistent drumbeat of the less-than-ethical sellers of promised riches and focus on working hard to create a business where you can do what you love, serve your customers, and make money at the same time — for the long term, not overnight.

For the latest home-based business opportunities, take a look at Chapter 3.

You Can't Make Any Money

Money magazine commissioned a study of the earnings of home-based businesses in 1996 and found that 20 percent of home businesses reported gross business incomes between $100,000 and $500,000 a year. Similarly, when Paul and Sarah and Lisa Roberts did a nationwide survey in preparing their book *The Entrepreneurial Parent* in 2001, they found that while over half of the over 600 respondents worked fewer than 40 hours a week, one in seven claimed earnings of over $100,000 a year. Most recently, the research firm IDC found the average income for income-generating home office households to be $63,000 a year.

Can you make any money with a home-based business? The answer is an unequivocal yes! How? The key is to provide something people will pay for and then pour your heart and soul into it.

Home-Based Businesses Aren't Real Businesses

What is a business? According to *Webster's New World Dictionary,* a business is "a commercial or industrial establishment; store, factory, etc." Today, a commercial or industrial establishment can be found anywhere, from traditional storefronts and mini-malls to suburban basements and urban lofts. Real businesses aren't defined in terms of how many cash registers they have or whether they're located in a shopping center or mall. Real businesses are measured by the attitudes of those people who own and run them, and by their results. In fact, the term "brick and mortar" had to be coined to distinguish traditional storefront businesses from the growing number of home-based and virtual ones.

The fact is, home-based businesses are just as real as any other. If you don't believe it, ask any home-based business owner who is making enough money to be his own boss and follow his dreams.

Home-Based Businesses Are Cheap

Sure, some home-based businesses can be started on a shoestring, using tools and equipment that you might already have (a phone, a computer, wrenches, and so forth). But some do require a substantial investment of both time and money to get off the ground. Here are some startup estimates for a few types of home-based businesses:

- **Computer consultant:** $4,700 to $12,050
- **Gift-basket business:** $2,655 to $9,770
- **Home inspector:** $4,925 to $12,600
- **Medical transcription service:** $2,670 to $8,700
- **Image consultant:** $3,080 to $9,650

As you can see, even at the bottom end of their ranges, starting some kinds of home-based business — while usually not as costly as a car — is not an inexpensive proposition. In fact, it can be quite the opposite. If your primary reason for starting a home-based business is because you think you can make a lot of money for little or no investment, you will want to select a type of business that doesn't require much cash to get off the ground.

But if you buy a franchise; start a business that requires significant training, such as medical coding or information brokering; or begin one that requires special equipment, such as mobile pet grooming or medical transcription, you may need to invest $10,000 to $20,000 or more. Even businesses with low entry costs require you to cover your cost of living — rent, food, health insurance — until you generate enough revenue to pay yourself. This can take months or sometimes years.

It's a good rule of thumb to expect your startup costs to be three times what you calculate them to be.

There's No Going Back

Here's another popular — but patently untrue — myth about home-based businesses: After you get out of the regular 9-to-5 world of working for someone else and start your own business, you can never go back. Indeed, many potential home-based businesspeople decide to defer or even forget about their plans because they're afraid that if they leave the regular world of work, they won't ever get another job.

The truth is that if for some reason your home-based business doesn't work out, you always have the option of returning to the good-old 9-to-5. In fact, depending on the kind of home-based business you start and the amount of experience and clients you gain, you may find yourself in even more demand than before you started your own business.

If You're at Home, You Must Not Be Working

We are convinced that every home-based business owner feels the effects of this myth from time to time. Because you're working at home — and not in an office or store or workshop — you're not really working at all. But as anyone who works at home will tell you, nothing could be farther from the truth.

That fact still doesn't stop your friends, relatives, and acquaintances from calling on the phone, visiting and carrying on as though you had nothing better to do all afternoon than talk, talk, talk. If you find that people don't believe that you're working when you're at work in your home-based business, give these ideas a try:

✔ Set regular business hours, and let all your friends, relatives, and acquaintances know what they are.

✔ Set up separate phone lines for your business and your home. Answer only your business line during your regular business hours.

✔ Don't fall into the trap of taking on people's errands during your work-day just to be nice. This means not agreeing to babysit someone's kids or pick them up from school every day!

✔ Don't be shy! Be polite, but firmly let your nonbusiness callers know that you're busy and that you'll get back to them when you take a break or after work. Remember: Time *is* money!

The sooner you treat your home-based business like the business it is, the sooner everyone else will.

You Can Write Off Everything

This one makes us laugh, but unfortunately, it's an all-too-common myth. Sure, being able to write a variety of expenses (including a home office) off of your taxes is one of the great things about having a home-based business, but there *are* limits. You can write off business-related travel, computer purchases, postage, and office supplies, and you may be able to deduct a prorated share of your rent or mortgage expenses (see Chapter 10).

But one thing is for sure — you can't write off *everything!* That means you can't deduct that trip to a local tavern with your pals to watch "Monday Night Football." You can't write off that flashy new car you bought for your spouse. And you definitely can't deduct the timeshare Maui condo.

If you're especially excited about the prospect of having a home-office deduc-tion on your taxes, be sure to consult a good tax accountant or CPA first. She will be able to explain exactly what expenses you can and can't legally deduct, and guide you through the process in a way that will keep you and your business out of trouble.

You Can Run around in Your Pajamas All Day Long

Actually, this one isn't a myth. In many cases, you can have a home-based business and work all day in your pajamas or bathrobe, and no one would be the wiser. It's really up to you — what you're most comfortable wearing and what's appropriate for the kind of business you've chosen. If your home-based business is a cleaning service, and you spend a lot of time at customer sites, pajamas probably aren't appropriate, much less comfortable. But if you provide bookkeeping services and rarely meet with clients at your work site, pajamas may work out just fine. Name another business that allows you the freedom to do that!

Long story short, it's really up to you — you're the boss, and you get to make the rules! (Which is exactly why so many people establish their own home-based businesses.)

Chapter 20

Ten Things to Do if Times Get Tough

. . . .

In This Chapter

▶ Finding ways to cut expenses and manage cash flow

▶ Communicating with customers and offering special promotions

▶ Getting customers to pay their bills

. . . .

*N*o one ever said that starting and operating a home-based business — and making a profit — was easy. Although failure rates for home-based businesses aren't nearly as bad as many have been led to believe (see Chapter 6 for details), more than a few give up every year. Why? Because even the best of plans sometimes go awry, if only for a short time. Due to your business's inherent smallness, you may not have enough clients to manage the financial roller coaster that can result when a customer goes bankrupt, puts you on a slow-pay plan, or switches vendors.

Good planning can help you see far enough out on the horizon to anticipate the most serious financial shortfalls — and then take steps to avoid them — but it is impossible to anticipate each and every bump in the road and miss them when they arrive. When that's the case, use the ten tips in this chapter to help you weather the storm and emerge stronger than ever.

Save for a Rainy Day

Even if you find yourself making a lot of money for some period of time — for weeks, or even months — every business owner knows that there are no guarantees, and tough times can be right around the corner. One of the best things you can do is put aside money when times are good. Although it's tempting to run out and purchase the fastest new computer or a new furniture setup when the money is rolling in, first be sure that you set aside cash in your business savings account or money-market fund.

Here's a goal that will help you weather a storm when it arrives: Build a cash reserve sufficient to run the business for a minimum of three months, preferably six to twelve months. After you have your cash reserve established and funded, go out and buy that fun stuff you've had your eyes on.

Manage Your Cash Flow

Cash flow — more specifically, maintaining a *positive* cash flow — is by far the number-one financial issue facing every small business owner. And if you rely 100 percent on the proceeds of your home-based business to support you and your family or significant other and to pay for health care and other essential benefits, without the kind of steady income that a regular job brings, a shortfall in cash can quickly bring financial disaster.

The solution is to manage your cash flow (see Chapter 7), which means make a habit of doing the following:

- **Keep an eye on your net cash flow.** List all the cash you expect to receive (cash inflows) during a specific period of time, and compare that with the cash you expect to pay out (cash outflows) during the same period of time. Study this information religiously, at least once a week. Many popular business accounting programs, such as QuickBooks, have a built-in function for monitoring cash flow. Use it!

- **Be proactive in bringing cash into your business as quickly as possible.** The goal is to be paid as soon as you can after you provide a product or service, if not before. Don't sit around waiting for customers to get around to paying you; get your money as soon as you can. Try to get paid when you deliver your products or services, rather than invoicing your customers after the fact. You can do this by requiring customers to pay by credit card or by negotiating advance payments with them. Or simply require payment by cash or check upon delivery. If you sell over the Internet or through an online-store host (such as Yahoo! Store), most customers already expect to pay by credit card.

- **Pay your bills only when they are due, but in time to avoid interest and penalties.** There's really no advantage for you to pay your bills before they are due. Once you pay, you lose the advantage of having the cash in your own bank account. If payment on a vendor invoice isn't due for 30 days from today, don't pay it tomorrow. Pay it when it is due. The idea is to be paid by your clients before you have to turn around and make payments to your vendors. By paying as late as you possibly can — while still paying on time — you can optimize your cash flow.

Keep in Touch with Your Customers

Business is all about relationships: More than just a few businesses have found incredible success because of the close relationships their owners have established with their clients and customers. After all, given the option, wouldn't you rather work with someone you like than someone you don't like?

When times get tough, your first priority should be to ensure that your current customer relationships are *solid.* Drop in for a visit, schedule a lunch, do whatever you can to keep your relationship on the front burner. And while you're busy keeping your relationship active, let your customers know that you're actively seeking more work. This gentle reminder that you're out there will often lead customers to send more work your way — exactly what you need when times are tough!

Push Your Clients to Pay Their Bills

On the long list of things that home-based businesspeople enjoy least about their jobs is having to call clients to encourage them to pay their bills. But no matter how great your customers are, there are going to be times when you've got to do just that.

So how do you know when payments due to your business are running behind? You can figure this out by monitoring *receivables* — the money owed to your company by your clients and customers. QuickBooks and other business accounting programs have built in receivables *aging reports* that make the task easy. And when you discover that one of your client's payments is overdue, act immediately — especially when the amount owed is substantial.

Here are some tried-and-true ways for collecting your money:

> ✔ **Call or visit your customer, and ask for payment.** The direct approach is often the best when it comes to getting customers to pay an overdue invoice. Don't simply rubber-stamp a copy of the invoice with a note like *We value your business — we hope you'll pay soon* or *Second notice — we would really like to be paid now.* Chances are these halfhearted efforts will be ignored. You won't be ignored if you make a personal appeal for payment.

> ✔ **Offer to help.** More times than most companies like to admit, a payment gets held up because the accounting department loses an invoice, doesn't have proof of delivery, or can't find the purchase order that authorized the item in the first place. Find out what's holding up payment, and offer to assist in getting what the customer needs.

> ✔ **As a last resort — and only if you aren't concerned about getting any future business from your client — turn the matter over to a collections agency.** If your client is taking no action to pay you and is ignoring your phone calls, take action quickly. Sometimes all the client needs is a gentle nudge by a good agency to free up your payment right away.

Whatever you do, when a payment is late, get on it immediately — don't wait for days or weeks (or months!), hoping that it will come in. Keeping the money coming in on time should be one of your key concerns, and this task needs your immediate attention.

Minimize Expenses

When times get tough, you have essentially two ways to hunker down: increasing the amount of money that comes into your business or decreasing the amount of money that goes out (or both). Minimizing expenses is one of the quickest ways to help weather the storm, and you should act immediately when you go into survival mode.

Before you buy anything, ask yourself whether you could survive without it for a while. Can the expense be deferred for a few days, a few weeks, or even a few months? Can you borrow or rent equipment instead of purchasing it? Can you barter your services or products in exchange for the products and services of other businesses?

Be careful, however, about exactly what expenses you cut. Do *not* cut expenses that will bring more money into your business; instead, you may need to increase them.

Offer a Special Promotion

By far the best way to turn things around when you're in tough times financially is to bring in more business. Cutting expenses certainly helps, but it is not the best long-term solution. The best long-term solution is selling more of your products and services.

To quickly generate more business, offer your customers a special offer on your products or services — perhaps 10 percent off of all orders during July or a two-for-the-price-of-one offer. The exact form of your promotion will vary, depending on the nature of your business, but you should be clear to your customers that they need to act quickly to take advantage of the special offer.

Alternatively, offer your clients and customers a premium — a value-added product or service — for placing an order during a specific period of time. For example, every customer who places an order of at least $100 during February receives a gift certificate for $10 worth of merchandise or a free video. You can offer a special price to customers who are willing to commit to a contract. Be creative!

Subcontract for Others

Many home-based businesses — especially those with only one employee (you!) — are subject to extreme swings in business. One month, the business can be overwhelmed with orders; the next month, the phone may never ring.

That's why you should develop a network of business contacts — perhaps other home-based businesses — to subcontract your work out to in times of feast and to subcontract work *from* in times of famine. Sure, it may sound a bit strange to turn work over to a competitor, but it actually makes good business sense. The key is for you to remain the primary contact with the client and to ensure that the work is of the same high quality that you would insist on if you did it yourself.

Volunteer

Every business has times when business is down. Down times are perfect for developing new contacts who may turn into customers or who may refer you to future customers. If you still have time left after servicing your current customers, you may consider doing volunteer work in your community.

Not only can volunteering be a terrific way to put your skills to work for your community, but it's also a good way to increase your network of potential clients. And as that network expands, so will your future business. Believe us, you never know who you'll meet when you volunteer in your community. That woman next to you in the soup kitchen may be the president of a local bank or the purchasing manager of a large manufacturer.

Moonlight

When starting your business, it's not a bad idea to keep your day job — at least until your home-based business is generating enough income to allow you to pay your bills. But even after your business is established, you may find that moonlighting — in the form of a part-time job — offers a number of benefits, including the following:

 ✔ Creating a steady source of income that you can rely on, independent of the ups and downs of your business income.

 ✔ Providing a range of benefits that your own business does not, including health and dental insurance, life insurance, 401(k), stock options, and more.

 ✔ Being a potential source of work for your home-based business.

If you do decide to moonlight, be sure you're not taking too much time away from your own business — time that you could devote to building higher levels of sales or expanding your business.

Refuse to Give Up!

When times are tough, you may be tempted to throw in the towel and give up. What's much more challenging — but ultimately much more rewarding — is to fight for your business and refuse to give up, *no matter what.* When interviewed and surveyed, successful entrepreneurs most consistently attribute their good fortune to *persistence.*

You can fail only if you allow yourself to do so. By refusing to consider giving up as an option, you'll force yourself to focus on doing the things that help pull you through your tough times — things like the other nine items on this list.

Index

• F •

• Q •

• R •

TV
distracting, 271, 320
promoting business, 81
24-hour office, avoiding, 320–321
Tyson, Eric (*Taxes For Dummies*), 192

• *U* •

UFOC (uniform franchise offering circular),
30–31
*The Ultimate Guide to Dog Training: How to
Bring Out the Best in Your Pet*
(Margolis), 287
unemployment insurance, 186
unique identity, 42
uniqueness cache, 59, 86
United States Personal Chef Association, 46
United States Tour Operators Association
(USTOA), 48
universal connectivity, 49–50
unserved markets, 70
unwanted work, pricing for, 171
upline, multi-level marketing, 35
URL (Uniform Resource Locator), 102–103
U.S. *See also* FTC; SBA
government job scams, 253
luxury goods, sales of, 59
maturing population in, 45
rules and regulations, 115–116
tutoring assistance in, 55
US Patent and Trademark Office, 129,
225, 227
US Postal Service warnings, 258
USTOA (United States Tour Operators
Association), 48
utilities, living off the grid, 53

• *V* •

vacations, 189, 289
value, creating, 166–167, 337
valuing business, 306
vandalism insurance, 116
variance, zoning, 230
VAs (virtual assistants), 53
vehicle
insurance, 117
tax deduction, 209

vendors
described, 39
trade accounts, 236–237
vest pocket or micro farming, 58
virtual assistants (VAs), 53
virtual retirement communities, 48
virtual storefront, 50
vision coverage, 185
voice mail, 289
volume discounts, 174
volunteering
during down time, 337
word of mouth marketing, 73

• *W* •

The Wall Street Journal, 165
Walters, Dottie and Lilly (*Speak and Grow
Rich*), 162
warehouse superstores, 236
Web
auctions, pricing from, 168
bidding for work, 87–90
business opportunities, finding, 10
competition, researching, 164–165
customers, 98
e-learning, 56
etiquette for building good relationships,
95–96
fraudulent business opportunities, 258
merchant or auction/trader, 50
networking, 20
newspapers and journals, reading
online, 165
online forums, 93–94
scams and ripoffs, 251
social networking sites, 94
startup funding, finding, 126
Web site, business
as addendum from online bidding for
work, 89
advertising, 103
building, 100–101
contact information, capturing, 103
design, 103, 267
e-commerce, 81–83, 101
help starting business, 119
hiring someone to create and maintain,
99–100

● *X* ●

● *Y* ●

● *Z* ●

BUSINESS, CAREERS & PERSONAL FINANCE

0-7645-5307-0

0-7645-5331-3 *†

Also available:

- Accounting For Dummies †
  0-7645-5314-3
- Business Plans Kit For Dummies †
  0-7645-5365-8
- Cover Letters For Dummies
  0-7645-5224-4
- Frugal Living For Dummies
  0-7645-5403-4
- Leadership For Dummies
  0-7645-5176-0
- Managing For Dummies
  0-7645-1771-6

- Marketing For Dummies
  0-7645-5600-2
- Personal Finance For Dummies *
  0-7645-2590-5
- Project Management For Dummies
  0-7645-5283-X
- Resumes For Dummies †
  0-7645-5471-9
- Selling For Dummies
  0-7645-5363-1
- Small Business Kit For Dummies *†
  0-7645-5093-4

HOME & BUSINESS COMPUTER BASICS

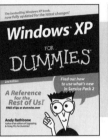

0-7645-4074-2

0-7645-3758-X

Also available:

- ACT! 6 For Dummies
  0-7645-2645-6
- iLife '04 All-in-One Desk Reference
  For Dummies
  0-7645-7347-0
- iPAQ For Dummies
  0-7645-6769-1
- Mac OS X Panther Timesaving
  Techniques For Dummies
  0-7645-5812-9
- Macs For Dummies
  0-7645-5656-8

- Microsoft Money 2004 For Dummies
  0-7645-4195-1
- Office 2003 All-in-One Desk Reference
  For Dummies
  0-7645-3883-7
- Outlook 2003 For Dummies
  0-7645-3759-8
- PCs For Dummies
  0-7645-4074-2
- TiVo For Dummies
  0-7645-6923-6
- Upgrading and Fixing PCs For Dummies
  0-7645-1665-5
- Windows XP Timesaving Techniques
  For Dummies
  0-7645-3748-2

FOOD, HOME, GARDEN, HOBBIES, MUSIC & PETS

0-7645-5295-3

0-7645-5232-5

Also available:

- Bass Guitar For Dummies
  0-7645-2487-9
- Diabetes Cookbook For Dummies
  0-7645-5230-9
- Gardening For Dummies *
  0-7645-5130-2
- Guitar For Dummies
  0-7645-5106-X
- Holiday Decorating For Dummies
  0-7645-2570-0
- Home Improvement All-in-One
  For Dummies
  0-7645-5680-0

- Knitting For Dummies
  0-7645-5395-X
- Piano For Dummies
  0-7645-5105-1
- Puppies For Dummies
  0-7645-5255-4
- Scrapbooking For Dummies
  0-7645-7208-3
- Senior Dogs For Dummies
  0-7645-5818-8
- Singing For Dummies
  0-7645-2475-5
- 30-Minute Meals For Dummies
  0-7645-2589-1

INTERNET & DIGITAL MEDIA

0-7645-1664-7

0-7645-6924-4

Also available:

- 2005 Online Shopping Directory
  For Dummies
  0-7645-7495-7
- CD & DVD Recording For Dummies
  0-7645-5956-7
- eBay For Dummies
  0-7645-5654-1
- Fighting Spam For Dummies
  0-7645-5965-6
- Genealogy Online For Dummies
  0-7645-5964-8
- Google For Dummies
  0-7645-4420-9

- Home Recording For Musicians
  For Dummies
  0-7645-1634-5
- The Internet For Dummies
  0-7645-4173-0
- iPod & iTunes For Dummies
  0-7645-7772-7
- Preventing Identity Theft For Dummies
  0-7645-7336-5
- Pro Tools All-in-One Desk Reference
  For Dummies
  0-7645-5714-9
- Roxio Easy Media Creator For Dummies
  0-7645-7131-1

SPORTS, FITNESS, PARENTING, RELIGION & SPIRITUALITY

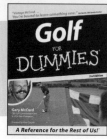

0-7645-5146-9

0-7645-5418-2

Also available:

- Adoption For Dummies
  0-7645-5488-3
- Basketball For Dummies
  0-7645-5248-1
- The Bible For Dummies
  0-7645-5296-1
- Buddhism For Dummies
  0-7645-5359-3
- Catholicism For Dummies
  0-7645-5391-7
- Hockey For Dummies
  0-7645-5228-7

- Judaism For Dummies
  0-7645-5299-6
- Martial Arts For Dummies
  0-7645-5358-5
- Pilates For Dummies
  0-7645-5397-6
- Religion For Dummies
  0-7645-5264-3
- Teaching Kids to Read For Dummies
  0-7645-4043-2
- Weight Training For Dummies
  0-7645-5168-X
- Yoga For Dummies
  0-7645-5117-5

TRAVEL

0-7645-5438-7

0-7645-5453-0

Also available:

- Alaska For Dummies
  0-7645-1761-9
- Arizona For Dummies
  0-7645-6938-4
- Cancún and the Yucatán For Dummies
  0-7645-2437-2
- Cruise Vacations For Dummies
  0-7645-6941-4
- Europe For Dummies
  0-7645-5456-5
- Ireland For Dummies
  0-7645-5455-7

- Las Vegas For Dummies
  0-7645-5448-4
- London For Dummies
  0-7645-4277-X
- New York City For Dummies
  0-7645-6945-7
- Paris For Dummies
  0-7645-5494-8
- RV Vacations For Dummies
  0-7645-5443-3
- Walt Disney World & Orlando For Dummies
  0-7645-6943-0

GRAPHICS, DESIGN & WEB DEVELOPMENT

0-7645-4345-8

0-7645-5589-8

Also available:

- Adobe Acrobat 6 PDF For Dummies
  0-7645-3760-1
- Building a Web Site For Dummies
  0-7645-7144-3
- Dreamweaver MX 2004 For Dummies
  0-7645-4342-3
- FrontPage 2003 For Dummies
  0-7645-3882-9
- HTML 4 For Dummies
  0-7645-1995-6
- Illustrator cs For Dummies
  0-7645-4084-X

- Macromedia Flash MX 2004 For Dummies
  0-7645-4358-X
- Photoshop 7 All-in-One Desk Reference For Dummies
  0-7645-1667-1
- Photoshop cs Timesaving Techniques For Dummies
  0-7645-6782-9
- PHP 5 For Dummies
  0-7645-4166-8
- PowerPoint 2003 For Dummies
  0-7645-3908-6
- QuarkXPress 6 For Dummies
  0-7645-2593-X

NETWORKING, SECURITY, PROGRAMMING & DATABASES

0-7645-6852-3

0-7645-5784-X

Also available:

- A+ Certification For Dummies
  0-7645-4187-0
- Access 2003 All-in-One Desk Reference For Dummies
  0-7645-3988-4
- Beginning Programming For Dummies
  0-7645-4997-9
- C For Dummies
  0-7645-7068-4
- Firewalls For Dummies
  0-7645-4048-3
- Home Networking For Dummies
  0-7645-42796

- Network Security For Dummies
  0-7645-1679-5
- Networking For Dummies
  0-7645-1677-9
- TCP/IP For Dummies
  0-7645-1760-0
- VBA For Dummies
  0-7645-3989-2
- Wireless All In-One Desk Reference For Dummies
  0-7645-7496-5
- Wireless Home Networking For Dummies
  0-7645-3910-8

HEALTH & SELF-HELP

0-7645-6820-5 *†

0-7645-2566-2

Also available:

- Alzheimer's For Dummies
  0-7645-3899-3
- Asthma For Dummies
  0-7645-4233-8
- Controlling Cholesterol For Dummies
  0-7645-5440-9
- Depression For Dummies
  0-7645-3900-0
- Dieting For Dummies
  0-7645-4149-8
- Fertility For Dummies
  0-7645-2549-2

- Fibromyalgia For Dummies
  0-7645-5441-7
- Improving Your Memory For Dummies
  0-7645-5435-2
- Pregnancy For Dummies †
  0-7645-4483-7
- Quitting Smoking For Dummies
  0-7645-2629-4
- Relationships For Dummies
  0-7645-5384-4
- Thyroid For Dummies
  0-7645-5385-2

EDUCATION, HISTORY, REFERENCE & TEST PREPARATION

0-7645-5194-9

0-7645-4186-2

Also available:

- Algebra For Dummies
  0-7645-5325-9
- British History For Dummies
  0-7645-7021-8
- Calculus For Dummies
  0-7645-2498-4
- English Grammar For Dummies
  0-7645-5322-4
- Forensics For Dummies
  0-7645-5580-4
- The GMAT For Dummies
  0-7645-5251-1
- Inglés Para Dummies
  0-7645-5427-1

- Italian For Dummies
  0-7645-5196-5
- Latin For Dummies
  0-7645-5431-X
- Lewis & Clark For Dummies
  0-7645-2545-X
- Research Papers For Dummies
  0-7645-5426-3
- The SAT I For Dummies
  0-7645-7193-1
- Science Fair Projects For Dummies
  0-7645-5460-3
- U.S. History For Dummies
  0-7645-5249-X

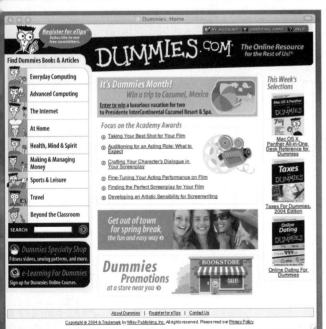

Get smart @ dummies.com®

- **Find a full list of Dummies titles**
- **Look into loads of FREE on-site articles**
- **Sign up for FREE eTips e-mailed to you weekly**
- **See what other products carry the Dummies name**
- **Shop directly from the Dummies bookstore**
- **Enter to win new prizes every month!**